How to
Paint Your Car

How to
Paint Your Car

Dennis W. Parks and David H. Jacobs, Jr.

Dedication

To my wife, Sandy, for putting up with me for all these years; to Roger Ward for knowing the answers to most of life's questions, and to J for inspiring me to write.

First published in 2003 by MBI Publishing Company and Motorbooks, an imprint of MBI Publishing Company, 400 1st Avenue North, Suite 300, Minneapolis, MN 55401 USA

Motorbooks titles are also available at discounts in bulk quantity for industrial or sales-promotional use. For details write to Special Sales Manager at MBI Publishing Company, 400 1st Avenue North, Suite 300, Minneapolis, MN 55401 USA.

To find out more about our books, join us online at www.motorbooks.com.

On the title page: Longtime custom car painter Roger Ward painted his 1932 Ford roadster Nissan Taupe (light tan) at a time when every one else was painting their hot rods Porsche Red. His roadster stood out from the sea of red, and still seems timeless when all of those other cars have been repainted a time or two already.

On the back cover: I know what you are thinking … It must have been a girl who picked out the colors on this 1969 Camaro. Who else would paint a Camaro pearl white with peach colored stripes? JoAnn Peters's impressive "girl's car" received a first place or Best of Show award in all but the first of the 23 shows in which it was entered in 2001.

About the authors: Dennis W. Parks began his professional publishing career as a freelance magazine photographer/writer in 1985. His work has been seen in more than 160 articles in *Street Rodder, Rod & Custom, Hot Rod, Rodder's Digest, Super Chevy,* and *Custom Classic Trucks,* as well as several other publications. Dennis is the author of *How to Build a Hot Rod Model A Ford* and *How to Build a Hot Rod.* Currently employed as a technical writer for a worldwide automotive service equipment company, Dennis lives with his wife in a suburb of St. Louis, Missouri.

David H. Jacobs Jr., has been busy writing books about different automotive topics since the 1980s. He likes to talk to and hang around with experts in the field to learn how they best accomplish their work in automotive detailing, bodywork, painting, and the like. He appreciates and especially enjoys writing about their tips, advice, and tricks of the trade.

Library of Congress Cataloging-in-Publication Data

Parks, Dennis, 1959-
  How to paint your car / by Dennis W. Parks, David H. Jacobs, Jr.
    p. cm. -- (Motorbooks workshop)
  ISBN 978-0-7603-1583-5
  1. Automobiles--Painting. I. Jacobs, David H. II. Title. III. Series.

TL255.2.P35 2003
629.2'6--dc21

Edited by Kris Palmer and Peter Bodensteiner
Designed by Chris Fayers

To find out more about our books, join us online at www.motorbooks.com

Printed in Hong K[...]

CONTENTS

FOREWORD

How To Paint Your Car is an informative, well-written book that will help the first-time painter, the novice hobbyist, or even the professional custom car painter. There are many pitfalls in this business, whether it is a business or a hobby, and the way you react can make or break a paint job. Paint products change so frequently that it is vitally important to read and understand the latest tech sheets for all the products you are using.

To the novice painter: always try to do the next job better than the one you just finished, and you're on your way. Remember that good taste and simplicity always work. Good luck.

—*Roger Ward*

PREFACE

The original version of *How To Paint Your Car* was written by David H. Jacobs Jr. and published by MBI in 1991. The information contained within was current and correct . . . at that time. However, in the 12 years since, a lot of changes have been made in the automobile paint industry, both in application and especially in health and safety aspects. The original book was a bestseller, and I've done my best to preserve and enhance all that made it so useful and popular. I thank the original edition's author for his excellent research and writing, which provided a solid foundation for this updated book. Thanks, too, to editor Peter Bodensteiner for choosing me for this project.

I must also thank my longtime friend, Roger Ward, who has taught me most of what I know about auto painting. Roger painted his first car at age 14, and has been refining his skills for close to 50 years now. Roger has seen a new development or two in the painting industry, has

earned a fair amount of magazine coverage, and most of all has been a truly great friend over the years.

Thanks also go to Keith Moritz at Morfab Customs, Kevin and Wendy Brinkley at The Paint Store, and Jim Miller and Duane Wissman at Jerry's Auto Body for opening up their shops to me for photos and for providing a wealth of information. I must also thank Randy Lenger at Rudy's Custom Works for providing photos of a flame job in progress when scheduling didn't allow me to shoot them in person. Lastly, I must thank Tim Herrington, color and compliance manager at Valspar Refinish, along with Doug Slattery, vice president, and Eric Waeckerle, sales manager, at Automotive Technology, Inc., for providing updated information.

Wishing you the best in your painting projects,

—*Dennis W. Parks*

INTRODUCTION

Even though automotive paint products and techniques have changed over the years, it is still possible to paint your own car or truck. With the products now available, you have perhaps the best opportunity ever to achieve a perfect paint job. What you must realize before you start is that there is much more to painting a car than squeezing the trigger on a paint spray gun.

How To Paint Your Car tells readers virtually everything they need to know before painting their car, from basic bodywork, such as patch panel installation and dent repair, to prepping the surface for primer. From that first coat of primer-surfacer to the last coat of paint, and beyond with polish and wax, this book explains everything you need to achieve that "I did it myself, and I'm proud of it" attitude. Whether you are planning to straighten some minor dents and repaint just the affected area, or repaint the entire car or truck, this book should tell you what you need to know to do the job correctly.

You must get the body as straight and as smooth as possible. Painting over imperfections is only going to highlight them, rather than cover them. You must also mix primers, hardeners, top coats, and catalysts as directed. The directions are included with each product—you just have to read them. If you can read and follow directions, you too can paint your car. The chemistry of automotive paint has already been determined for you. There is no reason for you to try to "improve" the characteristics of any paint product. Mix the components as directed, apply them as directed, and allow them to dry as directed before applying successive coats, and you can create a professional paint job on your car, once you've followed the guidelines outlined in this book for making the surface perfectly paint-ready.

You must also have the right tools, and as with most jobs, that also requires the correct safety equipment. Today's paint products are safe to use, but only when they are used properly. Correct safety equipment, such as respirators, rubber gloves, and painter's coveralls, is essential. Learn what safety equipment is required for each type of paint product. This book will also tell the differences between conventional, HVLP, touchup, siphon feed, and gravity feed spray guns, and which type is best for your particular needs.

Depending on the job at hand, paint can be applied to automobile bodies in more than one way. Initially, our automobiles roll off the assembly line with a fresh coat of paint. Eventually, our cars or trucks will begin to need slight touchups to keep small nicks or scratches from blemishing their fresh appearance. This is usually done with a small brush attached to the cap of a bottle of touchup paint. If wear and tear necessitates the painting of small body items or trim, you might use a spray can to bring that finish up to snuff. If your automobile has sustained collision damage, repair will usually involve repainting the affected panel(s) or sections with conventional paint spray guns.

The techniques used to apply automotive paint are determined by the type (and amount) of coverage needed and the condition of the existing surface material. You would not use a full-size spray gun to touch up a small scratch, or expect to use a touchup brush to refinish an entire panel. Likewise, paint from a spray can might be "close enough" in color match and texture to refinish or modify a trim panel, such as a grille or body molding. If the entire vehicle is going to be repainted, however, paint specifically meant for automotive refinishing should be used.

A small scratch on the sheet metal or the edges of this nameplate is the type of damage touchup paint is designed for. The small brush in the cap of a typical touchup bottle would work well to refinish this emblem, whether you remove it or not. If you had some bulk paint designed to be sprayed, you could pour some into a small container and then use a fine artist's paintbrush to touch up the emblem.

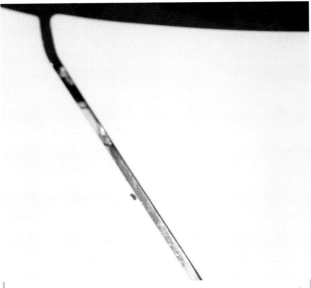

Very difficult to see in the photo, but readily apparent to the owner of this Oldsmobile, is a small chip on the top edge of the right front fender. About ⅛ inch wide and ⅜ inch long, it is typical of the kind of blemish that can be easily remedied with some touchup paint.

On the other hand, this rearview mirror is better suited to a spray can of touchup paint. It would be better to remove the mirror to avoid a substantial masking job. Sanding the surface with 400-grit sandpaper, cleaning it with wax and grease remover, and then spraying on a couple of thin coats of touchup would work wonders.

This late-model Ford pickup truck is in for a total repaint. All trim, lights, door handles, bumpers, and virtually anything else that can be removed will be, rather than masked. Something to remember with pickup trucks is that for a complete paint job, the bed needs to be removed. This truck's bed will be before all of the prep work is completed.

Whenever you use spray paint, touchup or otherwise, the spray can should be warm for best results. This will help to thoroughly mix the ingredients of the paint and will give the propellant its maximum power. If you need to warm the spray paint, you can allow it to sit in a sink of warm water prior to use. Just make sure that you do not heat spray cans over their recommended safety temperature, which is clearly indicated on the label. Never hold the can over a flame!

To achieve a visually acceptable, compatible, and durable paint job, you must use products designed to suit the existing paint finishes or undercoat preparations. The finest paint job in the world will not last if the various layers of body filler, primer, sealers, and final top coat are not compatible. Simply put, do not try to be a chemist when it comes to repainting your car.

DETERMINING THE TYPE OF PAINT ON YOUR CAR

Before the advent of high-tech polyurethane paint products, cars were painted with either enamel or lacquer. Each had its own distinct characteristics. Enamels were quick and easy, generally covering in one or two coats and not requiring any clear coats or rubbing out. Lacquer, on the other hand, required multiple coats, but allowed imperfections to be easily rubbed out and quickly repainted. Its fast drying time afforded painters the opportunity to fix blemishes almost immediately.

Although both paint products offer specific benefits, they cannot be used together on car bodies because they are not compatible. It would be all right, under proper conditions, to spray enamel over lacquer when surfaces are properly prepared, but lacquer applied over enamel will almost always result in wrinkling or other severe finish damage. This is because the solvent base for lacquer paint (lacquer thinner) is much too potent for the rather soft materials used in enamel products.

Product compatibility factors are also extremely important today. This is not confined to just enamel, lacquer, or urethane bases. Every product in an entire paint system must be compatible with the surface material to which it

This Dodge sedan suffered some minor damage to the driver's side doors and rear quarter panel. None of the damage was severe, and almost all of it could be repaired by the hobbyist. Careful attention to detail during the body repair and prep work will go a long way toward making this sedan look like new, once the repairs are completed.

The VIN tag on this pickup truck gives a code that can be deciphered by an auto paint jobber to provide the correct color of paint. Before mixing the paint, it would be a good idea to confirm that the new paint is going to be blue (in this case), just to verify that the vehicle hasn't been repainted or mistagged.

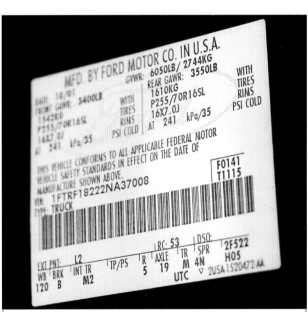

Newer vehicles use paint and options tags to provide the paint code. On some vehicles, the VIN is included on this tag, while on others, it is located elsewhere. If you are having difficulty finding the paint and options tag, your auto paint and supply store should be able to offer assistance in determining where it is located on your particular vehicle.

will be applied, as well as with every other product in the system. For example, using a PPG reducer with a BASF hardener in a DuPont paint product is asking for trouble. The individual products were not designed as parts of a single compatible paint system, and as a result, the color, adhesion, and surface flow of that combination could be adversely affected. More coverage of paint chemistry and compatibility is found in Chapter Two.

Before arbitrarily purchasing paint for you car, you need to determine what type of material currently exists on the

vehicle's surface: enamel, lacquer, or urethane. Note that on newer vehicles, factory paint jobs are all going to be urethane based, as enamels and lacquers are quickly becoming history. For your specific vehicle, it will be worth asking your local paint supply jobber for information on what kind of paint was applied at the factory. For those cars still clad in factory paint jobs, specific paint codes are listed on their identification tags. In addition, autobody paint and supply store jobbers can determine the exact type of paint and color from the vehicle identification number (VIN) on older vehicles, or from a separate paint and options tag on newer vehicles. This makes material identification easy when you plan to match existing paint.

If your car or truck has been repainted with a type of paint or a color different from its original factory job, you will have to obtain paint code numbers from a paint can used during the repaint or from some other source, like the painter who completed the job. Hopefully, that person kept track of this information and will make it available to you.

Should you not be able to determine specific paint codes or information relating to the type of paint used on your car, you will have to test an inconspicuous spot on the vehicle body with lacquer thinner; you could also test a spot on an area already slated for repaint. Dab a clean, white cloth with lacquer thinner and rub a spot of paint. If color comes off immediately or the spot begins to wrinkle, the paint type is enamel. Should color wipe off onto the cloth after vigorous rubbing, lacquer paint is present. If nothing wipes off, the paint is probably a type of urethane.

To determine if finishes include coats of clear paint over their base color, sand an inconspicuous spot with 600-grit or finer sandpaper. White sanding residue indicates the existence of a clear coat finish, whereas a color residue demonstrates that the body was painted with a color material only.

I can't place too much emphasis on the importance of determining the type of paint currently covering the surface of your car before you apply new coats of fresh paint. About the only exceptions would be those vehicle bodies that have been stripped to bare metal in preparation for complete new paint system applications. If you are still unsure about the type of paint on your car after this test, or if you have any other related questions or problems, consult a professional auto body paint and supply store jobber. Be up front and attentive with that person in order to receive definitive answers and patient assistance. Remember, applying mismatched coatings to an existing finish can ruin the whole paint job.

NICK AND SCRATCH REPAIR

Minor nicks and scratches can sometimes be polished or buffed out. They must be shallow and expose only paint at their deepest point. If primer or bare metal is visible, you must apply new paint.

An easy and inexpensive way to repair nicks involves the use of touchup paint. Small bottles of stock factory colors are commonly available at auto body paint and supply stores and a number of auto parts houses. Mostly supplied for newer cars, these touchup paints match the paint code on your vehicle's ID tag. They are applied using a small brush attached to the bottle's cap or with an artist's fine paintbrush. For years, auto enthusiasts have successfully used the clean ends of paper matchsticks to apply touchup paint. The choice is yours.

It is imperative to cover nicks as soon as possible, especially when bare metal is exposed. Oxidation quickly attacks bare metal to begin a rust and corrosion process. Like a cancer, oxidation spreads undetected beneath paint until damage is so extensive that flakes of paint peel off at random. Prior to the advent of convenient touchup paint bottles, auto enthusiasts applied dabs of clear fingernail polish to nicks in an effort to protect bare metal and deter the progress of oxidation, rust, and corrosion.

Compared to tiny nicks, long, deep scratches may pose more serious problems. Although minor scratches may be touched up in basically the same fashion as nicks, long strokes with a touchup paintbrush may be too rough or noticeable. Depending on the color and type of paint finish, you may be better off carefully sanding scratches smooth and then feathering in new layers of fresh paint with an aerosol touchup can (available at some auto parts stores and auto body paint and supply outlets) or a regular spray paint device.

PANEL PAINTING

With the possible exception of a few special automobiles, most vehicles are composed of a number of separate sections welded or bolted together to make single motorized units. Professional auto body people generally refer to these sections as panels—for example, quarter panels, and rear body panels. In addition, cars and trucks have roofs, hoods, fenders, and doors.

In a lot of body collision or simple repaint situations, painters have to spray complete panels in lieu of spraying specific spots. The determination of whether to spot paint or cover entire panels depends upon the type and style of the existing paint finish, size of the repair area, and the ability to blend new paint into the surrounding body paint.

Spot painting a number of minor ding repairs scattered over an entire hood panel would probably turn out looking something like a spotted leopard. This work would be much easier and the finished look much more uniform and professional if the entire hood was completely prepared and painted all at one time. The same holds true for other panels in need of more than just a spot or two of new paint.

Some situations allow for painting just parts of panels, as opposed to entire units. These might include lower panel sections up to featured grooves, ridges, or trim lines on

This Dodge sedan is almost masked sufficiently for the application of primer/surfacer, which will extend beyond the actual repair area, yet not completely to the masked edge. The color coat will cover the entire left rear quarter panel, and both doors will be painted. To match the rest of the car, the painter may need to blend clear onto the trunk, the roof, and the front fender.

The areas of body filler show that this sedan had four small dents (two in each driver's side door) and a larger dent above the left rear wheel. If they were repainted separately, this car would have a spotted appearance so the entire side will be repainted.

doors, fenders, or quarter panels. Special graphics or vinyl stripes might also serve as perimeters to cordon off particular areas, allowing for partial panel repaints. A ridge or trim line draws the eye away from the paint itself, making very minor color variations unnoticeable.

With the advent of base coat/clear coat paint systems, blending has all but eliminated panel painting. Even though the correct paint code may be known, the surface prepped properly, and the paint applied flawlessly, any panels painted separately from others will most likely not match the rest of the vehicle. Blending can be done with single stage paint products also; however, base coat/clear coat is recommended for the novice. Although the actual color of the repaired area may not match the adjacent

This is your typical fender-bender that could be repaired by a novice body man. It is slightly wrinkled, but there are no major creases in the sheet metal. In days gone by, it would be necessary to remove the inner fender panel (and whatever accessories were in the way) and hammer the dent out from behind. Stud guns available now would allow you to weld small studs onto the outside of the fender, and then use a slide hammer to pull the dent out. With either method of straightening the metal, it would require at least a skim coat of body filler to finish the repair.

On this Dodge truck, a small portion of the passenger door required attention, and the roof had to be replaced because a tree fell across it. The small area of the door requiring bodywork was masked off from the rest of the door, although the entire door will receive paint before the repair is completed. When masking for actual paint application, the door or any other panel would never be masked with a square like this, unless the desired paint scheme called for a checkerboard pattern.

panels exactly, the blend will create the illusion that the affected area was never damaged. On the other hand, two adjacent panels that are painted separately are quite noticeable when reinstalled on the vehicle.

Color blending and uniform paint feathering are of utmost importance when you paint panels. Your ultimate goal is to apply paint in such a way that no definitive edges are visible, making that area appear as if it had never been repaired or repainted. Some single-panel repaint jobs require that adjacent panels on either side be lightly sprayed with feather coats of paint. This is done to help a primary painted panel's new finish blend in with surrounding panels.

COMPLETE PAINT JOB

On a partial repaint job, approximately 70 percent of the work involved is surface preparation, and only 30 percent is related to actual paint application. However, for a complete paint job, approximately 95 percent of the work is surface preparation, while only 5 percent is spent applying paint.

Many people do not understand that the condition of body surfaces prior to paint application directly affects the outcome of a paint job. Every speck of dirt, sanding scratch, pinhole, or other tiny blemish is magnified to a great extent after paint has been applied over it. The flawless, even quality of the surrounding paint draws the viewer's eye directly to the imperfection. Automotive paint, even in multiple layers, is still a very thin coating and it simply will not cover up even minor flaws the way,

for example, house paint might. If it isn't smooth, don't spray it!

Complete paint jobs call for all exterior body trim to be removed. You should take off door handles, trim pieces, mirrors, emblems, badges, key locks, radio antennae, and anything else attached to your car's body. This effort alleviates the need for intricate masking and will prevent accidental overspray onto these pieces as a result of inadequate masking. Likewise, it allows paint to cover all vehicle body parts evenly and greatly reduces the chance of paint build-up or thin coat coverage on areas obstructed with handles, adornments, and add-ons.

Removing body trim and accessories will require the use of hand tools to loosen nuts, bolts, and screws. Other pieces held in place by adhesives or double-backed tape may require the use of an adhesive remover product. You must take your time and remove items in a controlled manner so that none of them are broken or damaged during disassembly.

Once you start taking parts off your car, you will probably be surprised at the amount collected. In addition to door handles, key locks and trim, you'll be removing light assemblies, reflectors, grille pieces, bumpers, license plates, mudguards, and a lot more. Therefore, develop a systematic storage plan so nothing gets lost or broken.

Have plenty of sturdy boxes on hand to store related parts as you take them off specific body areas. Keep fender parts together in one box, door items in another, and so forth. This way, when you start replacing them after paint

Before painting, and even prior to most of the surface preparation, the bumpers, grille, door handles, mirrors, and everything else that could be, was removed from this Ford pickup truck. The headlights will be left on in this case, as masking paper will eventually cover the entire front of the vehicle.

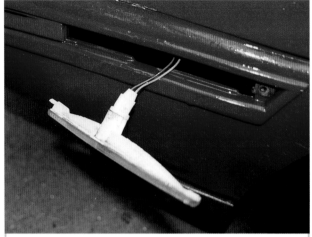

Most side marker lights are held into place by one or two small screws. Where Phillips screws were once common for this application, Torx head screws are typically found now. Make sure that you use the proper type of screwdriver or tool for the fasteners on your vehicle. This particular light uses only one screw. The tab on one end is positioned into the opening, and then the single screw holds the assembly in place. To completely remove the lens assembly, simply twist the bulb's socket while holding the lens assembly. The wires and the bulb can then be stuffed down into the opening in the fender to keep them out of the way.

work is completed, you will be able to quickly and easily locate all necessary body and trim pieces, as well as their fastening nuts, bolts, screws, clips, and so on. In addition to boxes, resealable freezer bags work well for temporary storage of small pieces and parts. Use a magic marker to note the contents on the storage label.

Expect to spend plenty of time sanding every square inch of your car or truck's body surface before picking up a spray paint gun. All imperfections must be smoothed or repaired to give paint a blemish-free bonding base. By itself, paint is not thick enough to hide sand scratch swelling or pinholes. For those problems, products like primer-surfacers are used, which also have to be sanded and smoothed to perfection if paint is expected to lay down evenly and be visually attractive.

Color Change Paint Job

Changing the color of a vehicle involves additional considerations. This is more difficult on some vehicles than others. For a complete color change, it will be necessary to paint the engine compartment, the doorjambs, and the interior. Unless you are extremely good with a detail gun and masking procedures, it will be necessary to remove the engine to repaint the engine compartment. If you are repainting a vehicle that the engine is already out of, this is of little consequence, other than the additional sanding and

Although much of the sheet metal in the engine compartment is blocked from plain view by the engine, accessories, and trim panels, it would be quite noticeable if it were a different color from the rest of the car. For that reason, you should think twice before attempting a color change paint job on a vehicle that is not going to be completely disassembled. To paint the engine compartment correctly, you would remove the engine and accessories, steam clean the compartment, and then perform the standard sheet metal prep work. On a vintage restoration or hot rod project, that would be standard procedure, while on a daily driver it most likely wouldn't be practical.

surface preparation. This also holds true for the interior, although much of the interior will be covered by upholstery.

COLOR SELECTION

A very important part of any paint job is picking the right color. If you are simply repairing and refinishing a dented fender on a late-model vehicle, this is not a big deal. However, if you are building that long-awaited hot rod or custom, the choice of a color may be more difficult than you would think. No matter what you are painting, or how you go about choosing the color, look at your anticipated color under as many different lighting conditions as possible to make sure it is the right color for your vehicle.

Because there are so many different automotive paint colors to choose from, it may become confusing or downright frustrating trying to pick just one dynamic color for your car. Have patience. Look at issues of car and truck magazines to get ideas of the colors other enthusiasts are using. Attend car shows and talk to fellow car buffs about how they arrived at certain paint schemes. These conversations may lead you to good suppliers and products, and also help you avoid mistakes your fellow enthusiasts have already made.

Many times, especially for older classic and vintage automobiles, certain color schemes prove more appealing than others. While a pink 1957 Thunderbird may be a head turner, an equally pink 1956 Oldsmobile may look out of place. Experienced car painters have a knack for envisioning the outcome of cars painted specific colors. From their experience around body shops and car shows, and through reading thousands of auto magazines, they know which colors look best and are in style for most types of vehicles, from sports cars to pickups, and late-model sedans to classic coupes.

True auto enthusiasts can be found in a variety of places. One of the best places is car clubs. Members have a keen interest in automobiles—why else would they belong to such an organization? Many clubs specialize in certain types of vehicles, like 1955 through 1957 Chevrolets, 1960s vintage Corvettes, all Mustangs, particular Ford F-100 trucks, MGs, and so on. If yours is an older project car that is finally ready for paint and you find yourself in a quandary as to what color to paint it, locate a local club whose members share an interest in the same make, model, or general vintage. A few casual conversations with them should help you to at least narrow your color choices to a select few. If there's any chance you may someday sell the vehicle, picking a color that's somehow in keeping with its style and vintage may make it a hotter prospect at that time.

Matching the Old

Choosing the right color for blending in repaint areas on newer cars is easy. You simply go by the vehicle's ID tag

Whether your vehicle is a bone stocker or is highly modified, with a minimal amount of searching you are bound to find at least one magazine that caters to your same automotive interests. These magazines can be a great source of ideas for paint schemes and colors.

Contrary to popular belief, you don't always need flashy colors to stand out in a crowd. Longtime custom car painter Roger Ward painted his 1932 Ford roadster Nissan Taupe light tan at a time when every one else was painting their hot rods Porsche Red. His roadster stood out from the sea of red, and still seems timeless when all of those other cars have been repainted a time or two already.

color code or let an auto body paint and supply store jobber decipher that information from its VIN or its color and options tag.

A word of caution about color codes printed on VIN or color and options tags is in order. Believe it or not, occasionally the codes do not actually match the color that was really sprayed on the vehicle at the factory. With the vast number of automobiles that are manufactured each year, the percentage that have incorrect codes is very small, yet it is a somewhat alarming number of vehicles. When you take the color code from your vehicle to the local automotive

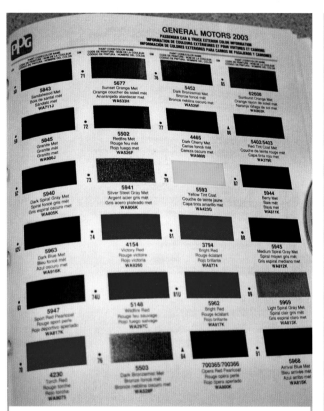

This photo of a 2003 General Motors color chart shows five different shades of red that are very similar, and other colors also have similar shades. The "plain" red for a Chevrolet may be different from the red on a Buick or a Pontiac. Although they may look the same on a paint chip book, they can be noticeably different when sprayed side by side. Some colors shown in the sample book are for under hood or interior use, and therefore will not have as much gloss. Before you select a color, view it in sunlight, not just the store's florescent lighting.

paint retailer to purchase paint, you should tell them that the basic color of the vehicle is blue, red, green, or whatever. If the color code that you supply yields yellow paint, but your car is black, the paint jobber will want to know before mixing a gallon or two of paint that you won't actually be able to use.

If this happens, you can choose a color from a large selection of paint selection charts. Automotive paint jobbers have volumes of OEM paint chips categorized by year and vehicle manufacturer. If you are looking for paint to match a 2003 Chevrolet Monte Carlo for example, you could go to the 2003 General Motors portion of the paint selection chart and probably find what you are looking for. Realize that similar colors from different years or manufacturers may be close, yet somewhat different. When you find a color that looks close, ask the paint store jobber if the color you selected is actually for a Monte Carlo. The color you selected may be for a Camaro or a Corvette, but not the correct color for your Monte Carlo. When there were fewer colors for cars, finding an exact match was much easier.

Another reality to be aware of when ordering paint is that for each color code, there are multiple actual formulas that will provide paint that is acceptable by the vehicle manufacturer for any specific color. The reasoning for this is due to the robotic paint process in use by the vehicle manufacturers. As an example, the first 10 vehicles going down the paint line are supposed to be black, followed by 10 that are supposed to be white, followed by 10 that are supposed to be red, the next 10 to be yellow, and the next 10 to be blue. By computer control, the paint spraying system is purged at each color change. In our example, 9 of the first 10 vehicles will be black, yet the 10th vehicle will be slightly lighter than the 9 before it. The first 2 or 3 white vehicles will be slightly grayer than the middle "white" vehicles, while those at the end of the white session will be slightly pink, due to the red in the system. Of the red vehicles, the first few won't be as vibrant as the heart of the run, while the end of the run will have more of a yellow cast, or orange appearance to them. Of course, the yellow vehicles are affected also. The first few may yield a "dirty" yellow when compared to the middle of the batch or the slightly green appearing vehicles that would result from the end of the yellow run.

This characteristic is not limited to any one manufacturer or color, although certain colors of certain vehicles are more commonplace. For any color code entered into the paint formula database by a paint supply jobber, a prime formula is displayed. Formulas for all known variants of this same color code are also displayed. Each variant has a code that indicates such properties as "less red, more yellow" or "less white, more red." Some color codes may not have variant codes, while some may have 10. When a color code has variant color codes listed, the person mixing the paint will always supply the paint from the prime formula if the paint is intended for a complete paint job. If the paint is for a repair, color chips from each of the variant colors must be compared to the vehicle that is to be repaired to obtain the correct color.

A second method of determining the paint formula for virtually any color found on an automobile involves the use of a color spectrometer. This is a very expensive tool that the average paint retailer will not have, yet they may be able to gain access to one through their paint distributor. If you are trying to match a specific color that cannot be found through available paint codes, the extra effort of finding a color spectrometer may be the answer.

A portion of the vehicle with the desired paint color is scanned using the color spectrometer. The information gathered by the spectrometer is then downloaded into a computer, which deciphers the color and then displays the appropriate paint formula. Although paint matching cannot be 100 percent accurate all of the time, this process

These two paint formulas are both for Bright White for a 1999 Chrysler product. The formula on the left is the prime color, while the one on the right is for a variant that is lighter/redder than prime. Either one of these paint formulas, along with two or three other formulas for this particular color, would yield a paint color that is within specifications for this particular vehicle color. When you purchase paint using a particular formula that has variant formulas, the paint supplier will provide you with the prime formula, unless you specify one of the variant shades. The paint supplier will probably know if the particular vehicle you are painting has a variant formula. If they provide you with the prime formula and your new paint doesn't match, they can probably still determine which variant should be used and alter your paint to match the actual vehicle. Please note that variant paint formulas are not restricted to any one vehicle manufacturer or any particular colors. The Paint Store

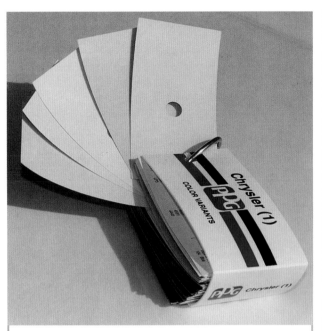

Although difficult to distinguish in the photo, all five variant chips are slightly different, but are all for the same paint code. You place the card on your car and compare its color to the surrounding shade through the hole in the middle. After you have determined that the vehicle you are painting is actually the prime color, or a variant thereof, you should make note of it for future reference, should you need to purchase additional paint for that vehicle at some other time.

is extremely accurate on single-stage or two-stage paints. However, it is not designed for nor capable of determining the formula of tristage paints, or finishes that include special effect additives, such as pearl or metallic.

Selecting a New Color

Selecting a new color for the complete repaint of a vehicle might not be quite as easy. Valspar Refinish already has 100,000 different automotive paint colors on file, and its engineers are kept busy using computer science and experience in graphic arts to develop new hues. The days of walking into a paint store and simply asking for a quart of red paint are gone. Today, there are easily more than 600 different shades of red, so customers must be a lot more specific. They need to pick out a certain color chip from any number of color catalogs or have a particular paint code number available. Most other colors have as many variations.

One way to decide on a new paint color is to visit local automobile dealerships. When you find a car or truck with a paint scheme that you like, copy the vehicle's numeric paint code and take it to your local auto body paint and supply store. In lieu of actual paint codes, proper paint mixing formulas may be located on computer files with just the year, make, and model of most any newer vehicle. Customers can

confirm particular colors by comparing that information with corresponding color chips from paint color catalogs.

Custom Finishes

Along with color selection, you may want to investigate special custom paint additives. Metallics have improved since their heyday in the 1960s. Now, instead of large, bold flakes loudly accenting a car body, you can add specific doses of tiny microflakes to make an otherwise bland color light up to a magnificent and brilliant finish. A good number of newer car paint finishes include tiny metallics. You can see them firsthand on automobiles at almost any new car dealership or on color chips at your local auto body paint and supply store.

Pearl additives are another means by which you can make a solid color look custom. In years past, fish scales were used to give stock colors a pearlescent appearance that made them look different shades when viewed from various angles. In essence, a vehicle that might appear white when viewed straight on, may offer a bright pink or blue shade when seen from a lower angle, or viewed from the front or back.

Today's pearl additives are made by applying oxide pigments to milaceous iron oxide (mica) or aluminum. These tiny chips may be painted on one side, while remaining clear on the other. Depending on the pearl color selected and the angle of light reflection from one's viewpoint, these paint jobs can offer truly unique perspectives. With improvements in pearl products and stricter standards, they are now easier to blend for spot repairs than just a few years ago. It used to be that manufacturers would frequently advise painters to repaint the entire affected side of the vehicle from headlight to taillight. This is so each part of the full side will display identical tints from all directions and not cause clouds of varying degrees between panels or parts of panels. Today, the only real drawback to a pearl finish is that it absolutely must be clear coated for long-term color stability.

CONSULTANTS

Besides choosing what color to paint your car or truck, possibly the biggest decision is whether to paint it yourself, or to pay someone else to do the work. Before you simply jump in (and possibly get in way over your head before you know it), you should first find out what your choices are and what they will cost. If you want to get your daily driver painted, but don't have the proper equipment or the necessary time, you may be better off, quite honestly, to have the work done by a reputable shop.

However, whether it is your daily driver or a project vehicle, by reading this book you must have at least a more than casual interest in learning how to do it yourself. If you are willing to purchase, rent, or borrow the proper equipment (for both paint application and safety), *and* have the

If you are not looking to match an OEM color and are not looking for a metallic or pearl, you may decide to go with a fleet color for your repainting project. This is a sample book of virtually every color of vehicle paint imaginable, although they will all be solid colors, no pearls, metallics, or other "custom" additives. This is just one page of predominately red paints, with a few more pages of reds in the book, and several other pages of predominately yellows, blues, and shades of gray.

time and workplace to make your investment worthwhile, we encourage you to go for it. Whether your repaint job consists of straightening or replacing a fender, painting a new set of steel wheels, or a complete color change, having done it yourself with pleasing results will increase your self-esteem. Before jumping in, talk with those in the business to get a better feel for what your specific project will entail.

Talking with a Professional Auto Painter

Automobile owners with little or no knowledge of the auto body repair and paint business are frequently surprised at the cost of a quality paint job. They have no idea of the amount of work involved during preparation stages before painting, nor of the cost of materials such as primers, sealers, reducers, hardeners, and paint. Uninformed car owners have a difficult time understanding why some companies can paint cars for as little as $99.95, while other shops might charge around $5,000 or more for a top-notch, complete paint job. Of course, there is no real ceiling for the price of a paint job, as the labor involved will vary greatly, depending on what you need to have done.

Should you decide to have a professional paint your car, remember that you get what you pay for. Outfits that specialize in cheap paint jobs cannot afford to spend a lot of time preparing or masking cars. Their business relies on volume. The more cars they paint, the more money they make. Therefore, sanding and masking work is normally minimal.

Close inspection of vehicles that have been repainted by inexpensive paint shops generally reveals overspray on fender wells, leaf springs, emblems, badges, window trim, spare tires under pickup truck beds, and the like, due to minimal masking. Rough surface spots may receive a quick pass or two with sandpaper, but extra time cannot be allotted for definitive sanding and feathering needs. These

shops are not going to remove the bed from your pickup truck to paint the back of the cab either.

Now, should you want a much more thorough paint job than the one just described, and most people do, these shops can provide better quality service. This will, of course, cost you more, with the price of "extras" quickly approaching that of a more thorough, lower volume shop. Inexpensive paint shops are forced to use bulk supplies. Color choices are usually limited to the colors on hand in 55-gallon barrels. Frequently, shops like these will buy out paint manufacturers' supplies of discontinued colors at huge discounts. They pass this savings on to you. In many cases, enamel-based products are used because they cover in one or two coats and do not require rubbing out or polishing work afterward.

Auto paint shops that specialize in overall quality and customer satisfaction are vastly different from high-volume shops. You will have to pay more for their service, but your car or truck will be meticulously prepared and then painted with a high-quality, durable, and long-lasting paint product. All exterior accessories will be removed, including the bumpers and grille. Masking will be complete and the work required after spray painting will be accomplished professionally.

Skeptics may still not completely understand the enormous differences between paint jobs that cost only a few hundred dollars and those that command thousands. Simply put, professional paint technicians spend hours and hours sanding surfaces to perfection. Then they apply required coats of primer-surfacer to fill in tiny sand scratches and other minute blemishes. Those surfaces are also sanded to perfection.

The amount of prep work performed is what raises the price of an automotive paint job. This prep work is what distinguishes the final quality and longevity of the paint job

Body filler and primer-surfacers must be allowed to dry fully before you apply additional fillers or top coats. Painters often use heat lamps to speed up the process. This GM truck has had some sheet metal straightened, some body filler added, and some primer-surfacer applied. The current coat of primer-surfacer is being dried with a heat lamp.

as well. It is very important to remember this, whether you are doing the work yourself or farming it out.

Once the surface has been meticulously smoothed, coats of sealer are sprayed on to protect undercoats from absorbing potent solvents included in paint. Sufficient drying time must be allotted. Professionals often use high-intensity heat lamps to speed this process. These lamps use a tremendous amount of electricity, which must be figured into estimates as part of the overhead costs.

After that phase has been completed, color coats are applied and then cured with assistance from heat lamps. Depending upon the type of paint system used, clear coats then might be sprayed over the entire vehicle. Normally, three coats are enough. When the clear has dried, painters carefully inspect car bodies for imperfections. Then 1,200- to 2,000-grit sandpaper is used to smooth blemishes, as needed, and additional coats of clear may be applied.

Satisfied that their job has turned out correctly, painters buff entire vehicle bodies with fine polish and a soft buffing pad. After all of that has been done, parts still have to be replaced. Again, this takes time, as gaskets and seals must be perfectly positioned to function as intended. Care must be taken so that parts are not bumped against newly painted finishes to cause nicks or scratches.

As if that were not enough, each vehicle is then detailed to perfection. I doubt many customers would pay their paint bill if glass, wheels, tires, weather stripping, and other parts of the car were dirty and covered with sanding dust when they arrived to pick it up from the shop. Most quality body

shop owners insist that their customers' cars be detailed before delivery. Their customers enjoy a freshly painted car, and can relish the fact that it has been cleaned to perfection. The car stands out, looks crisp, and is a pleasure to drive.

When shopping for a professional auto painter, be sure to ask if your car will be detailed before delivery. Ask if all exterior accessories will be removed for painting, and whether or not overspray to fender wells and suspension assemblies will be removed or painted over. Be certain that maximum attention will be given to masking, and that quality paint products will be used throughout the job.

Finding a professional auto paint shop with a reputable track record should not be too difficult. Word of mouth recommendations are generally reliable. If a friend or neighbor has recently had a car painted, ask how he or she feels about the quality of service. You can also talk to your auto insurance agent, fellow car enthusiasts, a local detailer, or your mechanic.

You might even ask the owner of a local specialty auto sales business. These folks are true auto enthusiasts—they have to be, in order to stay up-to-date on the latest classic car trends and make the best deals when it comes to the sale of classic and vintage automobiles. To them, a less than professional auto body shop is a nightmare. They expect to pay higher prices for quality work, but in return, demand that work be of the highest caliber. Dealers in this business get a lot of money for the cars they sell. They know that quality $5,000 paint jobs can easily raise values of special automobiles by $6,000 or more.

This small portion of the stock room at The Paint Store contains just about everything you could possibly need for painting your vehicle: sandpaper, masking tape, paint spray guns, respirators, paint, and primer.

Your telephone book's yellow pages are loaded with auto body repair and paint shop advertisements. Call a few of the shops to get a feel for their professionalism over the phone. As you cut your list to three or four, take time to visit selected facilities to see firsthand what kind of operations they conduct. You should expect courteous and knowledgeable estimators and organized, well-lighted, tidy work areas. Talk to estimators and ask direct questions. Get estimates from each shop before committing to one. At the end of the day, compare prices and select the shop that offers the best service for the most equitable price.

Auto Body Paint and Supply Stores

Auto body paint and supply stores are in business to keep body shops adequately supplied in paint products, body repair materials, and tools for both types of work. The jobbers who work in these stores are constantly updated with product information from manufacturers of paint and body repair supplies. Although some jobbers may never have actually painted cars, their technical knowledge of paint product use is second to none.

Novice auto painters can learn a great deal from jobbers when both parties fully comprehend the paint project at hand. Be up front and honest with the jobber. If possible, bring your car to the store's location so the jobber can see your project firsthand. This way, he or she can best recommend a proper paint system to use and supplies you will need to complete the job.

Don't expect jobbers to drop everything just to give you lessons in painting cars. Their primary job is to serve professional body shops, not teach auto painting. For the most part, Mondays and Fridays are their busiest days. Shop owners generally call in orders on Monday for supplies they will need for the week's work. On Friday, shops may need special deliveries of materials to complete jobs that customers expect to pick up that afternoon. So, plan to visit an auto body supply store during midweek, when jobbers may have more time to converse with you.

In addition to stocking everything from paint guns to sandpaper, auto body paint and supply stores carry information sheets and application guides on almost all of the paint-related products they sell. Paint manufacturers provide this material. You can get sheets on the use and application of primer-surfacers, sealers, and tristage paint systems, as well as just about every other product that you might ever put on your car's body. They are free, and you are advised to take one for every product you intend to use.

Auto body paint and supply stores can match almost any color of automotive paint. However, if you want a specific color that is not displayed in any color chart or paint chip catalog, realize that it will have to be made by hand using trial and error methods. Expect to pay a lot more for this service than for stock colors, because of the added labor involved.

This situation arises when customers request a color match with a repainted car and they have no idea what color was used or who did the work. In those cases, jobbers simply ask customers to search through volumes of color chips until the closest match is found. Then, he or she

Virtually any color that you could imagine could be mixed from the toners on these shelves. After choosing a color, you could decide to have it in a base/clear system, a single-stage urethane, acrylic lacquer, or acrylic enamel. Very few colors are actually stocked in a ready-to-use mix, as shelf space would quickly be depleted.

works with specific tints until a suitable color is produced. Unless a paint chip can be found that perfectly matches the paint on that car, jobbers mix by hand until a match is accomplished, a process that may require hours and hours of work. This is why special, hand-matched colors cost a lot more than standard quantities of those colors whose formulas are stored in company computers.

Unless you have experience painting cars, you might ask your auto body paint and supply jobber how much sandpaper of which grit you will need to properly prepare your car's finish for new paint. Sanding chores are different with each job, and fine-grit paper does not last as long as one might expect. Along with sandpaper, plenty of automotive paint masking tape and paper should be purchased. Two-inch tape works great for some chores, while ¾-inch and ⅛-inch works better for more detailed tasks.

By and large, your auto body paint and supply store jobber can be a fountain of information. Take advantage of this person's knowledge by being polite and courteous, and by asking intelligent questions. Be aware of the store's busiest hours and plan to visit during slack times.

SPECIAL CONSIDERATIONS
Automotive painting has surely become a high-tech business. Not only do painters have to be concerned about the finished product, they must also be keenly aware of personal safety hazards involved with potent chemicals used in paint bases and hardeners. Where filter masks were considered to be health-conscious aids a few years ago, positive-pressure respirators are the state of the art now. Be aware of fire hazards, especially pilot lights on hot water heaters and home heating systems. Thinners and reducers are highly flammable, so be sure cigarettes and other sources of ignition are kept far away from your project.

Special paint systems utilizing metallics and pearls can be satisfactorily applied by novice painters who follow all label instructions and tips from application guides. Take advantage of this wealth of information at your fingertips to make your paint job progress as expected.

Be sure to spend an adequate amount of time preparing your car or truck's surface for paint. Too many times, enthusiastic novice painters get ahead of themselves. They believe that a thick coat of paint will hide blemishes or flaws. Don't settle for that. Plan on spending a day or two just to prepare your car's body surface for paint. Be sure that the paint system you employ is compatible with surrounding paint. And, decide early on that you will practice on an old hood or trunk lid before starting work on your favorite automobile.

Automotive paint manufacturing is a highly technical and scientific business. Along with satisfying customers' needs with quality products, paint manufacturers must conform to increasing health, safety, and environmental standards and regulations. When a new product is developed for the auto paint industry, it must meet all of the strict regulations related to personal user safety and overall environmental pollution criteria.

Just because a fantastic new product might be able to cover car bodies in one easy step, shine forever without wax or polish, and resist oxidation and other debilitating factors does not guarantee it would be safe to use. It may require a different kind of application procedure or special high-tech filtering system to prevent deadly fumes from injuring users or poisoning the atmosphere. Therefore, an even balance has to be found for every paint product that will not only serve its intended function, but also be safe for users and the environment.

The research required to develop quality paint products includes continuing studies by paint manufacturers through their teams of scientists and engineers. In addition to the development of new and vibrant colors, researchers in this field conduct tests to determine the amount of hazardous materials created by various paint products and their application techniques. These scientists and engineers, along with those from related fields, have invented some water-based automotive paint products, although they are mostly undercoat materials.

In addition, a relatively new system of paint application has been developed that incorporates a high-volume spray with very low pressure. This system, referred to as High Volume Low Pressure (HVLP), allows more paint to adhere to vehicle bodies with far less overspray than encountered with conventional spray paint systems. In essence, since more material sticks to properly prepared sheet metal surfaces, much less is lost to the atmosphere through clouds of overspray that ricochet off body panels into the air.

Through increased safety awareness and continued research, manufacturers are determined to eventually develop environmentally safe paint materials that can be satisfactorily applied by a means that will almost completely eliminate overspray and hopefully reduce pollution to practically nothing. This effort has taken time to design, develop, and implement, yet it should be on retailers' shelves in the very near future. *[For more information on roller-applied primer, refer to Chapter 5: Bodywork.]* Meanwhile, automotive painters must be especially aware of potential user hazards and take advantage of all recommended safety procedures and equipment. This includes the use of positive-pressure full-face respirators, protective hoods, quality rubber gloves, and painters' coveralls.

The chemistry surrounding automotive paint materials is quite complex. You can certainly learn a lot more, should you want to, about the molecular structures, atomic weights, and other chemical compositions of these products through voluminous tomes at a library. Although that information may be of interest to certain scientific folks, it really won't be of much help to those who simply want to learn how to paint their car or truck. But you should understand some automotive paint properties in order to choose the proper products and achieve a professional-looking and long-lasting paint finish on your vehicle.

BASIC INGREDIENTS

Auto paint is made up of pigments, binders, and solvents. Pigments give paint material its color. Binders are used to hold pigment materials together and keep them in a state that remains solidly attached to vehicle bodies. Solvents are those liquid media (thinners and reducers) that transform solid pigment and binder materials into sprayable liquids. Solvents are, for the most part, the materials that evaporate into the atmosphere and cause pollution concerns.

Various pigment, binder, and solvent combinations produce different types of paint. Their differences are reflected in coverage techniques, drying times, reparability, and durability. In general, all paint materials are basically solid substances that have been mixed with a solvent and changed into liquid forms in order to be sprayed. Once solvents have evaporated, pigments and binders harden into colorful sheets that strongly adhere to auto body surfaces to offer pleasant appearances and oxidation protection for underlying metal.

In years past, auto painters were limited to either straight enamel- or lacquer-based paints. Enamels were relatively easy to apply and covered in just one or two coats. They did not have to be rubbed out, and they lasted a long time. Nitrocellulose lacquer paint required many thin coats and numerous clear coats over color bases, which had to be rubbed out in order to gain a deep, lustrous shine. It dried fast and allowed minor flaws to be gently wet-sanded and then painted over just minutes after the paint was applied.

Advances in paint chemistry brought new kinds of enamel and lacquer paint, referred to as acrylic. Acrylic simply means plastic. Although acrylic enamel and acrylic

VOC Compliant Products for The National Rule
Undercoats

Product	Mixing Ratio	Hardener	Reducer	VOC Lbs/gal
Pretreatment VOC Limit 6.5 lbs/gal				
Priomat® 1:1 Primer 3688	1:1	3689	N/A	6.4
Priomat® 1 K Primer Surfacer 4080	N/A	N/A	+50% 3363 or 3365	6.1
Priomat® Primer 3255	N/A	N/A	+50% 3363	6.3
Primer/Primer Surfacer VOC Limit 4.8 lbs/gal				
Permahyd® Primer Surfacer 4100	N/A	N/A	0-10% 6000	1.5
Permasolid® H.S. Surfacer plus 5110	4:1	3100,3050,3040 3030,3368,3324	N/A	4.4
Permacron® Vario Surfacer 8590	2:1	3100,3050,3040 3030,3368,3324	+5-10% 8580 3363,3365,3366	4.7
Permacron® Tinting surfacer 5100 (mixed 2:1 with color)	4:1	3100,3050,3040 3030,3368	+10% 8580 3363,3365	4.8
Primer Sealer VOC Limit 4.6 lbs/gal				
Permacron® Non Sanding Surfacer 5030	2:1	3050,3040 3030,3368	+15% 8580 3363,3365,3366	4.6
Permacron® Vario Surfacer 8590	2:1	3050,3040 3030,3368	+15 % 8580	4.6
Permacron® Transparent Surfacer 8550	2:1	3050,3040 3030,3368	+15 % 8580,3365	4.6
Specialty Coating VOC Limit 7.0 lbs/gal				
Priomat® Elastic Primer 3304	N/A	N/A	N/A	7.0
Priomat® Elastic Primer Filler 3305	N/A	N/A	+50% 8581	6.5
Permacron® 1:1 Elastic Primer Surfacer 3300	1:1	3301	N/A	5.6

All Product VOC's and Product Combinations are as of November 1998

VOC Compliant Products for The National Rule
Topcoats

Product	Mixing Ratio	Hardener	Reducer	VOC
Single stage Topcoat VOC Limit **5.0 lbs/gal**				
Permacron® Acrylic Urethane Series 257	2:1	3050, 3040, 3030 3368, 3324	+5-10% 8580 3363, 3365, 3366	**4.9**
2-Stage Multistage System VOC Limit **5.0 lbs/gal**				
Permacron® Base Coat Series 293/295	N/A	N/A	+50% 3055, 3056 or +65% 3054	**5.9 - 6.6** (Depending on Formula)
Followed by:				
Permasolid® HS Clear Coat 8030	2:1	3309, 3310, 3315, 3320	N/A	**3.7**
Permasolid® HS Clear Coat 8030	2:1	3310, 3315, 3320	+0-5% 3363, 3365, 3366, 8580	**3.9**
Permasolid® HS Clear Coat 8030 (Use with base coat equal to or less than 6.1 lbs/gal before reduction)	2:1	3309, 3310, 3315, 3320	+10-30% 9030 Accelerator	**4.3**
Permacron® MS Vario Clear Coat 8000 (Use with base coat equal to or less than 5.8 lbs/gal before reduction)	3:1	3309, 3310, 3315, 3320	+2% 8580, 3363, 3365, 3366	**4.4**
3-Stage Multistage System VOC Limit **5.2 lbs/gal**				
Permacron® Base Coat Series 293/295	N/A	N/A	+50% 3055, 3056 or +65% 3054	**5.9 - 6.6** (Depending on Formula)
Followed by:				
Permasolid® HS Clear Coat 8030	2:1	3309, 3310,3315,3320	N/A	**3.7**
Additional Information				

- No record keeping required for coating usage.
- No HVLP spray equipment necessary.
- No limits for surface preparation materials.

In 1998, the federal government issued a national rule concerning the VOC (volatile organic compound) content of coatings used to refinish automobiles in the United States. The regulation establishes maximum VOC limits and is broken down into eight different categories: pretreatment wash primers, primers/primer-surfacers, primer-sealers, single-stage top coats, two-stage top coats, three- and four-stage top coats, multicolored top coats, and specialty coatings. Each category is limited to a certain weight of VOCs per ready-to-spray gallon of product. Under the regulation, paint manufacturers must produce compliant products. Spies Hecker

DELTRON® 2000 BASECOAT #2
This material is designed for application only by professional, trained personnel using proper equipment under controlled conditions, and is not intended for sale to the general public.
IMPORTANT: This product must be blended before application. Be sure you understand the warnings on all containers since the mixture will have the hazards of all its parts.
PHOTOCHEMICALLY REACTIVE
WARNING! HARMFUL OR FATAL IF SWALLOWED. CONTAINS LEAD. DRIED FILM HARMFUL IF EATEN OR CHEWED. MAY CAUSE MODERATE SKIN IRRITATION, SEVERE EYE IRRITATION AND MAY BE ABSORBED THROUGH THE SKIN. PROLONGED OR REPEATED CONTACT MAY CAUSE AN ALLERGIC SKIN REACTION. VAPOR AND SPRAY MIST, SANDING AND GRINDING DUSTS MAY BE HARMFUL IF INHALED. VAPOR IRRITATES EYES, NOSE AND THROAT.
FLAMMABLE: Keep away from heat, sparks and flame.

Contact with flame or hot surfaces may produce toxic decomposition products.
CONTAINS: CHROMIUM COMPOUNDS, LEAD, PIGMENTS, PETROLEUM DISTILLATES, XYLENE, TOLUENE, ESTERS, KETONES, HIGH BOILING AROMATICS, ADDITIVES, RESINS.
This product contains an insoluble form of chromium (6+) compound. NTP and IARC associate these materials with an increased risk of cancer.
Avoid contact with skin and eyes and avoid breathing of vapors and spray mist. Repeated exposure may cause permanent damage to the kidney, liver, blood forming tissues, brain/nervous system, and respiratory tract irritation. Eye watering, headaches, nausea, dizziness and loss of coordination are indications that solvent levels are too high. Intentional misuse by deliberately concentrating and inhaling the contents can be harmful or fatal.
Do not apply on interior surfaces or other surfaces to which children may be commonly exposed.
Wear chemical-type splash goggles or full face shield and protective clothing, including impermeable apron and

gloves. USE WITH ADEQUATE VENTILATION. Overexposure to vapors may be prevented by ensuring ventilation controls, vapor exhaust or fresh air entry. NIOSH/MSHA-approved (TC-23C) paint spray or air supplied (TC-19C-) respirators may also reduce exposure. Follow directions for respirator use and wear until all vapors are gone.
FIRST AID: In case of skin contact, flush with plenty of water; for contact with eyes, immediately flush with plenty of water for 15 minutes. If affected by inhalation of vapor or spray mist, remove to fresh air. Apply artificial respiration if necessary. If swallowed, DO NOT induce vomiting. If ingested or if other difficulties persist or occur later, contact a POISON CONTROL CENTER, EMERGENCY ROOM OR PHYSICIAN IMMEDIATELY. Have label information available.
SEE MATERIAL SAFETY DATA SHEET.

KEEP OUT OF REACH OF CHILDREN
Emergency Medical or Spill Control Information
(304) 843-1300; In Canada (514) 645-1320

Distributed by PPG Finishes, Delaware, Ohio 43015, United States and PPG Canada Inc., Mississauga, Ontario L5J 2Z5, Canada.

COUCHE DE BASE DELTRONᴹᴰ **2000** #2
Ce produit est conçu pour être appliqué seulement par du personnel professionnel spécialement formé, utilisant l'équipement qu'il faut, dans des conditions contrôlées, et n'est pas conçu pour la vente au grand public.
IMPORTANT: Ce produit doit être mélangé avant l'application. S'assurer de comprendre les avertissements figurant sur tous les contenants, car toutes les parties de ce mélange présentent des risques.
PRODUIT PHOTOCHIMIQUEMENT RÉACTIF
AVERTISSEMENT! NOCIF OU MORTEL EN CAS D'INGESTION. CONTIENT DU PLOMB. LA PELLICULE SÈCHE EST NOCIVE SI ON LA MANGE OU SI ON LA MÂCHE. PEUT CAUSER UNE IRRITATION MODÉRÉE DE LA PEAU, UNE IRRITATION GRAVE DES YEUX ET PEUT ÊTRE ABSORBÉ PAR LA PEAU. L'EXPOSITION PROLONGÉE OU RÉPÉTÉE AU PRODUIT PEUT CAUSER UNE RÉACTION CUTANÉE ALLERGIQUE. LA VAPEUR, LE BROUILLARD VAPORISÉ ET LA POUSSIÈRE DE PONÇAGE ET LE MEULAGE PEUVENT ÊTRE NOCIFS EN CAS D'INHALATION. LA VAPEUR IRRITE LES YEUX, LE NEZ ET LA GORGE.
INFLAMMABLE: Tenir loin de toute source de chaleur, des étincelles et de la flamme. Le contact avec la flamme

ou des surfaces chaudes peut dégager des produits de décomposition toxiques.
CONTIENT: COMPOSÉS DE CHROME, PLOMB, PIGMENTS, DISTILLATS DE PÉTROLE, XYLENE, TOLUÈNE, ESTERS, CÉTONES, AROMATIQUES À POINT D'ÉBULLITION ÉLEVÉ, ADDITIFS, RÉSINES.
Ce produit contient un composé de chrome insoluble (6+). La NTP et l'IARC associent ces produits avec une augmentation du risque de cancer.
Éviter tout contact avec la peau et les yeux, ainsi que l'aspiration des vapeurs et du brouillard vaporisé. L'exposition répétée peut causer le dommage permanent des reins, du foie, et des tissus sanguins, et des lésions du cerveau et du système nerveux, et peut irriter l'appareil respiratoire. Le larmoiement, les maux de tête, les nausées, l'étourdissement et la perte de coordination sont des indices démontrant que les taux de solvant sont trop élevés. L'usage abusif intentionnel par la concentration et l'inhalation délibérées du contenu peut être nocif ou mortel.
Ne pas appliquer sur des surfaces intérieures ni sur des surfaces auxquelles les enfants risquent d'être couramment exposés.
Porter des lunettes de protection résistantes aux produits chimiques ou un masque couvrant le visage et des vêtements protecteurs, y compris un tablier et des gants imperméables.

UTILISER DANS UN ESPACE BIEN AÉRÉ. On peut prévenir la surexposition aux vapeurs en assurant des contrôles d'aération, l'évacuation des vapeurs ou l'entrée d'air frais. Les respirateurs purificateurs d'air (TC-23C-) où à canalisation d'air (TC-19C-), approuvés par NIOSH/MSHA, peuvent également minimiser le risque. Suivre les instructions pour l'utilisation du respirateur et le porter jusqu'à ce que toutes les vapeurs se soient dissipées.
PREMIERS SOINS: En cas de contact avec la peau, rincer à grande eau; en cas de contact avec les yeux, rincer immédiatement à grande eau pendant 15 minutes. En cas d'asphyxie par l'inhalation de vapeur ou du brouillard vaporisé, porter la personne incommodée au grand air. Pratiquer la respiration artificielle si nécessaire. En cas d'ingestion, NE PAS faire vomir. En cas d'ingestion, ou si d'autres difficultés persistent ou se produisent plus tard, contacter IMMÉDIATEMENT UN CENTRE ANTIPOISONS, LE SERVICE D'URGENCE D'UN HÔPITAL OU UN MÉDECIN. Lui montrer les renseignements donnés sur l'étiquette.
VOIR LA FICHE SIGNALÉTIQUE.

TENIR HORS DE LA PORTÉE DES ENFANTS
Renseignements médicaux en cas d'urgence ou pour le contrôle en cas de déversement
(304) 843-1300; Au Canada (514) 645-1320

Distribué par PPG Finishes, Delaware, Ohio 43015, États-Unis et PPG Canada Inc., Mississauga, Ontario L5J 2Z5, Canada.

PPG PPG Industries, Inc., PPG Finishes, 19699 Progress Drive, Strongsville, Ohio 44136
Made in U.S.A./Fabriqué aux États-Unis.
FORM/FORMULAIRE 1675   DBC #2

As do all paint product labels, this label from a gallon of PPG Deltron 2000 Base coat provides critical safety warnings, product information, and first aid information. PPG Finishes

lacquer retain their same basic application and benefit characteristics, their durability and ultraviolet sun ray resistance have been greatly improved.

As acrylic enamels and lacquers underwent improvement, a new type of paint was introduced. Urethane paint products, and more recently polyurethane, combined advantages of both enamels and lacquers to offer quick-drying ingredients that could cover in one to three coats, and could allow blemish repair soon after a coat was sprayed on. One of the biggest advantages urethanes offer is durability. In a sense, they were developed to resist the hazards of today's harsh airborne pollutants, acid rain, and other oxidizing elements.

Once again, although basic ingredients remain the same—pigment, binder, and solvent—their chemical compositions give each paint its own individual characteristics. The addition of chemical hardeners plays a significant role by improving the way pigments and binders bond together and adhere to painted surfaces.

Liquid hardeners (catalysts) are added to paint and solvent mixtures in established proportions as recommended by label instructions and informational guidelines. Instructions for hardeners, as well as their labels and information sheets, emphasize that fresh air respirators must be employed whenever hardeners are used. This is

Opposite: *These are the technical details of the SATAjet 2000 high volume, low pressure (HVLP) spray gun. HVLP spray guns apply paint products at lower air pressure than their conventional counterparts, allowing the user to put more paint on the vehicle's surface and less in the air as overspray. As stricter controls regulate the use of high-pressure spray paint systems to reduce overspray pollutants, use of HVLP systems will continue to increase.* Automotive Technology, Inc.

SATAjet 2000 HVLP - Technical Details

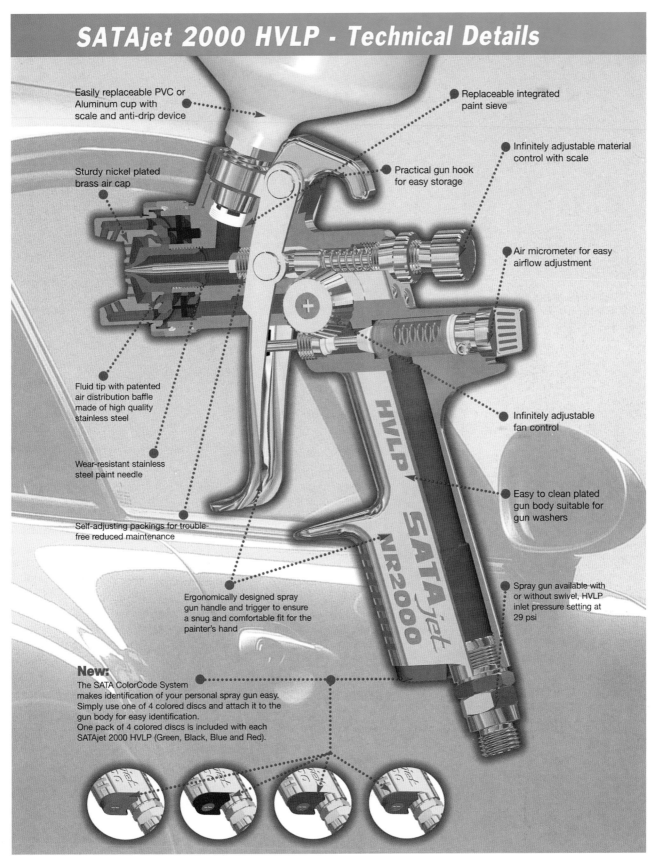

Easily replaceable PVC or Aluminum cup with scale and anti-drip device

Sturdy nickel plated brass air cap

Fluid tip with patented air distribution baffle made of high quality stainless steel

Wear-resistant stainless steel paint needle

Self-adjusting packings for trouble-free reduced maintenance

Replaceable integrated paint sieve

Infinitely adjustable material control with scale

Practical gun hook for easy storage

Air micrometer for easy airflow adjustment

Infinitely adjustable fan control

Easy to clean plated gun body suitable for gun washers

Spray gun available with or without swivel, HVLP inlet pressure setting at 29 psi

Ergonomically designed spray gun handle and trigger to ensure a snug and comfortable fit for the painter's hand

New:
The SATA ColorCode System makes identification of your personal spray gun easy. Simply use one of 4 colored discs and attach it to the gun body for easy identification.
One pack of 4 colored discs is included with each SATAjet 2000 HVLP (Green, Black, Blue and Red).

P-200 Effective 4/99

Directions for Use

DCU2002

Preparation

Where VOC limits allow a maximum of 5.0 #/US Gal. for multi stage systems, reduce DBU Color 150% with DRR Reducer or DBC Color 100% with DT Reducer. Refer to the Product Information Bulletin of the color system for its application and dry times.

Mixing Ratios

DCU2002	DT REDUCER	DCX HARDENER
4 :	1 :	1

Pot Life of mixture is 4 hours at 70°F (21°C).

DCU2002	DT REDUCER	DFX11
5 :	1 :	5

Pot Life of mixture is 3 hours at 70°F (21°C).

Application and Dry Times

Apply:	2 wet coats
Fluid Tip:	1.3 - 1.5 mm or equivalent
Air pressure	8-10 PSI at the cap HVLP guns 45-50 PSI for conventional guns
Flash Time	10-15 min. with DCX hardeners 5-10 minutes with DFX11

Dry Times 70°F (21°C).	DCX8	DCX9	DCX61	DFX11
Dust Free:	80-90 min.	100 min.	70 min.	15-20 min.
Tack Free:	3-4 hrs.	3½-4 hrs.	2¾-3 hrs.	1-1¼ hrs.
Tape Time:	5-6 hrs.	6 hrs.	6 hrs.	12 hrs.

Air Dry	16 hrs. 70°F(21°C)
Force Dry:	Purge 0-5 min.
	Bake DCX hardeners 30 min. at 140°F (60°C)
	DFX11 15-30 min. at 120-140°F (49-60°C)

Polishing

Air Dry:	DCX hardener - 16 hrs. at 70°F (21°C). DFX11 - 12 hrs. at 70°F (21°C)
Force Dry:	DCX hardener- cool down + 4-8 hrs. DFX11 - cool down + 4-6 hrs.

Repair and Recoat

DCX - force dry/cool cycle or 16 hrs. air dry 70°F (21°C)
DFX11 - force dry/cool cycle or 5 hrs. air dry 70°F (21°C)
After 3 days, DCU2002 must be sanded before recoating with primer, color or clear.

Painting Flexible Parts

Full panel only when part is off the vehicle. It is not necessary to add DX814 when the part is mounted on the vehicle.

DCU2002	DT REDUCER	DCX HARDENER	DX814
4 :	1 :	2 :	2

Pot life of flexiblilized DCU2002 is 1-2 hours at 70°F (21°C)

DCU2002/DT/DCX9 (4:1:1)
May be used on flexible parts without DX814

This is the information provided on the P-sheet (product information sheet) for PPG's Concept 2002 Polyurethane Clear. Along with undercoat and color coat information, it includes mixing, application, air pressure, and drying time instructions. PPG Finishes

Other than the necessary undercoat products, this photo shows typical products required for a PPG base coat/clear coat paint system compared to a PPG single-stage paint system. DCU2021 Clear would be mixed with DT885 Reducer and DCX61 Hardener to provide a clear coat. DBC9700 Base (color) would be reduced with the same DT885 Reducer, minimizing the number of different products necessary. For a single-stage system, DCC9000 (color) would be mixed with DT885 Reducer and DCX61 Hardener.

because hardeners contain isocyanate chemicals, which have been deemed health hazards when inhaled or absorbed through the skin.

Currently, three basic types of automotive paint are being produced: acrylic enamel, acrylic lacquer, and urethane. Kevin Brinkley, sales manager of The Paint Store, says 99.5 percent of his paint sales are for urethane-based products. Any sales of acrylic enamel or acrylic lacquer are usually for restoration projects. Kevin and most professional painters strongly suggest that anyone painting his or her own car use urethane products, with base coat/clear coat being the first choice over single stage.

Acrylic Enamel

No automobile painting book would be complete without some mention of lacquers and enamels, if only for historical perspective. For all intents and purposes, their use in automobile painting is obsolete.

According to PPG's *Refinish Manual,* "Alkyd (natural-based) and acrylic (plastic-based) enamels dry first by evaporation of the reducers, then by oxidation of the resin (binder)." This means that although the paint finish may appear to dry quickly through evaporation of its solvent base, the material continues to harden as resins combine with oxygen in the air. Heat from infrared lamps helps to speed this process.

As the curing process continues, a dry synthetic film solidifies over the top of the finish to offer a tough, shiny color coat. Wet sanding this coat to remove bits of dirt or debris will destroy that film and require touchup painting to repair blemishes.

When compared to the durability of urethane products, alkyd and acrylic enamels fall short. Although they can

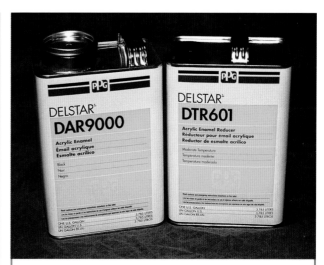

Acrylic enamel, such as PPG's DAR9000, does not use a hardener or a coat of clear. It is mixed with a reducer, such as DTR601 (depending on temperature) prior to spraying. Acrylic enamel dries first by evaporation of the reducers, then by oxidation of the resin (binder). Heat curing ovens or heat from infrared lamps help to speed up the curing process, making the painted surface harder.

cover in just one or two coats and do not require the use of isocyanate-based hardeners, they cannot hold up to the same kind of harsh environments or impact hazards. In addition, the application of any lacquer-based product over enamel will result in surface wrinkling or crazing. This is because the materials in enamel cannot hold up to the strong chemicals in lacquer.

In order for an enamel paint to accept a top coat of lacquer material, as for custom flames or other artwork, a special sealer has to be applied first to prevent lacquer solvents from penetrating and ruining enamel bases. For situations such as this, you must consult an auto body paint and supply jobber for advice and recommendations that apply to your specific job.

Acrylic Lacquer

Acrylic lacquer resists ultraviolet sun rays, cracking, dulling, and yellowing much better than nitrocellulose lacquer. It has been a favorite paint among auto enthusiasts for years because it is easy to mix, can be applied at relatively low pressures, dries quickly, and can generally be repaired and recoated within 10 to 20 minutes after the last coat has been sprayed.

By its nature, lacquer requires that a number of coats be applied to achieve color and coverage expectations. After that, coats of clear lacquer are sprayed over color bases for protection and for required buffing. If painters were to buff lacquer color coats, tints would be adversely affected. Therefore, clear coats are applied so that buffing shines them to a deep gloss without disturbing any underlying color characteristics. The process requires more time than enamel applications, but the extra deep shine and lustrous finish are worth the effort.

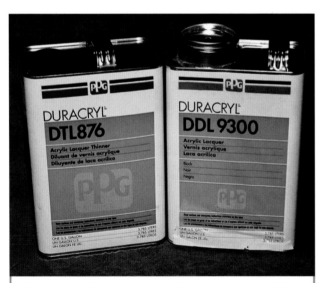

Although it has almost vanished now due to government restrictions, acrylic lacquer was at one time the most common paint system used by custom painters. Acrylic lacquer, such as PPG's DDL9300 would be thinned with DTL876 or other temperature thinner, and then several coats of color applied. Since the acrylic lacquer dried quickly, nibs of dirt, runs, or other blemishes could be sanded out, and another coat of color added fairly quickly. After several coats of color had been applied (and sanded in between), several coats of clear would also be added to provide protection to the color beneath. The high buildup of paint involved in acrylic lacquer finishes can cause the surface to resemble an alligator's skin if not properly applied and maintained.

Lacquer has also been used by a lot of custom painters because of its quick-drying nature. Frequently, custom designs require multiple masking in order to achieve unique paint schemes. Because lacquer dries in 10 to 20 minutes during warm weather, painters can apply masking tape over new paint and continue with their custom project without much interruption. To do the same thing in enamel, painters might have to wait for days until paint is dry enough to accept strips of masking tape without subsequent damage to its top film layer.

Years ago, most professional auto body painters would recommend novices start out using lacquer-based paint. This allowed then to repair defects almost immediately and continue with their work. Lacquer is forgiving in that regard. Repaint efforts to repair scratches and cover areas exposed by bodywork are also easy to match on lacquer paint jobs. After mixing and spraying the matching original-finish paint color, painters can revive gloss and texture by polishing and buffing the finish.

Because of the amount of volatile organic compounds (VOCs) emitted by lacquer solvents, regulatory agencies have minimized the use of lacquer paint or required that it only be sprayed in down-draft paint booths equipped with special filters and air-purifying systems. This is a factor to consider when contemplating a complete paint job for your car. Be sure to talk it over with your auto body paint and supply jobber, as he or she should be one of the first auto paint professionals to learn of any new restrictions.

Urethane

Perhaps one of the more familiar brands of urethane paint today is PPG's Deltron. Urethane enamels differ from alkyd and acrylic enamels in that their resins react chemically with isocyanates in the hardener. PPG's *Refinish Manual* states, "Urethane enamels dry by evaporation of the reducers and by a chemical reaction between the two principal base components (hydroxyls and polyisocyanates), which harden the paint film." In addition to maximum coverage and immediate high gloss without buffing, urethane enamels offer a much harder and more durable finish.

Acrylic urethanes are very versatile. They cover in just a few coats, dry quickly, can be wet sanded to repair minor defects or blemishes, and offer a very durable finish with maximum scratch, impact, and ultraviolet light resistance.

Urethane paint products dry much better when subjected to heat. Professional auto painters frequently use paint booths equipped with heaters or infrared lamps to help urethanes cure to their maximum strength in a short time.

At the factory, urethane paint jobs are baked at temperatures around 450 degrees Fahrenheit. This can be done because car bodies are bare and do not include any plastic pieces that would melt under those conditions. This

Although base coat/clear coat is strongly recommended by most professional auto painters, single-stage urethanes are also available. These do not rely on clear to provide gloss; however, any scratches or other damage therefore occurs directly to the color. Single-stage urethane is mixed with reducer, along with a hardener to provide durability and gloss with just one application. The actual number of coats to cover will vary, depending on the color used. Single-stage urethane must be applied to properly prepared undercoats, just as with multistage paint systems.

A high-dollar, state-of-the-art down draft spray booth isn't mandatory for a high-quality paint job, but it does make getting there much easier. A spray booth is fully enclosed and therefore much cleaner than spraying paint while outside. Exhaust fans dispose of the fumes and the overspray, reducing the risk to your health and making it easier to see what you are doing. Lots of light and the ability to force dry the paint are additional benefits.

baking process further hardens paint pigments and additives, and then helps them adhere to body surfaces better than ever before. Baked-on factory finishes provide a solid base for repainting as long as the finish is properly prepared and scuffed.

For repaint jobs, auto painters generally use heaters or lamps at temperatures below 140 degrees Fahrenheit for about 30 minutes. Higher temperatures could damage sensitive engine computers or melt plastic assemblies. Product information sheets list specific heat application times for particular temperature ranges.

Along with DuPont and PPG, other paint manufacturers, including Glasurit, House of Kolor, and Metalflake, offer their own brands of urethane products. All of these companies believe they have the best products. Likewise, auto painters all have their own personal preferences. But, just as with wax and polish brands, you can seldom get two auto enthusiasts to agree that one kind is better than all the rest. These decisions are based on all kinds of experiences.

One painter may have applied a certain product over an incompatible base to cause a less than satisfactory result; another may have used the same product differently to arrive at a perfect finish with plenty of gloss and adhesion. As much as users may disagree as to which brand is best, manufacturers are adamant about two things: First, painters must always use only those products included together as one paint system. In other words, if you decide to apply PPG paint on your car, be sure to use PPG reducer, hardener, primer, sealer, primer-surfacer, cleaner, and paint throughout the project.

Never mix those products with any different brand. All products listed as part of a manufacturer's paint system are designed to be used together. Chemical bases and other important chemical combinations have been thoroughly tested and researched to give users the best results for their money. Inadvertently mixing brands is asking for trouble. Should you mix brands, you are taking the risk that the new paint finish on your car or truck will wrinkle, craze, mottle, orange-peel, or otherwise suffer damage that cannot be repaired.

Painters' second area of emphatic agreement pertains to the use of all recommended personal safety equipment. In addition to spraying paint in well-ventilated areas away from all sources of heat and flame, they insist that you wear respirators and augment that protection with a hood, rubber gloves, and painter's coveralls. These recommendations are clearly printed on paint product labels, which even go so far as to mention the kind of NIOSH (National Institute for Occupational Safety and Health)-approved respirator to use when applying that particular material.

Because paint manufacturers must meet strict regulations and exacting product standards, it is quite safe to say that all of their products should perform as expected when

properly mixed and applied. To further ensure that the paint finish on your vehicle exhibits the deep shine and excellent adhesion expected, be absolutely certain you follow all recommended surface preparation instructions. If you don't, the new paint you carefully spray onto your car's surface could dry to a separate film that would be easily peeled off in long sheets.

Remember, baked-on urethanes offer durable, hard paint finishes. Because of this, new paint solvents might not penetrate their surface to guarantee quality adhesion. You will be required to scuff the paint with 180–220-grit sandpaper before applying new paint so that the new paint can bond to the old. Information of this nature must be confirmed with your auto body paint and supply jobber for the specific job you are contemplating.

SPECIAL EFFECT ADDITIVES

Although there are more than enough colors to choose from for making your vehicle stand out from the crowd, there are also additives that can be mixed with the paint to provide special effects. The most common additives are metallic and pearl. Their use is not necessarily difficult, yet it does add another variable to the equation. If this is the first vehicle you have ever painted, you may choose to stick with a solid color. Yet, if you are repairing a fender-bender, including metallic or pearl to match the existing paint might be necessary.

Metallic

Many newer cars sport brilliant metallic paint finishes. Unlike custom paint jobs of the 1960s, these newer paint products suspend tiny metallic flakes so small that you have to look at the surface from just a few inches away to distinguish their presence. Along with a pleasant color base, metallic particles offer extra shine and gloss to many paint schemes, adding a flair of custom character to vehicles.

Painters can add recommended doses of metallic flakes to almost any paint base. They do this by scooping out small amounts of flake material with a spoon. Then, according to mixture instructions, they add ounces or fractions of ounces to the paint blend. A test panel is sprayed to check the outcome. If flakes are spaced too far apart, a little more may be added. Painters always start out with minimal metallic doses. This is because more flakes can always be added, but none can be taken out.

Often, the type of flakes may require a special spray gun for application, such as one with a large orifice. Otherwise, the spray gun may become clogged by the flakes. Keep this in mind if you are purchasing a new spray gun and plan to spray metallic.

If you order a specific metallic paint from an auto body paint and supply store, flakes will be added in during the mixing process. Paint codes used by auto body paint suppliers

If you request a paint code for a metallic paint, those metallic flakes will be mixed in with the paint when you receive it from your paint supplier. Should you choose to customize a solid color, you may add metallic flakes on your own. Add metallic flakes in small, measured portions and do a test spray each time to determine if you've reached the desired effect. Measuring—and recording the amount of flakes you added—ensures that you can reproduce the effect easily once you find the right mix.

account for all additives required to make new paint mixes match original standards, including metallic flakes.

When applying metallic paints, vigorously shake paint containers before filling spray gun cups to ensure that all metallic particles are equally suspended in the solution. If necessary, visit the auto body paint and supply store just before painting and ask them to shake your paint container on their heavy-duty paint-shaking machine. While doing spray paint work, most professional painters shake their paint gun after each pass to ensure all particles remain thoroughly suspended and dispersed. This ensures uniform metallic coverage over all parts of the vehicle being painted.

For do-it-yourself painters who want to mix their own metallics, flakes are sold separately at most auto body paint and supply stores. They are displayed in small jars as a dry material; they do not come mixed with a paste or a liquid. You can purchase metallic flakes in different sizes and colors. You can also order metallic materials through custom auto paint outlets, like the Metalflake Corporation and Jon Kosmoski's House of Kolor.

Pearl

Have you ever glanced at a custom car and perceived it as white, and then during a subsequent glance realized it was light blue or pink? Chances are, your eyes are not failing you. Instead, the automobile in question has probably been painted with a pearl additive mixed with the paint.

This material consists of tiny chips of synthetic inorganic crystalline substances that are painted on one side and are clear on the other. Concentrates of pearl are sold at auto body paint and supply stores. Chips come mixed in a paste. They are added to gallons of paint in amounts of from two to four ounces. Small measuring spoons are used to remove material from jars and then transfer it to the paint mixture.

When viewed from different angles, light reflection off pearl finishes causes painted surfaces to reflect different colors. The color presented is determined by the color of the pearl additive. You have to check paint chips at the paint and supply store to select which combination of color paint base and pearl additive to use for whatever color you desire. Now, if your car was originally painted with a pearl-type paint color at the factory, a paint and supply store should automatically include the prescribed pearl dose to your paint mixture. To be sure, ask the jobber at the time you place your paint order.

If you are trying to jazz up a stock paint color by adding pearl yourself, you must verify that pearl is compatible with the paint product you intend to use. In most cases, pearl works well with just about any paint base. But why take a chance on ruining an otherwise clean paint job when all you have to do is ask an auto body paint jobber? Other than that, it is recommended you add just a bit less pearl than the prescribed amount listed on the information sheet or container label. Then, shoot a test panel and visually inspect the results. If more pearl is needed, add a little. This way, you should not have to worry about putting in too much pearl, which could ruin your paint job by making it look washed out or milky.

For the ultimate in special effects, paint manufacturers have designed paints that change colors, depending on the angle from which they are viewed. This is similar to the effect that pearl additives give, yet is much more pronounced. A common application changes from green to purple, while another application changes from blue to pink. This paint is a premixed product, rather than the result from the end user adding a special effect additive. PPG markets its two color-changing paints as *Radiance* and *Harlequin*, while DuPont markets its as *ChromaLusion*. Like pearl and metallic additives, these products are best left to professional painters.

CLEAR

Clear paint is just that, clear. It is sprayed over the top of certain color coats to serve as a protective film, which can be polished to perfection without the disruption of an underlying base of color, pearl, or metallic. Years ago, clear was used almost exclusively over lacquer paint jobs, because polishing lacquer color coats could disrupt their color uniformity. It also added resistance to sun rays and potential paint finish hazards.

Today, clear coats are commonly found on stock factory paint jobs. According to PPG's *Refinish Manual*, there were two reasons for introducing base coat/clear coat finishes. First, the application of clear paint over light-colored metallic paint finishes greatly increased their durability. Second, this process reduced the solvent needs for paint color applications to help manufacturers meet the government's emission standards. In essence, base coat/clear coat paint systems allowed painters to apply only a 1-mil thickness of color when it was covered with 2 mils of clear. Conventional paint color applications normally call for 2 to 3 mils of coverage.

Custom paint jobs almost always call for protective coats of clear paint. This is so polishing and waxing will not directly touch or adversely affect exotic color blends, metallic flakes, pearl additives, or custom graphics. Along with that, certain clear coat products contain chemical ingredients that are designed to ward off the harmful effects of ultraviolet sun rays and help color coats resist premature fading.

To determine if your car has been painted with a base coat/clear coat system, take the color code numbers from your factory-painted car to the auto body paint and supply store. Information in their paint books or computer will quickly tell what system was applied. If yours is a repaint, sand an inconspicuous spot with 600-grit or finer sandpaper. White residue is an indication of clear paint in most cases, providing, of course, that the vehicle is not painted white.

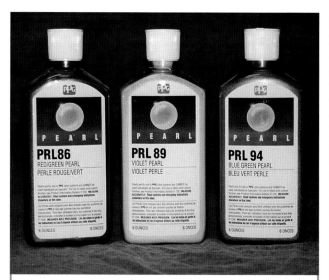

These are just three of the pearl additive colors available from PPG. With a few exceptions, pearl can be added to the clear used in most paint systems to provide a special effect with most any color. You should check with your paint and supply jobber for special mixing and application instructions. You should also add slightly less pearl than called for, then spray a test panel to view the results. It's easy to add more to the mix, but you can't take it back.

Clear is mixed with an appropriate temperature reducer to make it sprayable, and with a hardener to increase its durability and gloss. Some clear products are designed for use in a downdraft spray booth, while others are more compatible with an air-dry situation. For this reason, you should inform your paint and product supplier of the conditions in which you will be using the product.

Base coat/clear coat paint systems have clearly become the favorite of contemporary custom painters, and with their ease of use, they are highly recommended for novices as well. If you can accurately mix the ingredients, urethane base coat/clear coat paint systems are as easy to spray as lacquer and more durable than enamel. Base coat (color) is mixed with a reducer appropriate for shop temperatures. Clear coat is mixed with the same reducer and a hardener to increase gloss and durability.

MULTISTAGE SYSTEMS

Years ago, vehicles were primed and then painted with single-stage paints. There were no clear coats to protect the color, or metallic or pearl additives to enhance it. Plain, solid colors, with little protection (other than owner-applied wax) were commonplace. For the most part, the automobile factories have gotten away from single-stage paint. By using multistage paint systems, they can provide a wider variety of color effects, while providing a more durable paint finish.

Base coat/Clear coat

A base coat/clear coat paint system could also be referred to as a two-step paint system. One step involves color application, while the second refers to the application of clear paint. In theory, base coat/clear coat paint systems are the modern day equivalent of the old practice of spraying lacquer color coats, and then coating them with additional coats of clear. The base coats of color are applied to achieve coverage (the number of coats necessary differs with each color). After obtaining coverage, typically two or three coats of clear are applied. These are then sanded and buffed to achieve superior shine.

Tristage

Some new colors may require three steps—a fact that can be determined by color code deciphering or paint chip selection at an auto body paint and supply store.

Candy paint jobs require that a base coat of gold or silver be applied before toners or another color are sprayed on. Basically, that base coat will always show through somewhat, as toners are a light mixture of color blended in with clear paint. The first toner coat may not seem to cover a gold base at all, but additional light coats of candy toners will eventually cover to an exciting degree, but still allow shades of the base to be observed. The final semitransparent effect is described as translucent. You can get an idea of this by holding a lollipop up to a well-lighted surface. Although the lollipop color dominates, the surface color behind it will add some degree of color.

The same basic premise holds true for tristage paint systems. A base coat of white will make a color coat of purple, for example, a different shade than a base coat of gold or silver. The desired final finish color, along with the paint system brand selected, will determine what base color must be applied to achieve the intended results. Application guides available at the auto body paint and supply store list recommended flash times between coats and any other pertinent information regarding use of that particular paint system.

The third step of a tristage paint system is the application of clear paint. With this type of system, wet sanding, rubbing out, or polishing a color coat that has been applied over a base coat could remove enough color pigment to cause parts of the base coat to show through, creating a break in an otherwise uniform paint application. Therefore, coats of clear paint not only protect underlying color coats, but also allow painters to buff and polish surfaces to a deep, lustrous shine without ever touching color.

Although base coat/clear coat paint systems are highly recommended for novice painters, the use of a tristage paint system is *not* recommended. With the number of variables associated with painting, such as mixing paint, application procedure, and correct time between coats, the addition of a third stage variable increases the chances for error exponentially.

VOLATILE ORGANIC COMPOUNDS (VOCs)

Many parts of our planet have become so polluted that government agencies and research institutes have taken bold steps to curtail the creation of any new pollution sources, as well as to drastically cut back on sources that have been in existence for years. The automotive paint industry is not immune to these emission standards and has, in fact, done a great deal to curb pollution caused by paint overspray and solvent evaporation.

Volatile organic compounds (VOCs) are chemical substances that rise into the atmosphere from paint overspray and solvent evaporation to unite with nitrous oxides and produce ozone. Ozone is a major component of smog. Basically, VOCs are those elements in cans of paint that evaporate. Since pigments and binders (resins) are solids that form films on auto body surfaces, it is the chemical solvents that are responsible for VOCs. Solvent is a generic term used to describe the material in paint that keeps the mixture in a liquid state; lacquer paints have lacquer thinner, while enamels and urethanes have reducers. Any gallon of paint could include up to 90 percent solvent. Thinners and reducers are 100 percent solvent.

States like California, New York, Texas, and New Jersey have passed laws relating to the emission of VOCs by local companies, including automotive paint shops. In addition to mandating that shops install high-tech paint booths with downdraft ventilation systems, they insist that these booths be equipped with special filtering systems designed to burn off or otherwise filter out VOCs.

To aid in stemming the amount of VOCs escaping into the air by way of paint overspray, some companies, such as Accuspray, have developed High Volume Low Pressure (HVLP) spray paint systems. These units are capable of producing 64 cfm (cubic feet per minute) of air at 5 psi (pounds per square inch). They also warm air to approximately 90 degrees Fahrenheit. Since the paint is being sprayed with less pressure, more of the paint is actually landing on the vehicle, instead of bouncing off it. This results in less overspray, thereby reducing the amount of product required by approximately 25 percent.

Paint manufacturers are striving to develop new paint products that will dramatically reduce the amount of VOCs escaping into the air. Water-borne paint products have been produced with mixed results, however, research and development continues. Existing research suggests that base coats will eventually be water-borne, and that single-stage, solid-shade base coats, and all clears will eventually be high solids. As far as lacquers are concerned, it's just not conceivable to get their VOC content down to the levels imposed by the new laws. Manufacturers have accepted that lacquers are going to be phased out completely. Shops have to accept that as well.

As confusing as this issue can be, the best way to stay on top of it is to maintain contact with your local auto body paint and supply store. Jobbers will be among the first to know of drastic changes in the auto paint industry. They will also be among the first to receive new and updated technical material on new paint products and compatible systems for use on previously painted automobiles in need of touchup. In the long run, rest assured that any new paint technology will be well researched and made compatible with paint systems used on today's vehicles.

OVERVIEW

If your car or truck is scheduled to be stripped to bare metal and you are contemplating a complete paint job, you can use almost any paint system. It could be single-stage urethane for relatively easy two- to three-coat coverage with no rubbing out or buffing requirements, or a complete base coat/clear coat system that will mean more spraying and rubbing-out work, but a much more durable and bullet-proof finish. Preparations will basically be the same. You'll have to treat bare metal to coats of epoxy primer and primer-surfacer, and then sand to perfection before applying either a single-stage or multistage system.

Concerns over personal safety while using hardeners with isocyanate ingredients may cause you to opt for a single-stage product. Since small specs of dirt or debris cannot be wet sanded smooth, you will have to apply paint in an extra-clean and dust-free environment.

By far, your best source for product information is your local auto body paint and supply store jobber. This person can address concerns about your car's existing paint surface and any special mixing or application techniques unique to the new paint system you have chosen. He or she can also supply useful information concerning local climates and weather conditions. Jobbers should also be aware of uncommon regional factors, which enable them to guide you through purchases of temperature-related thinners and reducers, and other specific techniques required for that area.

The process of painting cars would be a lot easier and a whole lot less technical if only one paint product were necessary for all automotive uses. Wouldn't it be nice if you only had to buy one gallon of product, and it would take care of all primer, sealer, and color concerns? Unfortunately, that is not the case. Along with the various paint bases that actually put color on vehicle bodies, numerous other products must be used in specific situations to guarantee maximum color longevity, adhesion, and sheet metal protection.

Spraying paint directly onto bare metal will not result in the smooth finish you expect. The color may wash out, the paint may peel or crack, and a host of other problems will quickly surface. Likewise, painting cars whose vinyl and rubber parts have been treated with lots of silicone will likely produce fish eye problems, because the silicone has settled on the metal and made it resistant to paint adhesion. And what about flexible urethane plastic parts, such as bumpers and ground effects? Without a flex-additive, the paint on these components would randomly peel and crack.

As they do with paint products, manufacturers supply auto body paint and supply stores with information sheets and application guides for their sealers, primers, primer/surfacers, paint removers, and cleaners. Mixing instructions and flash times are spelled out, just as they are for paint.

A complete paint system includes all the products needed to accomplish any paint job. Starting with wax and grease remover, paint manufacturers design all of their sealers, primers, thinners, retarders, reducers, and paints to be compatible with each other. Mixing sticks from each manufacturer are calibrated so that as parts of one item are mixed with others, the outcome will be a perfectly blended paint product that will serve the purposes of metal protection, paint adhesion, and color holdout as intended.

Paint support chemicals are all of the products you will need to prepare auto body surfaces for paint (undercoats), as well as those additives designed to be mixed with paint to overcome specific problems. Since it is impossible to depict every kind of paint-related problem for every vehicle and every circumstance, you may have to confer with a paint and supply jobber or professional auto painter for unique problems. By being up-front with jobbers about the kind of paint job you expect to apply and your lack of painting experience, you allow them an excellent opportunity to share their technical paint knowledge with you and possibly solve more problems than you knew you had.

WAX AND GREASE REMOVER

Before any surface is ready for an undercoat or top coat, it has to be as clean as possible. All traces of dirt, grease, oil, silicone, and other contaminants must be removed. After a

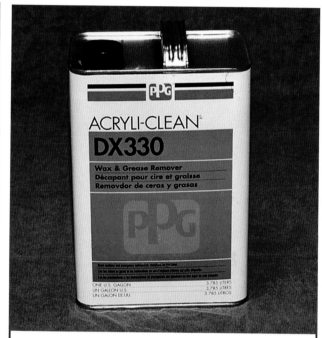

It is a simple fact that primer and paint will not stick to dirt, wax, or grease. Prior to sanding, after sanding, and between undercoats and top coats, use a wax and grease remover to clean the vehicle's surface. Wax and grease remover should be wiped onto each panel with a clean dry cloth, and then wiped off with a second cloth.

thorough and meticulous wash, car bodies must be wiped off with a wax and grease remover. Each paint system will have its own recommended product.

The best cleaning results can be obtained by using one cloth dampened with wax and grease remover to initially wipe surfaces with one hand, followed by a clean dry cloth in the other hand to remove lingering residue and moisture. Be absolutely certain that the cloths you use are clean and completely free from all traces of wax, polish, oil, or anything else. To be sure, you might buy a yard or two of soft flannel material at a fabric store, wash it in your washing machine, and then cut it into workable sizes about 2 feet square. It can then be folded into a handy size so fresh sides can be unfolded for use when one becomes soiled.

Every part of any surface to be painted must be cleaned with a wax and grease remover product. If this chore is not completed, you run the risk of contaminants on the surface ruining an otherwise professionally applied paint job. Be sure to follow label instructions, including the use of rubber gloves and any recommended protective respiratory device.

To ensure that auto body surfaces are as clean as can be, supplement wax and grease remover cleaning with an

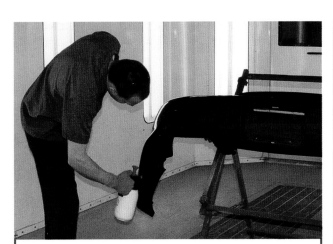

For convenience, body shops pour wax and grease remover into a spray bottle (just make sure that the bottle is labeled, as this is a clear liquid with few identifying characteristics). The wax and grease remover is sprayed, or wiped on with a clean cloth or new paper towel, and then wiped off with a second clean towel. Using anything less than a clean towel is simply defeating your purpose.

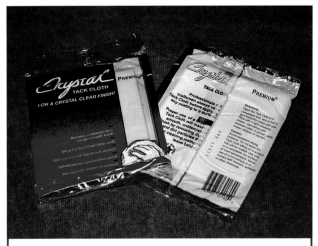

Use tack cloths to remove small particles of dust, dirt, or debris that may have been left behind by wax and grease remover. All surfaces should be cleaned with a tack cloth before you apply primer or paint. The less ideal your surroundings for spraying paint, the more you need to use a tack cloth.

additional wipe down using a glass cleaner. Ammonia in these glass-cleaning products helps to remove tiny traces of residual contaminant material and also assists in the removal of lingering moisture particles. Glass cleaner is simply sprayed onto surfaces and then wiped dry with a clean, soft, lint-free cloth.

TACK CLOTHS

The very last thing most painters do before actually spraying paint is wipe off body surfaces with a tack cloth. The special material used to make tack cloths allows them to pick up very fine particles of lint, dust, and other debris. As mentioned earlier, coats of paint almost always magnify imperfections on a primered surface. The process of wiping off body surfaces with a tack cloth helps ensure that bits of debris are removed so imperfections are not created. Do not rub tack cloths hard against the surface to be painted, as the residue may cause fish eyes.

You can buy tack cloths at any auto body paint and supply store. Their cost is minimal, especially when compared to the kind of intricate dust and lint removal they provide. It works best to open and unfold tack cloths and then lightly fold them back again. This sort of fluffs them up to make them more manageable. Be sure to take note of any package instructions or user recommendations to ensure adequate and complete cleaning.

THINNERS, REDUCERS, AND RETARDERS

In order for paint pigments and binders to cure and harden into a unified solid substance, the liquid parts of each paint mixture must evaporate. Those agents used to turn solid pigments and binders into liquids for sprayability are generically grouped and referred to as solvents. Thinners, reducers, and retarders all fall into the category of solvents.

The chemical makeup of various solvents, although similar in design and purpose, varies according to the type of pigments and binders used in particular paint products. Lacquer thinners are designed to work with lacquer-based products. Enamels require solvents containing different chemical blends, which are called enamel reducers. Lacquer thinner is not compatible with enamel products, and reducers are not generally compatible with lacquers. For all intents and purposes, the word thinner is associated with lacquer and the term reducer applies to enamels and urethanes.

A retarder is either a thinner or a reducer with an extra-slow evaporation time. Retarders are used for paint jobs that are sprayed during exceptionally hot weather, typically above 95 degrees Fahrenheit. Their function is to evaporate much more slowly than other thinners or reducers so paint does not dry too fast—which may cause checking, crazing, cracking, or other problems.

All of these paint solvent materials are designed for use under certain climatic conditions. They are related according to slow, medium, and fast evaporation abilities. In addition to temperature factors, you may need to use a specific solvent to compensate for very heavy or very light humidity. In essence, fast-evaporating solvents are used during paint work in cool temperatures, and slow ones employed during hot weather.

But using a fast solvent on a cool and very humid day could cause blushing, a condition in which moisture is trapped in paint after the fast solvent has evaporated. In

Thinners, reducers, and retarders all essentially do the same thing, however, it is extremely important that they be used with the correct product. Typically, thinners are used with lacquer-based products, while reducers are used with enamel- or urethane-based products. Using the correct product for the shop temperature is also very important. If, for instance, a reducer designed for hot weather (slows down the drying process) were used in a cooler temperature shop, the paint would not cure properly. On the other hand, if a cool temperature reducer (designed to speed drying times) was used in a warmer shop, the paint would blush, fade, or experience other problems.

that case, a medium thinner or reducer is needed to allow moisture time to evaporate along with solvent so that the resulting paint film dries completely and evenly.

Paint products are designed to be sprayed under climatic conditions of 70 degrees Fahrenheit and 30 percent humidity. These are perfect conditions under

The numbering of the product usually indicates the designed temperature range of slow, medium, and fast reducers. Fast reducers are designed for cooler temperatures, while slower reducers are for use in higher temperatures. As an example, DT860 is a fast reducer designed for use where the temperature is between 60 and 70 degrees Fahrenheit. DT885 should be used when the temperature is between 85 and 95 degrees Fahrenheit. These temperatures refer to the immediate spraying area (shop) where the product will be used, not the temperature outside.

which laboratory tests are conducted. You would have to paint cars in a controlled spray booth equipped with a dehumidifier and heater to achieve these perfect conditions all the time. To help you compensate for the lack of such a facility, which can easily cost $100,000 or more, paint chemists have designed various solvents that react differently under various atmospheric conditions.

To help inexperienced auto painters choose the correct solvent, labels on thinners, reducers, and retarders include the temperature range in which they are designed to be used.

To determine which rated solvent is best under the specific humidity conditions for the region you are working in, consult with an auto body paint and supply jobber. Jobbers are familiar with the atmospheric and climatic conditions in their areas. They want your paint job to result in a beautiful finish so you will be satisfied with their products and continue to buy merchandise from them in the future. Therefore, you should be able to rely on their advice about the use of various products and their application techniques.

Definitive information sheets and application guides, available at auto body paint and supply stores, will list specific paint-to-thinner and reducer mixing ratios. Although paint has already been mixed with certain amounts of solvent, since it is a liquid while in the can, even more solvent is needed to make the solution sprayable. Mixing sticks are used for this function according to product label instructions. The specific calibrations on mixing sticks are designed for use with certain bases and solvent. You must be sure to use a mixing stick designed specifically for the brand of paint product you use. Calibrated mixing sticks are readily available at auto body paint and supply stores—don't confuse them with wooden stir sticks!

PAINT REMOVERS

Automotive paint is removed from car bodies in basically three ways: sanding, media blasting, and chemical stripping. Auto body repairers remove paint from selected areas with coarse sanding discs on a high-speed sanding tool. More intense paint removal projects, like those for rusty and neglected hulks, require controlled media blasting. Both of these methods not only remove paint, they also take off undercoats and anything else covering bare metal.

Another method of removing paint down to bare metal is to use chemical strippers, which loosen paint material and make it easy to gently scrape off with a firm plastic squeegee or putty knife. The process is messy, as wet globs of paint are scraped off and fall to the floor. You must also be concerned about personal safety while using potent chemical strippers. Wear heavy-duty rubber gloves, eye protection, and a respirator as directed by the product label.

The use of chemical paint strippers is generally saved for complete new paint jobs, as opposed to auto body repair work to fix localized dents. For repair work, most auto body professionals quickly remove paint with a sander after the majority of dent repairs have been completed. This is because it is much easier to see surface imperfections, wrinkles, and low spots on painted body panels than on those with bare, shiny metal.

Sanding

For small projects or localized repair, an electric or pneumatic sander works quite well. You can easily remove paint from the immediate area that requires undercoat and paint application.

Using a 36- or 40-grit sanding disc, you can remove paint from a car body in no time. The extra-coarse discs also do a good job of removing all paint or body filler remnants from tiny dings and other hard to reach crevices. The heavy pattern of rather deep sanding scratches on sheet metal also serves as an excellent base for filler material adhesion.

Media Blasting

If you are completing a body-off restoration, or working on a relatively small part that can be removed from the vehicle, media blasting will probably be quicker than using a hand-held sander. This would be a more efficient way of removing paint and underlying primers from a complete body shell or chassis. With both media blasting and a hand-held sander, there is a down side. Either method, if concentrated on one area for too long, will cause excessive heat

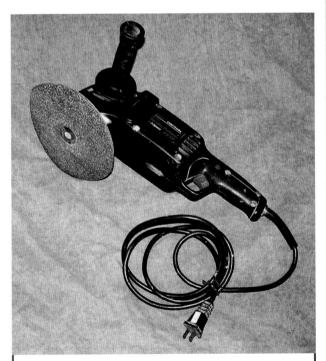

For the hobbyist, an electric sander/polisher such as this Craftsman model will work wonders.

buildup from friction, which can warp the sheet metal. You must then repair the warped metal before you can get back to your paint preparation.

Another drawback of media blasting is that, on a car body or truck cab, it is virtually impossible to remove all of the blasting media that accumulates between panels and within crevices. Some of this blasting media will eventually fall into your paint or interior upholstery, but will never be completely removed from the vehicle.

On the other hand, a good thing about media blasting is that with the correct media (plastic, walnut shells, etc.) and under the correct air pressure, it can be used on fiberglass or other nonsheet metal components. You must verify that the person who does your media blasting is competent in the various media available and the correct usage.

Chemical Stripping

Chemical paint removers work well on automobiles in need of a complete new paint job when the body is in almost perfect condition—in other words, when there is no compelling reason to roughen sheet metal with a sanding disc or take the chance that a mistake with sand-blasting equipment could cause panels to warp or otherwise be damaged by high-pressure media blasting away at its surface.

Although chemical strippers can easily damage nonmetallic items, such as rubber moldings or plastics, controlled applications and gentle material removal should result in a clean, shiny body surface with no ill effects. To further reduce the possibility of scratches or other scraping damage, consider using a heavy-duty plastic squeegee to remove wrinkled paint from body surfaces, instead of a metal putty knife.

A number of different brands of paint removers are available, but you might want to seek an auto body paint and supply salesperson's advice as to which particular product might be best suited to your needs. Use a sheet of heavy-duty plastic or cardboard under the edges of your car while removing chemically impregnated paint residue. This way, once the body is stripped, you can remove and discard the scrapings safely according to any local hazardous waste control regulations in effect in your area.

Chemical strippers are available in two basic forms, for dipping or brushing. When the body is going to be removed from the chassis, dipping it is a practical way to remove all paint and primer. For best results, everything to be dipped should be disassembled as completely as possible. This allows the chemical stripper to get into all of the places where rust may be hiding. This process removes all rust, leaving only shiny metal. Of course, if a band of rust is all that is holding the lower portion of a door or fender onto the upper portion, the lower portion may no longer be attached when the parts are lifted out of the rust removal vat.

Various types of products in bulk and in aerosol are available for removing paint. Some will be more effective than others, while some may cause surface damage to the material being stripped if not used on a compatible surface. Be sure to discuss your particular application with an expert at the paint and supply store to obtain the best product for the job.

Although the truck cab had been sandblasted (and all of the sand nearly impossible to remove), the doors for the author's one-time daily driver project were taken to Redi-Strip of Evansville (Indiana) to be chemically stripped. Upon their return, all paint, wax, grease, and most importantly rust had been eliminated. In their "like new" condition, surface preparation was the same as if they were new or reproduction parts.

Brushed-on chemical strippers should be reserved for relatively small jobs, such as a door or fender. Doing an entire vehicle by hand would be more expensive than disassembling it and having the components dipped.

PRIMER

There are many misperceptions about what primer is and does. Many believe this term simply refers to one product that adequately prepares car bodies for paint. Others think that a thick primer will hide dents and scratches, even out body surfaces, and allow paint to cover evenly. Some people even believe that primer will eliminate rust problems—quite the opposite is often true, as many primers (except epoxy primers) are actually very porous, therefore soaking up moisture. This works to increase the build-up of rust beneath the primer.

Simply put, primers are materials that are applied directly over properly prepared bare metal. Their category in the overall package of any paint system includes different products that are separately designed to provide a variety of surface preparation functions. Together, they could be clumped under the term undercoats: those materials applied to auto body surfaces in preparation for paint applications. Generally, these include epoxy primers, primer-surfacers, and sealers.

Epoxy Primer

Waterproof epoxy primers, like PPG's DP40LF, are used to protect bare metal from oxidation problems. Mixed with a hardener according to label instructions, catalyst-type epoxy primers are applied with a spray gun. One to two coats are normally recommended. Painters usually apply these kinds of primers to bare metal before the application of any other product. This is done for two reasons: first, since they are waterproof, they protect the sheet metal; second, epoxy primers offer excellent adhesion to metal, and they serve as perfect bases for additional undercoat products and top coats (paint).

As with other paint products, each manufacturer offers its own epoxy primer, and you are advised to use only those designed for the paint system you have chosen. Although the basic purpose of epoxy primers is to protect bare metal and offer quality adhesion bases, other catalyst-type primers in the same category are manufactured for different purposes. Some are designed to comply with strict military standards that require excellent corrosion resistance and exceptional adhesion capabilities. Others are made for aluminum surfaces or fiberglass materials.

In order to maximize oxidation, rust, and corrosion protection for sheet metal car bodies in regions with exceptionally harsh corrosion environments, like ocean coasts and areas where winter roads are salted, auto body painters have applied catalyzed epoxy primers to bare metal and

One of PPG's most popular products among hot rodders is its DP line of epoxy primers. Available in a variety of colors and now in a lead-free formula, it is an excellent choice for providing corrosion protection to bare metal. It is also suitable for use on other materials, as it greatly increases adhesion properties. It must be mixed with hardener DP401LF, for use with flexible parts, or DP402LF, for use as a sealer.

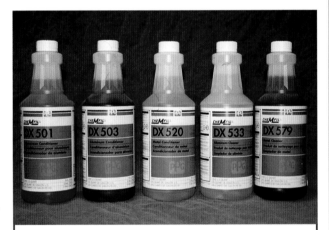

Metal and aluminum cleaners and conditioners are used to deep clean their respective surfaces to provide superior adhesion of subsequent primers and top coats, resulting in the best corrosion resistance. Each product has its own set of characteristics, so you should ask your paint and supply jobber for their recommendation on which to use for your particular application.

same company that produced the rest of the paint system. Because of their high solids content, primer-surfacers cover tiny imperfections and allow painters to sand the coated surfaces to smooth perfection.

These products must not be confused with body fillers, however. The materials used in body fillers offer a great deal more strength and durability than primer-surfacers. Where properly applied, fillers are designed to cover sheet metal imperfections up to ¼ inch in depth without cracking or chipping. Primer-surfacers are only intended to be sprayed on surfaces to fill very slight sand scratches or other tiny blemishes. They are a final means by which to smooth body surfaces to perfection.

Primer-surfacers are the final undercoat products that are designed to be sanded and smoothed. Undercoats applied after them are simply used to seal base materials against the absorption of paint solvents, or to increase overall paint adhesion. Therefore, it is imperative that their coats be applied uniformly and all sanding be executed in a controlled and systematic manner.

Although some primer-surfacers may resist moisture to a point where wet sanding can be completed with no problems, other products can actually absorb water. Therefore, while your car sports only a primer-surfacer finish, resist temptations to wash it or drive during periods of wet weather.

Should moisture find its way into primer-surfacer finishes, it could become trapped inside this porous, talc-based material and remain there after paint has been

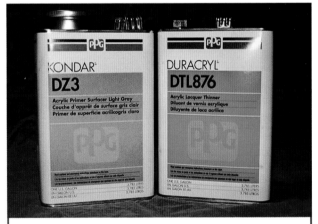

If your car needs any bodywork before painting, you will need to use at least some primer-surfacer and hardener. Although you should get the metal as straight as possible, and use body filler to further perfect the panel, a high-build primer-surfacer will be necessary to finish the task. Since you will be sanding much of the primer-surfacer off the vehicle anyway, some bodyshop professionals use a different color for each coat. This will help them determine high and low spots while sanding. Be sure your primer-surfacer is compatible with the primers below and your intended top coat.

then again over subsequent primer-surfacer undercoats. If you live in such an area, you should confirm the need, usefulness, and application procedure for additional epoxy primer coats with your auto body paint and supply jobber.

PRIMER-SURFACERS

After an automobile body has had its sheet metal repaired and received its required coats of epoxy primer, minor flaws might linger, such as sanding scratches. To cover them, painters use primer-surfacer products manufactured by the

SUPPORTING PRODUCTS

sprayed and cured. At that point, moisture could find its way to bare metal and start a rusting process, or, if thwarted in that direction by epoxy primer, it may travel toward the surface to cause problems with the paint finish.

Different primer-surfacers are designed for specific applications. While one may be best suited for use over an epoxy primer and serve as a base for a urethane top coat, another could be designed for use over aluminum or fiber-glass surfaces in preparation for lacquer paint. Be sure to read information sheets and application guides for any primer-surfacer product you intend to use, and remember that selection assistance can always be provided by auto body paint and supply store employees.

Be sure to purchase enough sandpaper of the proper grit to smooth the primer-surfacer after application. More than one sheet of sandpaper will be needed for just about every job, especially for those that entail entire full-body paint jobs. One coat of primer-surfacer is usually applied, and the cured surface block sanded with 150-grit. Another coat is then sprayed on over the first, and finish sanded with 320-grit and then perfected with 500-grit.

Most professionals use a guide coat (usually a black spray can enamel) over primer-surfacers. After adding the guide coat, you sand with a sanding block until all of the guide coat has been removed.

SEALERS

Paint manufacturers produce a number of sealers for an assortment of specific applications. Sealers protect under-coats from the materials and solvents in subsequently applied paint top coats, and add maximum adhesion capability for those top coats. Sealers also ensure uniform color match.

When applying new paint over an existing paint surface, you must consider the use of a sealer, especially when you are not exactly sure what type or brand of paint is currently on the vehicle's finish. Most sealers do not require sanding after they have been applied and cured. They simply form a sort of barrier between the undercoat and top coat.

Along with protecting undercoats from the absorption of paint solvents, sealers help to keep sand scratch swelling to a minimum. For example, let's say that some minor sand scratches are still present after you meticulously sanded the last coat of primer-surfacer. Absorption of a paint solvent will cause primer-surfacer sand scratches to swell and become more visible. As solvents evaporate, paint solids will fill the voids left behind by sand scratches to result in dull, scratchy-looking finishes.

Sealers also offer paint top coats a uniform base to maximize color uniformity. A properly prepared surface sprayed with an appropriate sealer, as your paint system requirements designate, gives paint its best chance of forming an even film with uniform solvent evaporation to ensure all painted areas exhibit the identical color without

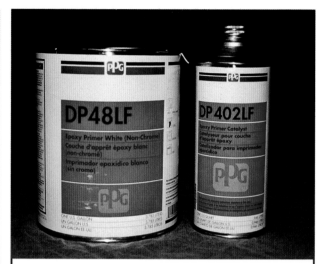

Regardless of whether you do any bodywork, apply sealer to the entire surface to be painted. This keeps solvents used with the top coats from seeping into the fillers or primers beneath and minimizes sand scratch swelling. The sealer coat should also provide a uniform color of primer for the paint to cover. If you were painting your vehicle a light color, it may take more coats to cover an area where dark-colored body filler was used. It would also take a different number of coats to cover darker primer as opposed to lighter primer. Since the sealer (usually a primer type of material with different mixing ratios) has good hiding qualities, it will cover most bodywork and differences in primer colors. The same amount of color can then be sprayed over the entire surface to be painted, resulting in maximum color uniformity. The color of the sealer will also have some effect on the color of the top coat. A white sealer will make brighter colors tend to jump off the vehicle, while darker sealers will make the paint look deeper.

blotches, clouds, or bleed-through. This is especially important when painting a light color over an existing dark hue.

Sealers are also advantageous for those jobs on which new paint will be sprayed over factory finishes that were baked on at temperatures around 450 degrees Fahrenheit. Because those stock paint jobs are so hard and durable, new paint may have a difficult time penetrating the surface to achieve maximum adhesion. A common mistake by inexperienced painters is to simply spray new paint directly over existing finishes without scuffing or sealing base surfaces. The results of this can range from massive random paint flaking, to the extreme, in which fresh paint layers can be peeled off in sheets.

Sealers can make the difference between an adequate paint job and an excellent one. Confirm with the paint and supply salesperson the exact kind of sealer product to use with your paint system. Be sure to refer to application guides and information sheets for mixing instructions and other pertinent product user recommendations.

SPECIAL ADDITIVES

A variety of additives are available to prevent or eliminate various problems that may present themselves as you paint your car or truck. Among these are fish eye eliminators, chip resistant coatings, and special additives for use on flexible components. For the most part, these additives should not be used unless your paint project involves the problems or circumstances they're designed to address.

Fish eye Eliminators

Tiny surface finish blemishes that resemble small circles of popped paint bubbles, which seem to occur almost as soon as paint hits an auto body surface, could be fish eyes. These flaws are generally caused by silicone residue. Small traces of silicone do not allow paint to settle evenly; rather, they cause material to encircle the speck of silicone and form a volcano-like shape.

Fish eye problems result from extended use of silicone-based vinyl dressings on body side moldings and other trim. Excessive dressing applications and their random overspray away from trim infiltrates surrounding paint surfaces to become embedded in finishes. Although these painted surfaces may be thoroughly cleaned before paint application, silicone particles commonly remain to cause fish eye problems.

Auto body paint protectants, like polyglycoats and other silicone-based materials, can also cause fish eye problems. In severe cases, silicone materials are absorbed by paint finishes to the point that underlying metal becomes saturated with silicone, making quality repaint efforts an almost impossible task.

Although fish eye preventers are available, their use is not widely recommended, as you are just fighting fire with fire, or actually silicone with silicone. The best way to eliminate fish eye problems is to thoroughly wash the entire vehicle before doing any paint prep work. A bucket of warm water with some ordinary dishwashing soap, such as Dove or Ivory, should be used to clean the entire painted surface of the vehicle. When it is clean and dry, you should then use a wax and grease remover to help remove any other residue. If you are going to be repainting the entire vehicle, a somewhat more aggressive cleanser such as Comet may be used to wash the vehicle to help eliminate fish eye problems.

For the extreme case in which thorough cleaning does not eliminate fish eyes, paint manufacturers have developed paint additives, which overcome the dilemma of fish eyes and allow paint to flow uniformly and cover evenly. Various paint manufacturing companies label their fish eye eliminators under certain names, like PPG's Omni AU MX194 Fish Eye Eliminator, Glasurit's Antisilicone Additive, and DuPont's Fish Eye Eliminator 9259S. Be sure to use only that product designed to be mixed with the paint being used; for example use PPG's Fish Eye Preventer with PPG paint products.

Fish eyes are caused by contaminants such as silicone on the paint surface. Fish eye eliminator contains much silicone, allowing the new paint to span over these contaminants. Once you have used fish eye eliminator, however, your paint spray gun is contaminated and fish eyes will always be a problem when you use that gun. For this reason, most professionals avoid fish eye eliminator. Instead of reaching for this product, you should thoroughly wash the vehicle with lots of water and some car wash soap (or even a heavier duty cleanser such as Comet or Ajax) to completely remove any contaminants from the vehicle's surface prior to doing any bodywork or surface preparation. Then use wax and grease remover.

Mixing instructions are provided on container labels. In addition, it is recommended you use the fish eye eliminator product throughout your entire paint job. Do not simply mix in a prescribed dose to paint one panel that seems to exhibit fish eye problems; rather, use that same mixture for the entire repaint to guarantee that color tints and coverage smoothness is the same.

To reduce fish eye problems during future paint touchups or repaints, use multipurpose vinyl dressings sparingly. Instead of spraying trim pieces directly, spray dressing on a soft cloth first and then wipe it on parts in a controlled fashion. Afterward, be sure to wash the entire car thoroughly with a high-quality car wash soap to remove traces of lingering silicone residue.

Flexible Additives

Newer cars frequently feature flexible urethane bumpers, spoilers, splash guards, and ground effects that are usually painted in body color. For the most part, paint products used to cover these pieces are the same as those used to paint bodies. However, since these types of parts are flexible, a special additive is mixed in with lacquer or enamel paint to allow its thin film to bend and conform along with the body part without cracking, peeling, or chipping. This

One of the most important things to do prior to sanding, priming, or painting, is to make sure your vehicle is as clean as it can be. Prior to doing any bodywork, the affected panels (or complete vehicle) should be thoroughly washed, using a mild car wash soap, or even dishwashing liquid, and plenty of water. Rinse just as thoroughly. Prior to even sanding any of the panels, use wax and grease remover. Quite simply, if the sheet metal isn't clean, body filler, primer, and paint are not going to adhere properly.

During the 1980s and 1990s, flexible components such as bumpers, spoilers, and fender flares became more common on vehicles. The paint products that were being used at that time required a flex additive to prevent them from cracking and peeling. Those flexible body components are still in use, yet most paints and applications no longer require additives.

kind of additive is critical if you want the painted finish on flexible parts to last. The use of flex additives is not as common as it was at one time. With lacquers and enamels, flex additives were a necessity; however, they are not required with urethane products.

According to PPG's *Full Line Catalog*, its Flexative Elastomeric Additive can be mixed directly with acrylic lacquers, acrylic enamels, urethane-modified acrylic enamels, and acrylic urethanes to repair flexible body parts. Specific instructions call for part surfaces to be clean and then sanded to promote paint adhesion. Once again, each paint manufacturer recommends its own brand of flexible additive to be used with its brand of paint products.

In addition to flexible painted bumpers and bumper guards, be alert to using a flexible additive when painting any other similar material. This includes flexible spoilers, fender flares, entire front nose pieces, and mud flaps.

ADDITIONAL ITEMS

OK, you have your wax and grease remover, primer, sealer, paint (color), clear, sandpaper, masking tape, a new spray gun, and the appropriate safety equipment. What could you have possibly forgotten? A few more items will make your painting job easier. Except for the cleanup solvent, these items are usually free, so you might as well use them.

Spray Out Cards

An extremely handy tool that will help you ensure proper paint coverage is a spray out card. They are available from your paint and supply jobber, and in most cases are free for

the asking. If there is a charge, it is minimal, and well worth the price. The spray out card is black and white, with some text printed on it.

Before spraying any paint on your vehicle, apply paint to the spray out card, using the same procedure as on your vehicle. Use the same overlap pattern, spray gun settings, and time between coats. Apply enough coats to the spray out card so that the black and white and text is completely covered. The number of coats required to do this is the number of coats that will be required when painting your car as well. This spray out card also serves as a test for color match.

Stir Sticks and Paint Strainers

You will also need stir sticks and paint strainers. Even though your paint products (undercoats or top coats) have been mixed at the factory, they will still require stirring by the end user. Paint retailers provide stir sticks free upon request.

Paint strainers filter out impurities or grit. Some professional painters strain paint products as they are being poured into the mixing cup, while others do not. However, they all strain the product as it goes into the spray gun cup. Whether you are spraying primer, sealer, or top coat, it must be strained to avoid getting dirt and debris in your spray gun.

Cleanup Thinner or Reducer

Ask your paint supplier what product to use for cleaning your spray gun. Instead of using the same expensive thinner or reducer that you are using with your paint products, most paint retailers have some less expensive products designed for that purpose. Some jobbers may not carry a less expensive product, but it is worth asking. Other than the expense, there is nothing wrong with using the same reducer for cleanup as you mix with paint. Just be sure that you have something to clean your spray gun with before you fill it up with a product that has a short pot life.

OVERVIEW

Compared to a decade ago, decisions regarding automobile painting have increased dramatically. Now, not only do you have tens of thousands of colors to choose from, you also have to determine which kind of solvent, primer, primer-surfacer, and sealer to use—and, for that matter, which products you do not need to use. The technology surrounding the auto paint industry has really become high-tech. Even professional painters sometimes have to suffer through difficult decisions relating to paint procedures on cars that have been repainted one or two times with an unknown type of paint, or worse yet, more than one type sprayed onto different body panels.

Before starting your paint job, research thoroughly what has to be done to prepare the vehicle's surface, and which paint products you'll need to complete the job safely, effectively, and with excellent results. Haphazardly starting a project with little concern over a systematic and organized

Even though you should ask your paint supplier to shake up your paint in the paint shaker, you will still need to stir it by the time you get to your painting location, so make sure you have some paint stir sticks. You will also need to stir up undercoat products, as those cans don't fit in the paint shaker. Stir sticks also come in handy for use as sanding blocks and as a means to check gaps between panels. Paint strainers are essential when pouring paint products into your spray gun cup. The slightest impurity in your spray gun can deal you more headaches than you can imagine.

approach will do nothing but delay the overall process and probably cause frustration over missed completion dates and the extra work needed to go over areas that were not properly serviced the first time.

Remember that all automotive paint products are potentially dangerous. Just about every product is flammable and you have to be keenly aware of all heat and flame sources whenever working with them. Flash fires involving clouds of flammable gases will quickly engulf your shop, garage, carport, and most importantly, you. Have a fire extinguisher available at all times just in case.

Personal safety has become an intense issue with the use of automotive painting chemicals. Every label of every product will clearly recommend the use of certain personal safety equipment. Heed those recommendations to protect your health. Should you have any questions about the intended use or function of any auto paint product or piece of related equipment, do not hesitate to consult an auto body paint and supply salesperson, manufacturer information sheet or application guide, professional auto painter, or paint manufacturer.

Spray out cards are the sliced bread of the auto painter's world. The one at the left is before paint (the yellow/green image is glare from an overhead light), while the other has received a few test coats of a particular blue paint. From the paint supplier, the cards are black and white, with some black text printed on the white portion. Prior to painting your car, you should apply enough coats (with proper drying times, spray gun settings, etc.) to achieve complete coverage of the black, white, and text. Whether it takes a single coat or several, this will tell you how many coats you'll need to apply to your vehicle. The spray out cards also serve as a final color matching check, instead of using an actual portion of the vehicle.

It is almost impossible to complete any job without the right tools, materials, and equipment. Automotive painting is no different from any other chore and you must expect to buy, borrow, or rent some rather specialized equipment if you expect to prepare an auto body surface properly and then paint it with results comparable to that of a professional.

Auto body paint and supply stores carry a wide selection of repair and painting tools and equipment. In most cases, this merchandise is designed for commercial use and will be of heavy-duty construction and quality. The cost may be high, but you could easily expect each item to last a long time with proper maintenance. You might opt instead to purchase required equipment from tool outlets or other stores that sell the items. These other places might carry items built a little less heavy-duty, which would cost less.

The Eastwood Company sells tools and equipment especially designed for both part-time and serious auto restorers, auto body repair technicians, and painters. All of the tools and equipment it sells are tested in its field laboratory, a quality shop where auto restoration and repair projects are ongoing. Eastwood advertises that each item listed in its catalog has been used in their shop with satisfactory results. Talk to other auto enthusiasts to see what equipment and suppliers they've had good luck with on their paint projects.

In lieu of purchasing or borrowing tools or equipment, you could rent items at a local rental shop. Although most rental shops make valiant attempts to keep all of their inventory in top condition, you may have some trouble finding paint guns that spray as expected. This is because tiny air and material ports are easily clogged with dry paint if they are not immediately cleaned after each use. Therefore, you might seriously consider spending a few dollars to buy your own paint spray gun so that you can guarantee it will be taken care of properly and will operate as expected every time.

WORK AREA

If you wanted to apply a nonskid paint job to your car that was rough enough to prevent a sheet of ice from falling off of it, you could apply almost any paint in a desert sandstorm and call it good. A little smoother texture, you say? Then try painting your car in a carport with a dirt and gravel floor. But, if what you really want is a smooth, blemish-free, lustrous, deep-shine paint job, consider renting a regular auto spray booth or spending a little time to devise a makeshift paint booth in your garage or workshop.

Because of the increasing restrictions regulating the auto paint industry, limitations are being placed on how and where auto paint can be sprayed. The advent of High Volume/Low Pressure (HVLP) systems is a great help, but along with them, painters in certain regions are required to

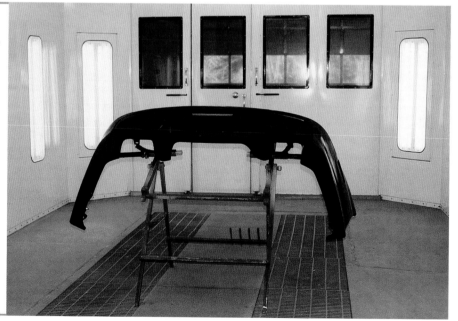

The essentials of a spray booth or paint spraying area are a sufficiently clean area, adequate lighting (too much is almost unheard of), room to move around without bumping into painted parts, a method of supporting or hanging parts, and an air supply for spraying the paint. If the area is not clean, air pressure will circulate dust, which will land on your freshly applied paint. Proper lighting is essential to verify that you have obtained complete paint coverage. And you need space so you don't rub the paint off of one piece with your backside while you are painting another. Small parts can usually be hung with welding wire or coat hangers, while larger pieces will need to be supported on saw horses, barrels, or whatever you have.

use high-tech spray booths equipped with downdraft ventilation systems and overspray capturing mechanisms.

To offset the staggering price of their booths, some paint shops make them available for rent—under supervised conditions, of course. You may be able to find rental booths through advertisements in your telephone book yellow pages under the heading "Auto Body Repair and Painting." You can also check with your auto body paint and supply jobber, auto parts store salesperson, and even make a few calls to local body shops to determine if they rent their booths, or know of any other body shops that offer theirs for rent.

A definite problem exists when renting paint booths, however, in that you have to transport your car to that location. Whether it is driven or towed, masking will have to be completed at that booth's location, along with possible part dismantling, such as lights, and required cleaning. Be sure transporting is done on a dry day with dry roads.

Should you decide to paint your vehicle at home, you must provide a suitable work area. A garage or shop should be fine. Plenty of air ventilation must be provided and overspray concerns accounted for. You will need an air compressor, lots of light, and an electrical source to operate a fresh air respirator compressor, if called for.

Rather than spray cars in an open garage and cover everything in the place with speckles of overspray, consider enclosing an area with sheets of clear plastic. Long, wide sheets of clear plastic sheeting are available at lumber yards and hardware stores. Roll an edge of plastic around strips of lath and nail them to the ceiling or rafters. Use heavy-duty duct tape to secure bottom edges to the floor. Consider placing plastic across open rafters as a makeshift ceiling to prevent dust from the attic space from falling onto your paint surface. Be sure not to put plastic too close to light fixtures, as hot bulbs could melt or ignite it.

To aid ventilation, put a large fan near the front of your work space. A hole can be cut in plastic for a fan to bring in fresh air from outside of the enclosure. Tape a thin, lint-free cloth over the fan's cage to trap dust or debris. Leave the garage door open to assist in ventilation, but be certain that local breezes will not flow directly from the outside in through the open door. If that is a problem, determine when breezes are minimal, maybe early in the morning, and plan to paint at that time.

If a gravel or dirt driveway is located right outside your garage or workshop, you will have to thoroughly wet it down to keep dust at an absolute minimum. You might even have to leave a light sprinkler spray in place during paint work to keep dust particles from being kicked up and blown all over your painting surface. It has often been suggested to wet down the floor in your paint enclosure to keep down dust. Under certain circumstances, this may be necessary, however, this practice should be avoided if possible. Wetting down the floor introduces humidity to your painting environment, which may cause more problems than what you are trying to eliminate. Be careful and avoid using electrical devices when working on a wet surface—doing so could get you electrocuted.

SAFETY REGULATIONS

Fortunately for users of most paint products, the paint manufacturers have been saddled with the responsibility of making their products environmentally safe and user-friendly. The manufacturers are continually striving to lower the amount of VOCs in their products. There is nothing that the user can do to lower the amount of VOCs in the paint itself, however, end users must obey local laws that govern the use and disposal of these products.

Protecting the Environment

Most federal and local laws governing the use of paint products are aimed at protecting the environment. In the United States, California has the most restrictive laws. Check with your local paint supply jobber for the latest laws in your area.

Painters in California are restricted to using waterborne products for most of their painting, along with downdraft spray booths for certain spraying operations. In the parts of the country that do not require the use of waterborne products, these products are typically not available in paint supply stores. The good thing about this is that you can use whatever product your favorite paint supply store has to offer. If the product is on the shelf, it has been deemed compliant with whatever local laws are in effect.

Most regulations are keyed to the amount of painting to be done. A shop that advertises and operates as an auto body repair and refinish business is obviously going to be under the watchful eye of the local authorities that govern that type of activity in your area. However, if you are purchasing only enough of those same products to repaint one car or truck, other than perhaps a pesky neighbor, no one is going to notice or care for the most part. To make your life easier though, you should use common sense, and not advertise the fact that you are using volatile chemicals to any of your neighbors who are not fond of your interest in automobiles. Remember too that these chemicals are regulated because of the dangers they pose to human health and the environment, and make your own health and safety and that of your neighbors paramount.

What do you do with the leftover paint products when the job is over? That will vary in your particular area, however, pouring it on the ground is a definite no-no. Some paint jobbers will dispose of your leftover paint products for a nominal fee, as they have to pay to have it disposed of. At least it will be disposed of properly. Information sheets for all paint products will provide disposal

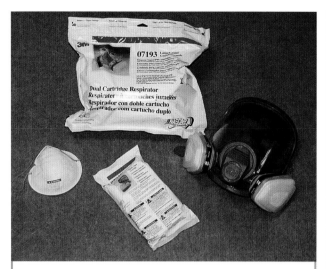

Different jobs require different types of protection. When sanding, a simple paper mask (sometimes referred to as a nuisance mask) will usually keep sanding dust out of your nose, and therefore out of your lungs and sinuses. At the minimum, you should use a half-mask that utilizes charcoal cartridges when spraying most automotive paint undercoat and top coat products. For additional protection, a full mask (which also uses charcoal cartridges) can be used at any time. When spraying any product that contains isocyanates, you must have a charcoal filtered mask and your eyes and skin completely covered. If using a half-mask, a head sock, goggles, and cap will provide the same protection as the full mask. Charcoal cartridges are replaceable on both types of masks, but it is less expensive simply to replace a half-mask. No matter which type of mask you use, the cartridges and/or the mask should be replaced after 24 hours of use.

recommendations. If you have any questions as to the correct procedure for product disposal, you can verify what is appropriate in your area by checking with your local paint jobber.

Protecting Yourself

Although the government may not care that you are spraying paint in your own garage, your body will. Decades ago, painters could get by with tying a bandana over their mouth and nose and be alright, as the prime concern was avoiding multicolored nose hair. Those days are now long gone.

You may not be breaking any laws if you do not wear the proper safety equipment as you spray paint, but violating this law will kill you in time. You may not die tomorrow or next week, but paint products are among the most dangerous available if proper precautions are not taken.

The paint manufacturers list the necessary safety equipment (breathing masks, skin protection, etc.,) and include precautions on the labels and information sheets for all of their products. It is imperative that you follow their recommendations.

Charcoal filter masks are suitable for most (but not all) undercoat products. These are relatively inexpensive for masks with replaceable cartridges, and disposable units are even less expensive. Charcoal filters should be replaced after 24 hours of use in a painting environment. When not in use, the entire mask should be stored in a resealable freezer bag.

Any paint product that contains isocyanates (epoxy primer, or any product that requires mixing with a hardener) requires the most complete protection. Isocyanates are not only inhaled, they are also absorbed through tear ducts in the eyes or through skin pores. A complete covering of the body with painter's coveralls, rubber gloves, goggles, and a hat are necessary to protect yourself when using these products.

If you're considering making a profession out of painting automobiles, I recommend a fresh air supplied hood. This is a hood that covers the entire head and face, and is connected to its own air compressor to supply fresh air to the user. When used in conjunction with painter's coverall's and rubber gloves, this offers the ultimate in protection from isocyanates. However, the cost for such a unit may be prohibitive for people who are painting their first vehicle.

As long as you are using a charcoal filtered mask (with fresh cartridges), and you are wearing goggles, a hat, rubber gloves, and a pair of painter's coveralls, you will be safe. As this is written, all of these can be purchased for around $50. This is an extremely small price to pay for health.

Paint products are most dangerous when they are being atomized, as when sprayed from a paint spray gun, however, they can be nearly as bad when the dried paint is being sanded. A filtered mask should be worn at that time as well.

Lighting

Except for extreme conditions, you cannot have too much light to paint. Light will reveal imperfections more clearly, allowing you to correct or remove them before they are painted over. Proper lighting will expose all areas of the parts or pieces that you are painting, providing you the opportunity for complete coverage with paint, and eliminating touch up later.

You must beware that your homebrewed lighting setup doesn't cause excessive localized heat that may cause blemishes in the paint. Most paint spray booths feature fluorescent light fixtures that are cooler than most other types of light.

Room to Work

Even though auto bodywork is dusty and dirty, your work area must not be cluttered. You must have room to walk around the vehicle or parts thereof that you are painting. Can you imagine the agony of straightening a fender or door to perfection, only to trip and fall into it just after applying a fresh coat of paint?

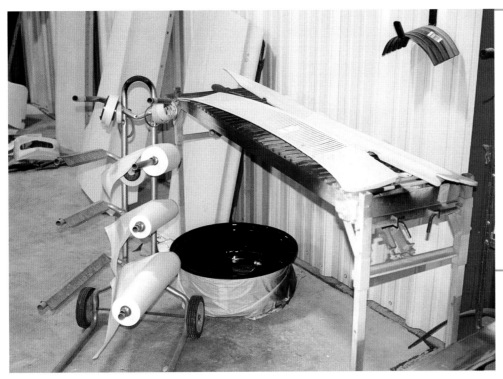

Your painting area should have adequate lighting, proper ventilation, a flat surface for mixing paint, and the means by which to hang small parts or subassemblies. Even if the situation is temporary, anything else that can be removed from your temporary spray booth should be.

SANDING

Quality paint jobs cannot be accomplished when paint is applied to improperly prepared surfaces. Paint products are not designed to fill cracks, crevices, or other surface irregularities. Rather, they will sink into these imperfections to magnify their depth and roughness. Therefore, you will have to spend as much time as necessary to sand all coats of primer-surfacer or existing paint surfaces to absolutely smooth perfection. All professional painters will quickly agree that by far most of their time is spent preparing cars for paint, rather than actually spraying them. A variety of sandpaper grits and useful hand tools are available for smoothing chores.

Sandpaper

Sandpaper is rated according to its relative coarseness, low numbers being coarsest and higher numbers finer. For example, 36-grit sandpaper is extremely coarse and 1,200-grit is superfine, almost smooth. Auto body paint and supply stores carry the widest selection of sandpaper grits, both in the type used for dry sanding only, and those that can be used dry or with water. Wet sanding is generally saved for those operations required to smooth blemishes on lacquer or urethane paints after they have been sprayed and cured.

To complement their assortment of sandpaper grits, paint and supply stores carry these products in various sizes and shapes. You can buy sheets of sandpaper measuring about a foot square that can be cut or folded to suit user needs. You can also take advantage of sandpaper strips with

Unless you have recently looked at the sandpaper at an autobody and paint supply store, you would not believe the variety of sanding products currently available. Where the choice used to be between open coat or wet or dry sandpaper, it now includes different backing types and shapes for a wide variety of sanding apparatus. Sandpaper can attach with a sticky backing or hook-and-loop type material on the paper itself, or with spring-loaded clips on the sanding device. Once you decide on what backing material you need for your sanding blocks, you still need to choose the correct grit for the job you are doing. Sandpaper ranges from 36-grit for roughing in body filler to 2,000-grit for final wet sanding.

or without adhesive backing for use on long sanding boards, or adhesive-backed discs for use with circular pads on dual-action (DA) sanders. Be sure to purchase enough sandpaper to complete your job, as one sheet is rarely enough for more than one small repair operation.

Sanding Blocks and Boards

For flat and even sanding, you must use a sanding block or board. Using your hand alone will result in minute low spots or grooves, caused by the hand's irregular shape and nonrigid nature. Knuckle protrusions featured on the palm side of your hand cause the sandpaper under them to dig in, while the rest of the sanding area receives only slight pressure and minimal smoothing. Sanding blocks and boards, on the other hand, provide flat, rigid bases that easily receive and disperse identical pressure over entire sanding surfaces.

Sanding blocks and boards are available at auto body paint and supply stores and some auto parts houses. Three sizes are commonly offered. The smallest, a little larger than the palm of your hand, is handy for reaching into tight areas confined by body designs or other obstructions. A medium size works great for sanding touchup areas that encompass small panel areas. Long blocks and boards work best for sanding chores on full panels, deck lids, and hoods. As a general rule of thumb, using the largest sanding board or block that will work within the area that you are sanding will give the best results.

One-Off Tools

Custom sanding blocks and boards have been designed for special applications. Rounded bases provide an excellent means for sanding curved body features, like grooves and arched fender flares. Small hand pads work best for smoothing imperfections near ridges, acute corners, and other unique spots too small for normal blocks or boards. Most of these items are also on display at your local auto body and paint supply store, and are available through auto-related equipment and tool outlets. Of course, when it comes to sanding, lots of oddball items found in the shop have been used to fit into a body seam or crevice. Everything from radiator hoses to paint stir sticks have been used as impromptu sanding blocks. As long as the sanding "block" and the body panel shape are compatible, whatever helps you achieve a smooth panel is precisely the tool you need at the time.

Sanding Machines

Sanding machines basically consist of pneumatic or electric hand sanders. Their use is not always required, especially for small jobs. However, on complete repaints or vehicles that have undergone body repair, these tools can help to cut the amount of time spent sanding. Beware, however, as a powerful sanding machine in the hands of an inexperienced operator can quickly do more harm than good.

High-speed rotary sanders are most commonly used to remove old paint, old body filler, and rust deposits on sheet metal panels. They can also be used to remove or smooth grossly jagged fingers of fiberglass that stick out from cracks and other collision damage to panels on fiberglass body vehicles. For the most part, these tools are employed by

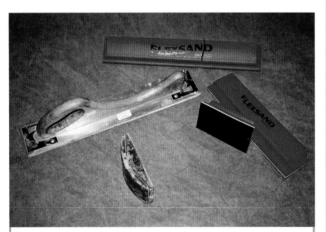

Sanding boards and blocks come in a variety of sizes and types. For large, flat panels, a rigid sanding board with a wooden handle should be used to eliminate waves and valleys. Sandpaper is usually attached by fitting under a clip on each end of the board. For areas that have broad curves, flexible blocks should be used. They are flexible enough to bend with the curvature of the panel, yet still eliminate waves and valleys. Sandpaper attaches to these particular blocks with a hook-and-loop system. A third type of sanding block is the rubber type, and is available in a variety of sizes. The largest possible sanding block that you can use will yield the best results.

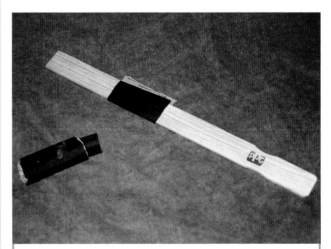

Don't throw away those used or extra paint stir sticks. Although you may need to cut them down, they work great as sanding blocks for small, intricate areas. You may also use pieces of radiator or heater hoses when sanding areas that have a small radius.

Although this Makita grinder is used more for welding projects, its smaller disc size (4 inches) makes it handy for many situations. For grinding away rust on heavy steel (such as a car chassis), the grinding disc as shown can be used. It can also be equipped with a wire brush attachment that could be used to strip paint off a car body.

auto body repair technicians, although painters do use them to remove years of accumulated paint and rust deposits from vehicles scheduled for full paint jobs.

With bases shaped like long sanding boards, air files make quick work of smoothing layers of plastic filler on wide panels, like door skins. Their internal mechanisms operate bases in a rapid back-and-forth direction. Users must constantly keep these tools moving because if allowed to rest on one spot, their forceful action will cause definite grooves, waves, or other imperfections. Like rotary sanders, air files can cut the amount of work required if used properly, or quickly cause more work if you are not careful.

Two pieces of equipment that you will find in any body shop are a DA sander (left) and an air file (right). The round pad on a DA sander is best used on curved surfaces, while the air file is best used on straight or flat panels. With the proper grit sandpaper attached, they can make short work of smoothing body filler when used properly. However, if used improperly, they can do more harm than good.

Dual-action (DA) sanders are a mainstay in professional auto paint shops. Their unique design causes a circular pad to move in orbital directions instead of just spinning in a high-speed circle. An offset counterweight working in conjunction with an oval-shaped mounting mechanism allows DA pads to be forced back and forth and side to side in a very fast movement. Speed controls allow for intricate sanding, and assortments of sandpaper grit discs can be used for anything from initial sanding to fine finishing.

DA sanders are available in different sizes and power ranges. Large tools work best for body repair jobs, and small ones are handiest for paint preparation work. You will find DAs at auto body paint and supply stores as well as some tool houses.

MASKING

No matter how skilled you are with a spray gun, any areas that are not to be painted must be covered with masking paper or tape. The time and effort to clean up overspray will quickly exceed that needed to mask off the area.

Tape

Almost everyone is familiar with masking tape. But did you know there is a drastic difference between the rolls of masking tape found at ordinary hardware stores and those specifically designed for automotive painting jobs? There is, and the difference in their designs could make a definite difference in the outcome of your paint job.

Ordinary household masking tape has not been treated to withstand potent auto paint solvents. Paint can penetrate weak tape to ruin the finishes underneath. In addition, adhesives used in ordinary masking tape are not designed to easily break loose from surfaces and can remain on painted bodies after the bulk of material has been pulled off. Lingering traces of tape and adhesive residue might require use of a mild solvent for complete removal, a chore that could threaten the finish or new paint applied next to it.

Whether your job consists of a very small paint touchup or complete paint job, you have to realize that automotive paint masking tape is the only product designed for such use. Using any other type of inexpensive alternative is just asking for problems and aggravation.

Auto body paint and supply stores sell masking tape in various widths. Sizes range from ⅛ inch up to a full 2 inches. Each masking job presents different needs, and having more than one size of masking tape on hand will help you accomplish those chores more quickly and easily. For example, it is much simpler to place a few strips of 2-inch-wide masking tape over a headlight, than having to maneuver a sheet of masking paper over that same relatively small area.

For masking designs, or to ensure perfect masking tape edges along trim and molding, many painters initially lay down a thin ⅛-inch wide strip of Fine Line plastic tape. Made

At least seven different widths (⅛-, ¼-, ⅜-, ½-, ¾-, 1-, and 2-inch) of masking tape are available from most autobody paint and supply stores. For the hobbyist, the ⅜-, ¾-, and 2-inch widths will probably suffice for most of your needs. Other sizes may be necessary, depending on your particular vehicle and your creativity. The smaller sizes are typically used for detailed masking of specific items that cannot be removed, while the wider sizes are for surfaces that are not large enough to justify masking paper. Generally, ¾- and 1-inch sizes are used for almost everything else and also for taping the seams of masking paper.

Plastic tape is different from masking tape, although its purpose is roughly the same. Although veteran painters can quickly tell the difference, plastic tape is usually blue to distinguish it from regular masking tape. Plastic tape is thinner and has more flex to it. Though not available in as many different widths as masking tape, each size of plastic tape can go around a tighter radius curve without kinking or bunching. For this reason, it is used for two distinct situations. When masking along an intricately shaped piece of trim, the plastic tape can more easily follow the outline to mask the edge. The second and perhaps more common use for plastic tape is for outline masking flames, scallops, or other artwork.

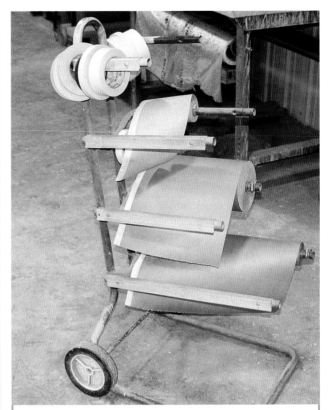

A masking paper rack makes masking chores much easier. Choosing among various widths of paper dispensed with masking tape already along one edge beats trying to hold down a piece of newspaper with one hand, while attaching masking tape with the other. Consider purchasing a masking paper rack before you attempt to do any masking on your vehicle. Even if you buy one that has only one size of paper, it will save you a fair amount of time. With a little bit of ingenuity, you could probably build a makeshift masking paper rack fairly easily.

by 3M, Fine Line is very maneuverable and will adhere securely around curves without bending or folding. It is easy to use as a primary masking edge along trim and molding edges. After you have the Fine Line in place, you can add ¾-inch or wider tape anywhere along it, sparing you the task of getting each piece right at the edge of the masked part.

Painters use more rolls of ¾-inch masking tape than any other. Its versatile size works great for securing paper and covering small items such as key locks. For a complete vehicle paint job, expect to use at least two rolls of 2-inch-wide tape and three rolls of ¾-inch. If you contemplate masking along trim or molding pieces, have a couple rolls of ⅛-inch Fine Line handy. Expect to pay anywhere from $2.50 to $5 per roll for quality automotive masking tape. Each roll is generally 60 yards long, the same as rolls of masking paper.

Paper

Seldom will you find professional auto painters using anything but treated masking paper for any masking job. Newspaper has been used by some inexperienced painters with mixed results. Although newspaper material may seem inexpensive and appropriate for paint masking chores, it is porous and can let paint seep through to mar surface finishes underneath.

Rolls of quality automotive paint masking paper are available at auto body paint and supply stores. Their widths range from 4 inches up to 3 feet, with 12-inch widths being the most frequently used size. This paper is chemically treated to prevent paint or solvent penetration, a most important asset. Two rolls of 12-inch paper should be enough for most jobs. You'll need a roll of wider paper to cover roofs, hoods and trunk lids in situations where they will not be painted at all, or will be sprayed a different color than body sides. A roll of 4- or 6-inch paper could be handy for intricate masking, as is necessary around doorjambs, trunk, and hood edges.

To make their masking jobs easier, professional painters use masking paper and tape racks designed to allow paper to be pulled off with tape already attached to the edge. The Eastwood Company offers a small, hand-held model that can accommodate paper widths up to 9 inches. To help you easily retrieve strips of masking paper, consider mounting a piece of heavy dowel on the side of your workbench with long brackets, so rolls can rotate freely as you pull off needed lengths.

AIR COMPRESSOR

You could buy the most expensive auto paint products made, spend weeks and weeks preparing your car or truck's surface to perfection, use the most highly advanced spray paint gun available, and then ruin your paint job by relying upon an inadequate air compressor or a holding tank loaded with moisture and oil residue.

One cannot overemphasize the importance of a clean, dry, and controlled source of air pressure for any spray paint job. Miniscule particles of water, oil, or rust will find their way from holding tanks to spray gun nozzles unless they are captured and retained somewhere between the compressor and spray gun. If allowed to accumulate, and eventually exit a spray gun's nozzle, these contaminants will blemish

This portable air compressor from Sears, a four-horsepower model with a 25-gallon tank, is typical of many units found in home shops. Comparable and slightly larger units are readily available for $300 or less. If you think you are going to be using an air compressor for anything other than airing up bicycle tires, buy the largest unit you can possibly afford. Bear in mind that some larger units will require 220-volt wiring, which may require special considerations in your particular shop. Developing a maximum air pressure of 150 psi, this compressor creates enough pressure for spraying paint, however, the 25-gallon tank is really too small for an HVLP spray gun. With the conventional spray gun that I use for spraying primer, it works well. When using my HVLP gun for spraying color, I have to let the air tank fill completely before I start spraying, or I quickly have to stop and let the compressor catch up.

A commercial body shop requires a substantial amount of air pressure, along with air volume. This unit is about 6 feet long, and serves the needs of an entire body shop. Although a home shop would not need an air compressor this large, plan ahead for future tool purchases when you are shopping for an air compressor. You may need only enough air for a spray gun now, yet you may later decide that you need an impact wrench, an air ratchet, and myriad other neat tools. Since you will probably just be using one at a time in a home shop, determine the air pressure and volume requirements of the air tool that requires the most, and then purchase an air compressor that will fill that need.

Minimum Pipe Size Recommendations

Compressor Size	Capacity	Main Air Line Length	Size
1½ & 2 hp	6 to 9 cfm	Over 50 ft.	¾ inch
3 & 5 hp	12 to 20 cfm	Up to 200 ft.	¾ inch
		Over 200 ft.	1 inch
5 to 10 hp	20 to 40 cfm	Up to 100 ft.	¾ inch
		Over 100 ft. to 200 ft.	1 inch
		Over 200 ft.	1¼ inch
10 to 15 hp	40 to 60 cfm	Up to 100 ft.	1 inch
		Over 100 ft. to 200 ft.	1¼ inch
		Over 200 ft.	1½ inch

The size and capacity of your air compressor, along with the distance the compressed air must travel from the compressor to the air tools that it operates, is a determining factor in the size of pipe that should be used. Copper or galvanized pipe should be used to plumb your air supply to where it will actually be used. PPG Finishes

the paint finish with fish eyes, dirt nibs, and possibly blushing problems all over the surface.

Most professional paint shops use a minimum 10-horsepower rated air compressor. These are big units that supply plenty of air for the operation of pneumatic tools and some painting equipment simultaneously. For the hobbyist, a smaller compressor may be satisfactory, as long as the compressor is rated at 5 horsepower or greater. This is not to say that smaller compressors cannot be expected to work fine for small jobs, but 5-horsepower compressors offer plenty of compressed air without having to run constantly to supply it.

The more a compressor works to maintain proper pressure, the hotter the air supply becomes. As heat generation continues, moisture is introduced into the air system through condensation inside piping. This is not good. You want your air compressor to build up a reserve of compressed air in its holding tank, and then shut off for a while to cool down.

Volume

About the best way to determine what size air compressor will work best for your needs is to compare the required cubic feet per minute (cfm) of air needed with your spray gun and the application of particular paint products, to the cfm rating on the compressor you plan to use. If the compressor can easily supply the required cfm at the prescribed application pressure, you should have no problem. But, for example, if you need 12 cfm for your spray gun and your 2-horsepower compressor can supply only a maximum of 9 cfm, you will need to rent or borrow a higher rated unit to meet the minimum 12-cfm requirement.

Your compressor must also have an adequate capacity. As an example, a 5-horsepower compressor with a 20-

gallon tank that supplies enough air for a conventional spray gun may not be able to keep up with the demands of an HVLP spray gun. Instead of being able to spray a complete coat of paint at one time, you may have to stop in the middle (or several times) to allow the air supply to catch up. The same 5-horsepower compressor with a 35-gallon tank may be more appropriate when using HVLP, or other high demand pneumatic tools.

Pressure

To ensure that you have the recommended air pressure at the tip of your spray gun, hold the trigger on your gun wide open while adjusting the air pressure regulator controls. Although a control gauge setting might show 40 psi while in a static condition, operating your paint gun may cause it to drop down to 30 or 35 psi. It is important to apply auto paint at the psi rating indicated on the container label or in the product's application guide literature.

Another factor that could cause false pressure gauge readings is the size of the air hose used to supply your paint gun. Small-diameter hoses will experience friction loss and cause pressures to dwindle once they arrive at the paint gun 25 feet away. PPG's *Refinish Manual* suggests ¼-inch hose is too small for standard production paint guns. It suggests a preferred hose size of ⁵⁄₁₆-inch inside diameter in maximum lengths of 25 feet. For HVLP spray guns, ⅜-inch inside diameter air hose is recommended.

Dry Air

After you have figured out which air compressor to use, consider installing a piping system with a water trap or air dryer at the end. Even for home use, a small air supply system with ¾-inch to 1-inch pipe could be advantageous. A copper or galvanized pipe running downhill away from a compressor toward a water trap or dryer will allow moisture accumulations in heated air to flow away from the compressor and toward the trap or dryer. Since the hot air will have time to cool inside pipes, moisture suspended in the air will condense into droplets that can be captured and retained as a liquid in the trap.

Do-it-yourself painters can run ¾- to 1-inch copper or galvanized pipe up from their compressor location to the ceiling, then attach a horizontal section to the riser and run it slightly downhill toward the opposite end of the garage or workshop. Another section then runs down the wall to a convenient point, where a water trap or air dryer can be mounted. Working air lines will connect at the trap or dryer to be used for pneumatic tools or spray guns.

To keep portable air compressors mobile and to prevent their operational vibration from causing damage to solid piping mounted to walls, it is recommended that you connect your compressor to your piping system with a short, flexible air hose. By doing this, you can easily disconnect the

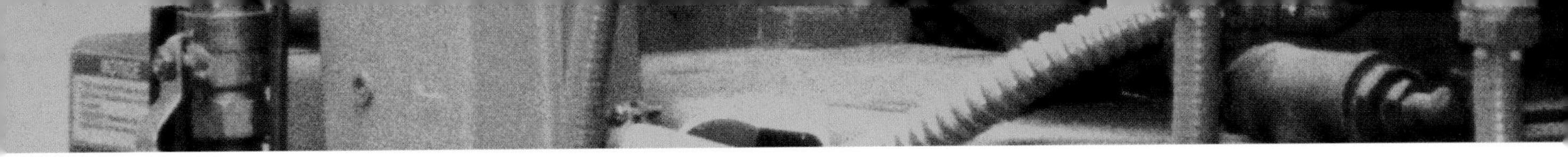

Table of Air Pressure Drop

AIR PRESSURE DROP AT SPRAY GUN

Size of Air Hose	5 foot length	10 foot length	15 foot length	20 foot length	25 foot length	50 foot length
Inside Diameter						
1/4 inch	**lbs.**	**lbs.**	**lbs.**	**lbs.**	**lbs.**	**lbs.**
at 40 lbs. pressure	6	8	9½	11	12¾	24
at 50 lbs. pressure	7½	10	12	14	16	28
at 60 lbs. pressure	9	12½	14½	16¾	19	31
at 70 lbs. pressure	10¾	14½	17	19½	22½	34
at 80 lbs. pressure	12¼	16½	19½	22½	25½	37
at 90 lbs. pressure	14	18¾	22	25¼	29	39-½
5/16 inch						
at 40 lbs. pressure	2¼	2¾	3¼	3½	4	8½
at 50 lbs. pressure	3	3½	4	4½	5	10
at 60 lbs. pressure	3¾	4½	5	5½	6	11½
at 70 lbs. pressure	4½	5¼	6	6¾	7¼	13
at 80 lbs. pressure	5½	6¼	7	8	8¾	14½
at 90 lbs. pressure	6½	7½	8½	9½	10½	16
3/8 inch						
at 40 lbs. pressure	1	1¼	1½	1¾	2	4
at 50 lbs. pressure	1½	1¾	2	2¼	3½	4½
at 60 lbs. pressure	2	2½	2¾	3½	4¼	5
at 70 lbs. pressure	2½	3	3¼	4	4¾	5½
at 80 lbs. pressure	3	3½	4	4½	5¼	6
at 90 lbs. pressure	3¾	4¼	4¾	5¼	5¾	6½

The inside diameter of air hoses can affect the amount of air pressure delivered to a paint spray gun. This chart shows some basic pressure drops for ¼-, 5⁄16-, and ⅜-inch inside diameter air hoses when used at specific lengths. Keep these calculations in mind when determining the correct pressure for spraying undercoats and paint, so you maintain the recommended gun pressure. PPG Finishes

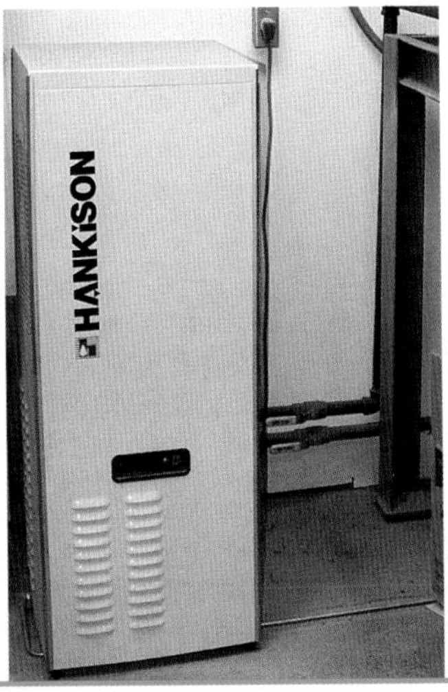

Drain moisture from your air compressor every day. To eliminate moisture in your air lines, install a water trap and air dryer between the air compressor and any point where you can connect an air hose or air tool. This commercial unit (about 3 feet high) is substantially larger and more expensive than what would be required for a home shop. Realize that moisture will wreak havoc with your paint job and will damage your air tools.

air compressor from the piping system to move it to wherever it is needed for other kinds of jobs.

PAINT GUNS

Sata, Sharpe, and DeVilbiss are three popular brands of automotive spray paint guns. You should be able to use equipment from any one of these name-brand manufacturers with good results. Two types of spray guns are available. The standard production model is biggest and generally features a one quart capacity cup. A smaller gun, referred to as a detail gun or jamb gun, features a 6- or 8-ounce capacity cup and has its trigger assembly mounted on top, as opposed to standard guns with handle grip triggers.

A full range of various spray paint guns and their accessories are available at auto body paint and supply stores. Prices start at about $60 and go upward, depending upon the brand and precision quality. Paint cups are generally extra, costing around $25 for detail gun cups, or around $35 for production models. Along with paint guns, you can purchase air valves that attach to spray guns in-line with their air supply. These valves help to fine-tune air pressure at the gun to perfect spray patterns.

Professional automobile painters rely on their paint guns to provide uniform spray patterns with each use. To achieve this, they clean their guns thoroughly after each use. Spray gun quality is a number one factor when considering such a purchase. Better to save up extra money to buy a top-of-the-line model than settle for second best on an unfamiliar import. The problems with cheap paint guns relate to inadequate spray patterns and difficulty in finding replacement parts. Take your paint gun purchase seriously and opt for long-lasting quality instead of make-do availability.

Just as professional photographers suggest buying a camera from a camera shop, professional painters will suggest buying your paint spray gun from an automotive paint and supply jobber. Cameras and paint spray guns are available at other outlets, however, a knowledgeable salesperson may not be. Having a knowledgeable person who has actually used a spray gun like the one they are selling you has some advantages. Product literature may suggest a particular setting for inlet air pressure, while real-world experience can assure you that a higher inlet pressure is necessary. If you do not have access to this firsthand knowledge, your brand-new spray gun may never operate as well as desired. Inlet air pressure settings are critical with HVLP spray guns, so it will be worth your while to ask someone who knows for their recommen-

dations, rather than relying solely on product literature. What works and what works best may not be the same.

Conventional

Conventional spray guns typically require air pressure of 60 psi or more. This relatively high pressure blasts paint at the surface with such force that over 65 percent of the material actually goes up in overspray. In addition to this overspray, the additional air pressure is more likely to stir up existing dirt and debris, and allow it to fall into fresh paint.

High Volume Low Pressure (HVLP)

Concern over atmospheric pollution has caused government agencies, civic groups, auto paint manufacturers, auto painters, and paint equipment companies to acknowledge paint VOCs, overspray, and material waste as pollution problems and they are therefore striving for solutions. One viable means of reducing VOC and overspray pollution is by use of High Volume/Low Pressure (HVLP) spray paint systems.

When HVLP spray paint systems were introduced, they were composed of a spray paint gun and a turbine system that replaced the conventional air compressor. Although the HVLP concept made good sense and was generally accepted as a good idea, the actual equipment met less than wide approval. The new turbine system caused the air pushing the paint onto the vehicle to get too hot, causing the paint to dry too soon, sometimes even before it was actually landing on the vehicle. The turbine systems have been redesigned so that they do not get as hot. However, perhaps a more practical solution is the development of HVLP spray guns that can be used with conventional air compressors. This allows experienced painters to use a system that is more familiar to them, and also makes the purchase of an air compressor easier to justify for the novice painter. The conventional air compressor is more versatile around the shop than an HVLP turbine paint system.

HVLP works by increasing the volume of paint that can uniformly pass through the spray gun's ports and nozzle, so that a relatively low pressure is all that is needed to propel the paint material. The end result is more adherence to auto surfaces and much less—up to 50 percent—waste through overspray from paint particles bouncing off surfaces at high pressure.

Much literature for HVLP spray guns recommends air pressure of 10 psi at the tip of the spray gun. This is not to be confused with the air pressure at the inlet of the spray gun where the hose connects. Depending on the design of the spray gun, the inlet pressure must sometimes be near 60 psi to obtain the suggested tip pressure.

Most painters who have used both conventional spray paint guns and HVLP systems agree that a vehicle that would take a complete gallon of paint when shot with a conventional gun can be completed with three quarts or less

This conventional spray gun from Campbell-Hausfeld has served the author well for spraying various coats of primer. It was modestly priced at a local discount retailer and will most likely last quite a while, as long as it is cleaned thoroughly after each use. As good as this spray gun works, you should seriously consider an HVLP model as your next spray gun purchase.

While I don't paint for a living, these three paint guns have served me well on a hobbyist level. The conventional gun at left is from Sears, the touchup gun from a discount store, and the HVLP gun is an inexpensive one from The Paint Store. None of them was very expensive in the grand scheme of things, with the HVLP gun paying for itself within a couple of uses by material savings alone. Hindsight being 20/20, my next spray gun will most likely be a medium-priced HVLP unit. No matter what kind of spray gun you use, it is important that you know how to adjust it properly AND keep it clean.

when an HVLP system is used. With the price of paint material alone being what it is, the purchase of an HVLP spray gun will certainly pay for itself in a couple of repaint jobs, if not on the first one. Not only are you saving paint material with an HVLP spray gun, you are going to have a great reduction in the amount of overspray, which should be of major importance to the part-time auto painter who is working in his residential garage or workshop. The fewer red flags that you send up to your neighbors, who may not approve of your car hobby anyway, the better off you will be.

Siphon Feed

Besides conventional or HVLP, spray guns can be further classified as siphon feed or gravity feed. Whether a production gun or a detail gun, a siphon feed gun's paint cup is mounted below the air nozzle. This design requires more air pressure to siphon the paint material up, out of the cup. With a non-HVLP siphon feed spray gun, approximately 75 percent of the paint material ends up as overspray.

Gravity Feed

As you might expect, a gravity feed spray gun has the paint cup mounted above the air nozzle. This allows gravity to do the work of some of the air pressure, allowing for the use of a lower inlet air pressure. However, on a non-HVLP spray gun, this will still result in approximately 65 percent of the paint material ending up as overspray.

Production Gun

If your painting is going to be limited to large body panels, such as doors, fenders, and hoods, a full-size production

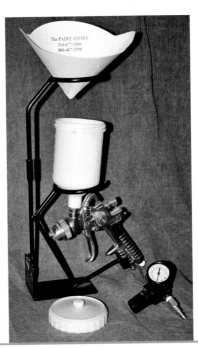

This is my gravity feed HVLP spray gun. Whether your gun is HVLP or conventional, gravity feed requires less air pressure than a siphon feed spray gun. This stand would typically be securely affixed to a workbench and hold the spray gun when paint is being poured into the paint cup. Although it was removed from the spray gun for this photo (it wouldn't fit into the stand), the air pressure regulator is installed in line between the air supply hose and the spray gun. A regulator installed at the gun is essential for HVLP and a great idea for all spray guns.

This detail gun, or jamb gun, is operated by pressing down on the lever at the top. Notice that it has a much smaller paint cup than the typical 1-quart size on a full-size production gun, making it more maneuverable for intricate, detailed areas or doorjambs.

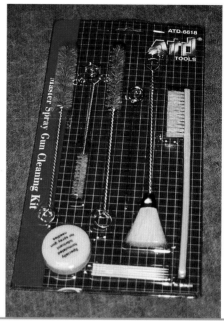

Spraying lots of the appropriate reducer or thinner for the paint product that you have just sprayed will clean most of the material out of your spray gun; sometimes some more vigorous cleaning will be necessary. Professional body shops often have cleaning cabinets where cleaning material is sprayed through the spray gun for relatively long periods of time to make sure that they are ready when needed. The hobbyist painter is not likely to have a cleaning cabinet, so an assortment of small brushes will have to suffice. Using liberal amounts of solvent and a small brush, you can gently scrub some of those thick built-up paint areas. Whatever you do, resist the urge to use any sort of metal object when cleaning the tiny orifices of your spray gun. Be sure you are wearing an appropriate respirator and rubber gloves.

gun will suit your needs. Commonly having a one-quart paint cup, this gun can spray a fair amount of material before you need to refill.

Detail Gun

The difference between the full-size production spray paint gun and the detail model is maneuverability. As the larger unit is perfect for complete paint jobs and panel repaints, the detail gun is perfect for intricate painting jobs, like small touchups requiring fine spray patterns and doorjamb painting. The top-mounted trigger on detail guns is operated by the full length of a user's index finger. This comfortable position allows painters to operate these lightweight units in confined spaces with maximum control.

Paint Gun Maintenance

Spray paint guns need consistent and conscientious cleaning and maintenance. Very small air and material passageways are easily clogged by bits of dry paint and debris. Once they become plugged, it is difficult to clear them.

Your spray gun must be cleaned after each use. Each paint system will have certain wash solvents designated as part of the overall paint system. Be sure that your auto body paint and supply jobber describes which cleaning product is best suited for the system that you are using.

Professional body shops have special enclosed cabinets they use for gun cleaning. Solvent is forced through gun assemblies under pressure while trigger units are maintained in an open position. Without a cleaning cabinet, you will have to fill your gun cup partly full with solvent, swish it around and empty it to remove the bulk of the remaining paint product. Then, refill it again with clean solvent and spray it through the unit. This should clear out the inner passageways.

Once you've done that, fill the cup about one-quarter full with clean solvent and spray it through the unit. Then, thoroughly clean the cup. Once that's done, spray clean thinner through the gun head again to be sure that nothing but clear solvent comes out. Use only those brushes designated for spray paint gun cleaning on housings, air caps, and other parts. *Never* use sharp objects to clear clogged air caps or other ports. The slightest scratch damage to finely machined spray gun parts can ruin otherwise perfect fan sprays.

Use a clean cloth, damp with the proper solvent, to clean bulk paint drips or splotches from exterior surfaces. When you're satisfied that interior ports and passageways are clean, run plenty of clean, dry air through the unit to remove lingering deposits of solvent. Hang or place guns in a vertical position for storing after completely drying them with clean cloths.

OVERALL SAFETY

Many veteran auto painters are realizing that they should have paid more attention to warning labels and other safety concerns during their apprentice years in the auto paint field. They are now fully comprehending the health hazards involved due to the amount of sanding dust, paint over-spray, and solvents they have inhaled over the years.

Inhalation

Especially with the advent of paint hardeners that contain isocyanates (present in all two-part paint products), painters must be keenly aware of all the respiratory protection that is available to them. Although many painters still spray cars while wearing only heavy-duty filter masks for protection, smart painters opt instead for full-face, fresh-air respiratory systems. These units may be a bit cumbersome, but whatever inconvenience they involve is easily overshadowed by the amount of personal safety they afford.

Because of increased awareness to hazardous materials, government agencies have demanded that chemical manufacturers comply with more and more standards relating to user safety. Therefore, you will commonly find recommendations of NIOSH-approved respiratory protection on almost all paint product containers. Be sure to read respirator package labels too. They will list the types of materials that the filter will hold out and those that are *not* filtered at all. Auto body paint and supply stores carry assortments of filter masks and fresh-air systems.

Osmosis

Since particles of paint overspray can readily enter your body through your eyes by way of moist tear ducts, manufacturers advise painters to wear goggles or full-face respirators. This is an important consideration during sanding as well. Most auto body paint and supply stores carry a selection of lightweight painter's goggles.

Skin Contact

You are encouraged to wear rubber gloves any time you handle thinners, reducers, hardeners, or any other paint product chemical. Because paint chemicals can enter painter's bodies through pores in their skin, paint manufactures have developed special impermeable coveralls. Designed to be used only once and then discarded, disposable coveralls serve two functions. First, they prevent paint chemicals from coming in contact with your skin. Second, the material used to make the coveralls is lint-free, which means that concerns over lint falling off of your clothes and onto paint finishes is greatly reduced.

This photo shows the basic equipment needed for painting your vehicle. Note that the safety equipment outnumbers the amount of painting equipment. Painting is safe, but the chemicals involved are fatal if you don't respect them. On the plus side, the necessary safety equipment is relatively inexpensive. Painter's coveralls are available in two different qualities; about $10 for a one-time use disposable suit or about $50 for a machine washable, reusable shoot suit. A full-face respirator that accepts replaceable charcoal cartridges and eliminates the need for goggles costs around $125. If you choose to not pay that amount, you can get by with a half-mask, a head sock, and goggles. A box of 100 rubber gloves costs about $6. So for less than $200, you can have more than adequate protection from paint for quite some time. That sure sounds like a bargain to me.

Professional painters who take full advantage of all personal safety equipment will suit up in the following way for maximum protection while painting: First to go on is a pair of painter's coveralls, and then rubber gloves. Both pant legs are taped closed around the ankles and both arm sleeves are taped around the wrist. Then comes a painter's hood, which covers the neck and entire head, except for the face. A full-face, fresh-air respiratory mask is next donned, which, when connected to its air compressor supply hose, will offer the user plenty of fresh, clean air.

This complete outfit gives painters full protection against harmful chemical liquids, paint overspray particles, and vapors. Serious consideration should be given to the use of all these protective items. None of them is very expensive, except for the fresh-air respiratory system. But, rental yards may have these kinds of respiratory units available at affordable rates.

CHAPTER 5
BODYWORK

This is not a bodywork book, but you will often be painting over bodywork, so we need to cover a few basic ideas and concepts. If you'd rather not do any bodywork—and, depending on what your car needs, that could be a reasonable decision—you can probably hire a professional bodyshop to make the necessary repairs. Realize that to do this, the bodyshop might actually charge you as much as it would to perform the paintwork to the affected panel(s) as well. An alternative might be to find a vocational school that teaches auto body repair. Perhaps an instructor there could connect you with a skilled student looking to make a couple dollars. You may also, through networking with other car enthusiasts, encounter someone willing and able to help you in this area.

COLLISION REPAIR

All too often, a minor fender-bender is the reason behind doing paintwork to your car in the first place. The paint was in decent shape, as you kept it washed and waxed on a regular basis. Everything is fine with your car's paint, and then someone bumps into it, causing more than minimal damage. You have the choice of ignoring the damage, but this was more than minimal, remember? You can pay a shop to make the repair. If this is your decision, you may have to wait longer than anticipated to get your car back, due to the shop's schedule. It may cost more than what you want to spend out of pocket or claim on your insurance.

The work may not turn out as well as you had hoped—or all of the above.

Unless you totaled the vehicle, chances are you can do the repair work yourself. If you are reading this book, you at least have some inclination to roll up your sleeves. If the panels are damaged slightly, they can be straightened. If

These are your very basic tools for doing bodywork. Shown are an air file, a DA sander, a small grinder, a dead blow hammer, a body hammer, sandpaper, and a pry bar. Experience is the best way to learn to use these tools. If the panel is already damaged, what have you got to lose by using it as practice material?

The damage to this sedan is typical of what can be easily repaired by the hobbyist. It consisted of a few small dents in the doors and rear quarter panel. No metal was creased or torn, and no glass was broken. Even if your sheet metal straightening skills are not the best, most of these repairs could be filled with body filler to a satisfactory degree. A deeper dent would simply take more layers of filler, as filler cannot be applied very thick in any one application.

they are damaged beyond your repair skills, they can be replaced, unless the damage is to the rear quarter panel or roof. Even that is not beyond repair, although replacing a rear quarter panel is beyond the scope of this book, since it involves cutting and welding.

Straightening a Panel

Before straightening a panel that has been damaged during a collision, you need to determine the original point of impact. Some of the damage is from the actual impact, while much of the damage is actually due to reactionary forces. Since a fender or door is basically secured around its perimeter, impact to the middle of that panel will cause deformation to the surrounding area, or cause the panel to separate itself from its mounting points.

To straighten the panel, you need to reverse the deformation process until the panel is straight again. Instead of trying to simply hammer out the dent from the back, you

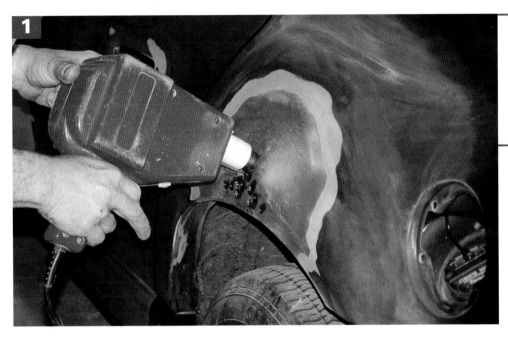

1

To straighten sheet metal, you often need to pull out a dent. To make this easier, this tool is used to temporarily weld small metal rods, about ⅛ inch diameter and 2½ inches long, to the sheet metal.

2

A slide hammer can then be slid over the rods one at a time, and then slid out to pull the sheet metal to its correct position. Sometimes you may need to tap the metal back in slightly with a hammer if you pulled it out too far.

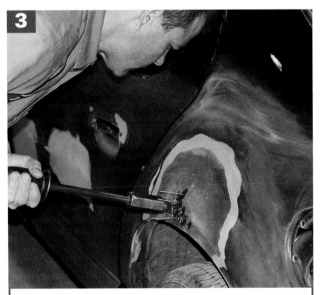

3

The slide hammer is moved to the next rod and then pulled out to undo the effects of the impact. Learning how to read dents and knowing where to pull is an art that takes practice.

4

After some pulling, check your progress to verify that the panel has been returned to its proper contour. You want to return the panel as closely as possible to its original shape, but you don't want any of the panel to be too high. High spots will need to be hammered back down, while subtle low spots can be filled.

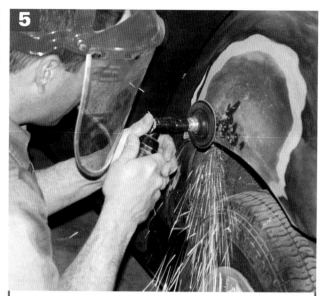

5

With the pulling completed, the rods can be cut off as close to the body as possible with a pair of diagonal cutters. The stubs are then ground away with a grinder and a coarse disc.

The lip of this fender, which is slightly low, is pulled out by using the slide hammer and a fender lip attachment.

6

should try to work from the outer perimeter of the damage toward the point of impact. This will be more difficult to do if there was more than one point of impact in any one panel, yet the theory is the same.

More than likely, a dent in one portion of the panel will cause another portion of that same panel to bulge outward. You should attempt to hammer this outward bulge back into the correct alignment, and then hammer the dented area to its original alignment. Attempting to straighten the dent first will actually cause the metal to stretch in the bulged area. In a complex repair, a shrinking hammer is used to minimize the effects of stretching the metal.

Ideally, you can straighten the panel to within approximately $1/16$ inch of its original contour. A skim coat of plastic

7

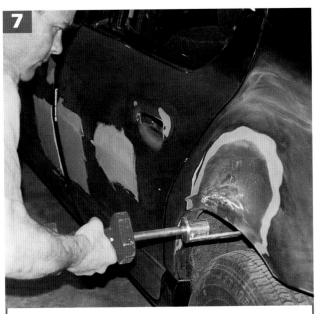

A couple more tugs with the slide hammer, and it should be pretty close.

8

Now that the metal has been straightened, the surface area can be smoothed with some body filler for most of the filling, and then a skim coat of glazing putty for the final surface. The mixing board shown in the middle of the photo has a tablet of disposable sheets for use when mixing filler or glaze. The filler is mixed and spread, and that sheet is torn off and thrown away. This is much more efficient than cleaning the old filler off the mixing board each time.

9

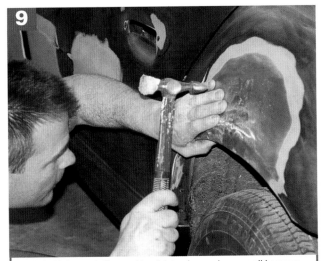

A slight high spot is finessed back into place using a small hammer. Older vehicles generally have thicker sheet metal, while newer vehicles generally have thinner, more pliable panels. The amount of brute strength and finesse necessary will depend largely on the vintage of the vehicle.

body filler will be able to cover any remaining imperfections. Obviously, unless you are able to metal finish the panel without using any filler, the repaired area needs to be slightly lower than the undamaged area. This will keep the body filler from building up above the surrounding area. Keep in mind that body filler should not be more than ⅛ inch thick at its deepest point, or it will be likely to sag or crack.

10

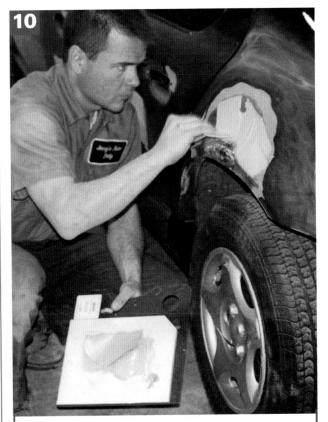

Using a flexible spreader and a careful eye, spread the filler to fill any low spots. Take care to minimize air bubbles. When the filler hardens, it can then be sanded to its final shape with 80- or 100-grit sandpaper.

11 *Looking at this filled area after the sanding has been completed, we can tell that filler (pale yellow) was used to cover the larger area, and a slight amount of glaze (light blue) was used to finish the edge of the wheelwell.*

Replacing a Panel

If the body damage was more severe than you can repair, or you have hammered the affected panel into oblivion while attempting to straighten it, you may need to replace the damaged panel. As long as the original panel is one that can be removed from the vehicle, this is always an option. If necessary, even a roof or quarter panel can be cut from a donor car and welded in place. The popularity of muscle cars has spawned an aftermarket industry that is reproducing many patch panels, including some rear quarter panels.

If you decide to replace a panel, you have a few different sources. These include new sheet metal replacement panels

This Ford truck will be receiving several new panels: new doors, front fenders, hood, roof, and one new bed side. When installing new panels, you must first determine if any of the mounting points need to be straightened or repaired. If a mounting bracket has been tweaked out of shape, the panel being attached to it won't fit correctly. You must also determine which existing panels are still aligned correctly, and match the new to the old.

These are the two doors taken off the Ford truck in the previous photo. The left door has a major dent in its midsection, a smaller deformity in the upright behind the window, and a tear in the front of the door. Although this door could probably be saved, it would be more labor intensive. If insurance is covering the cost, a replacement door is less expensive than the time necessary to fix it or the cost of a rental car for that time. If you are paying for the parts yourself, you may choose to repair some of the affected panels.

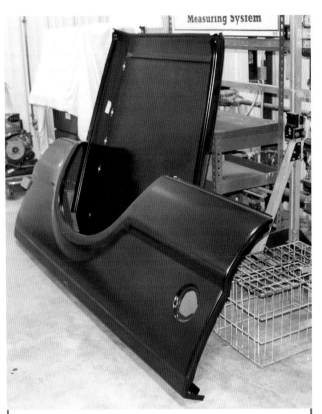

This is the bed side and roof to be installed on the Ford truck. On older trucks, it would not be an option to replace the roof, unless the old one was cut off, and a donor roof from another truck welded in place. Newer vehicles are designed with more of a component body system, allowing for easier panel replacement.

from the manufacturer of your vehicle, an aftermarket dealer of similar replacement panels, or a salvage yard.

Your vehicle dealer's body shop would use new, genuine replacement panels, if it was hired to make the repair. These replacement panels are brand new sheet metal, with the original mounting holes, light recesses, and contours. As you might expect, these are the most expensive to purchase, although their higher quality fit may save time and trouble.

Aftermarket panels can be great products, or they can be bad, depending on the manufacturer. These panels will usually have all of the necessary mounting holes and light recesses, and they will look just like the authentic panels they are designed to replace. Any problems with proper fit are not noticeable until after you have purchased the part, tried to install it, and found out that it doesn't fit. On the other hand, some of these replacement panels are superior. It pays to ask around before you buy.

If you resort to buying a replacement panel from a salvage yard, look around and try to find the best sheet metal that you can find that fits your vehicle. Buying a replacement panel that needs more work (collision or rust repair) than

what you already have defeats your purpose. Chances are, you won't be able to find a door or fender that fits and is the same color as your car, but you can take care of that. Any donor part from another vehicle will need to be tested for paint type and compatibility with the paint system that you anticipate using. Since this panel has not been installed on your vehicle, this would be a good time to have it chemically dipped or media blasted if necessary. Whether you are buying new or used, you will need to verify that any necessary mounting brackets, emblems, or trim are included with your order, or are still in useable condition from your car.

If the procedure for removing the affected panel from your vehicle is not obvious, consult a repair manual for your specific vehicle or a local body shop. As you remove the damaged panel, you can pretty well determine the manner in which the replacement panel should be installed.

Although the top coats of paint should be done after the panel is in place to allow for proper paint blending with adjacent panels, you should apply primer undercoats prior to installation. This allows for easier access to ensure that all areas of the panel are coated with epoxy primer.

This is another replacement fender, although its origin—new replacement, aftermarket, or salvage yard—is unknown. It should be checked for any signs of rust or damage before it's installed.

RUST REPAIR

Depending on what part of the country you live in (or where your project vehicle spent its past life), rust repair may be more necessary that collision repair. When dealing with rust, you will need to determine whether it is just surface rust, or corrosion that penetrates through the panel.

If it is mere surface rust, with solid metal beneath it, you can sand it off and apply epoxy primer. If the rust is more severe, with either complete rust through or severely pitted sheet metal, more extensive repairs are necessary before paint can be applied. This may necessitate media blasting or use of a chemical stripper, along with application of epoxy primer, followed by application of a high-build primer-surfacer. If rust is severe, it may be necessary to weld in patch panels.

Rust Removal by Sanding

To remove surface rust from otherwise solid sheet metal, block sand the panel with 80- or 100-grit sandpaper. When all of the rust has disappeared and either bare metal or painted metal is present, the panel should be wiped

The inner front fenders and radiator support of this vintage Ford Fairlane have been sandblasted to remove any signs of rust. It was then coated with an epoxy primer to prevent additional corrosion and to provide a suitable surface for primer-surfacer.

The steering column and other items that were protruding through the firewall of this vintage project were masked off, rather than removed. Later on in the project, they will be removed and fully detailed.

down with wax and grease remover, and then coated with epoxy primer. The sanding scratches from the course grit sandpaper will provide excellent adhesion for the epoxy primer. Any dents or dings should be repaired or filled, and then coated with a high-build primer-surfacer prior to block sanding.

Rust Removal by Panel Replacement

If a particular panel is damaged beyond repair by the spread of rust, a practical option is to discard the cancerous panel in favor of a new replacement. Panel replacement for rust repair is the same as for collision repair if you are replacing a complete panel, such as a door, deck lid, or fender. Whether you use genuine factory replacement panels, lesser-priced aftermarket units, or used parts, search out the best parts available for your cash.

For new replacement panels, surface preparation may be slightly different from the rest of the vehicle. The replacement panel(s) will need to be cleaned with wax and grease remover prior to anything else. Some scuffing of the surface will be

Front fenders, hood, deck lid, and other sheet metal components of this Fairlane have been prepped for paint. They are stored in an out-of-the-way corner of the shop to avoid possible damage.

necessary for proper primer or paint adhesion. Consult with your auto paint and supply jobber for their recommendations on the correct undercoat necessary to prep the panels for the paint system you will be using. If possible, primer undercoats should be applied before you install the panel. To allow for proper paint blending, top coats should be applied only after the panel has been installed and aligned, if possible.

Installing Patch Panels

Although patch panels are more commonly used on vintage restorations, their use is becoming more common on later model vehicles as the average vehicle age increases. Patch panels are used to repair a portion of a panel such as a lower door, fenderwell opening, or a portion of the main body, such as a cab corner or quarter panel.

The restoration aftermarket has become familiar with the typical rust-prone areas of the vehicles for which it supplies parts. Certain vehicles are known for their typical rust out over the headlights on front fenders, lower rear cab corners and cowls on pickup trucks, and trunk floors and floor pans on other vehicles. If you are working on a mainstream vehicle, chances are that the necessary patch panel

1 When installing a patch panel, you must first determine how much of the original panel should be removed. You should be able to remove all of the damaged or rusted area, but not so much that the patch doesn't cover the entire area. On this quarter panel of a Ford Model A coupe, Keith Moritz fits the panel in place, then scribes or marks a line on the original panel. Ultimately, the original panel below this line will be removed.

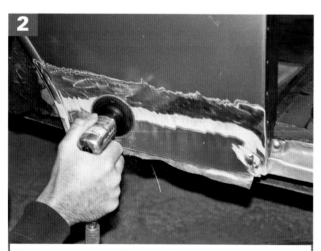

Since the patch panel will be welded into place, the existing paint (and body filler in this case) are ground away with a grinder. Approximately 2 inches of bare metal should surround the area to be welded.

Before cutting the original metal away, Moritz double-checks the fit of the patch panel, and then scribes the line along which the cut will be made. It pays to double-check the fit of the patch panel before cutting anything, so that you don't have to weld in a patch between the original metal and the patch panel you are installing. It is much easier to make a second cut than to add more material.

4

In this case, Moritz uses a die grinder with a cut-off wheel, however, a reciprocating saw or plasma arc cutter may be used to cut away the original panel. Accurately fitting the panel, marking the cut accordingly, and then accurately cutting out the panel will provide a better patch panel installation.

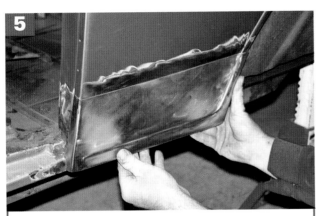

5

This is the opposite side of the same vehicle, receiving the same patch panel installation. After the defective area is cut out, the new patch panel is fit into position, making sure that all bodylines are correctly aligned. The patch can then be clamped into place to allow for welding.

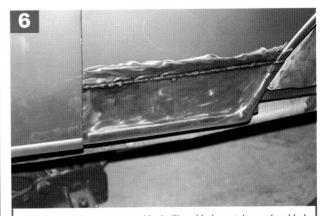

6

This is what the quarter panel looks like with the patch panel welded in place, prior to the welds being ground down. Notice that the bodylines are correctly aligned and the patch, along with an area above it, has been lightly ground to allow for proper adhesion of epoxy primer.

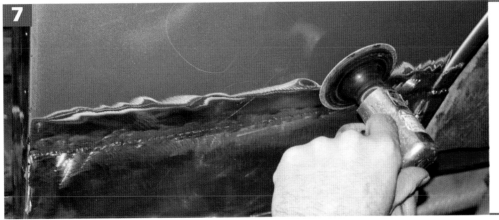

7

Moritz finishes the weld by grinding it down with a pneumatic grinder. When finished, it will be virtually impossible to tell where the seam is located. Depending on the condition of the surrounding area and the amount of previous bodywork, some body filler and primer-surfacer may be necessary to fully prep this area for paint.

BODYWORK

for your particular application is available. Even if available patch panels are not big enough to cover the entire area that needs to be repaired, one may be useful for repairing the intricate bodylines of the damaged area.

A patch panel is installed by first removing the damaged metal and then welding the patch in its place. When installing a patch panel, such as a lower door or quarter panel, compare the new panel to the area to be replaced to determine how much of the old metal to cut away. Using a plasma cutter, die grinder, reciprocating saw, or tin snips, cut out the damaged section. Set the patch panel in its place, check it for proper alignment, clamp it into its precise final location, and then weld. What type of weld to use depends upon the panel you're replacing, the type of welder available, and the operator's skills. When welding with a MIG welder, start with ⅛-inch tacks, and skip around to avoid getting the panel too hot, which would cause distortion. Another trick is to use your air hose with an air nozzle to blow cool air on the welds to keep them from getting too hot.

After completing all welding, clean the patched area with wax and grease remover, apply epoxy primer, and finish the bodywork to the surrounding area. Follow with primer-surfacer and block sand as necessary prior to applying sealer and top coats.

MODIFICATIONS

Body modifications know no bounds, and include everything from chopped tops, rounded hood and door corners, and filled cowl panels on older vehicles, to fender flares, hood scoops, and ground effects on later model vehicles. Depending on the skills of the customizer and depth of the pockets of whoever is paying the bill, these modifications can be done in metal, fiberglass, or carbon fiber.

Each material used in the modification (or even creation) of a vehicle will call for its own particular method of bodywork, surface preparation, undercoat application, and top coat application. Throughout the construction or modification process, you will need to verify the correct materials and methods necessary to prep for paint with your paint and supply jobber. Simply put, fiberglass preparation differs from that for sheet metal, which requires something different from carbon fiber.

GETTING IT ALL STRAIGHT

When doing bodywork to a vehicle, your main objective is to get the body, fenders, hood, doors, etc., as straight as possible. No, this does not mean removing all of the original recesses, bulges, or character lines so that all you have left is a slab-sided box. What it does mean, however, is that panels that are meant to be straight are like arrows, and panels that are meant to be curved are smooth curves. Any and all imperfections to the vehicle's sheet metal, aluminum, or composite body skin have been eliminated.

Any imperfections that you can find now will be greatly magnified after applying a new coat of paint.

Using Body Filler

Even if you don't have to use a body hammer to remove a dent, or so much as a piece of sandpaper to remove a spec of rust, there may still be some imperfections to the body. If the vehicle has ever been in a parking lot or a two-car driveway, there is bound to be at least one minor door ding. You may not notice it now, but after you have applied a fresh coat of paint, it will stick out like the proverbial sore thumb.

Most minor door dings (those less than ⅛ inch deep) can be eliminated by filling them with body filler. The dented area should be scuffed down to bare metal or epoxy primer. An appropriate amount of body filler—*and you always mix too much or too little*—is mixed with the appropriate amount of hardener, and then applied to the dented area with a body filler spreader. Read the instructions for the particular filler that you are using to determine when and how to begin working it. Some fillers require a cheese grater for rough shaping while the filler is tacky, while others are allowed to fully harden before sanding.

If necessary, a second coat of filler may be applied to completely fill the area. After rough shaping with a cheese grater or coarse (80 or 100-grit) sandpaper, sand the entire area with finer sandpaper until it blends into the surrounding area.

Aligning Panels and Fitting Gaps

OK, now that you have every door, hood, fender, and deck lid perfect, how do they fit with each other when installed

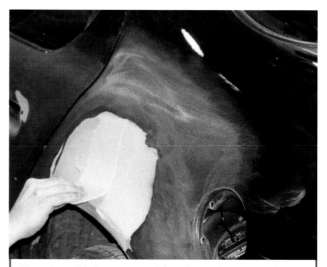

After using a slide hammer to straighten the metal to very near its original contour, the body person applies two or three thin coats of filler to match the final contour. Glazing putty can be used to fill any pinholes that remain in the sanded body filler. [see the glazed panel on page 66.]

1

Although the bedside of this pickup truck has a slight curve to it from top to bottom, it is straight from front to back. A long board is used when sanding to minimize any ripples.

2

After hand sanding with a relatively coarse (80 or 100) grit by hand, an air file with 200- to 320-grit sandpaper is used. When sanding a panel that curves in one direction but is straight in the opposite direction, sanding is mostly performed in the straight direction. Using a long board across the crown would tend to flatten the curve.

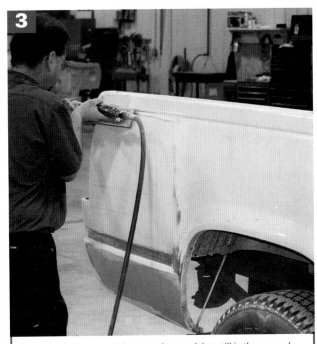

3

Move the air file up and down on the panel, but still in the general direction that the panel is running.

on the vehicle? Are the gaps between each panel consistent in width? Are the panels in line with one another, or does one stick out farther than the one adjacent to it? Some vehicles have better panel fit from the factory than others do, no doubt about it. How well they fit after you have painted the vehicle is up to you, and will be a great testimony to your attention to detail.

Whether they were present originally or not, it may be necessary to install shims behind some panels to get them to align properly with adjacent panels. Doors may have to be moved on their hinges somewhat to align the door latch mechanism or make the bodylines match. Most doors have a slight amount of adjustability built into accommodate for normal wear.

BODYWORK

4

Using a long board or an air file will also give you a better indication of high and low spots than a smaller sanding block. The smaller sanding block will simply ride over the wavy panel, while the longer board will span the high spots and bring them down to the same level as the low spots.

5

Sandpaper wrapped around a broken paint stick is used to sand the grooved area of this GM bed side. Although sanding blocks are available commercially in various shapes and sizes, you will often need to improvise to find a block suitable for the particular area that you are sanding.

6

The bluish-green areas indicate where a thin layer of glazing filler was used to fill a slightly low spot or fill some pinholes in the body filler. The glazing filler can be sanded with 400-grit or finer sandpaper to smooth the panel to your satisfaction.

7

A normal-sized sanding block is now used to touch up the edges of the filled area. You can never sand too much. What may look great in raw body filler will quickly show any pinholes or other blemishes when you apply a coat of primer-surfacer.

Hoods and deck lids may present the biggest problem, as any gap problem will need to be evenly split between the two sides. Doors and fenders should be fit as accurately as possible, however slight variations from one side to the other will not be as noticeable as a hood or deck lid that is biased to one side or the other.

Obtaining consistent gaps may require removing or adding material to a panel. Body shop professionals commonly shoot for a gap between panels that is as wide as a paint stir stick is thick, although this is not always possible. New vehicles generally have consistent gaps, but are two or three times the thickness of a paint stir stick. Consistency is the prime objective, while factory tolerances or tighter make a good target.

Any panels on which body filler has been applied are suspect when gaps are too tight. Getting the surface smooth may have required too much build-up. This usually

Any mirror will be smooth, but a mirror such as those found in an amusement park is wavy, distorting whatever it reflects. Bodywork can be smooth to the touch, but actually be full of minute waves that provide a distorted reflection. This 1947–1953 Chevy pickup truck is a great example of "flat" bodywork, judging by the reflections in its painted surface. To achieve this "flat" bodywork, somebody performed lots of block sanding.

happens when a portion of the area being filled was actually higher than it should have been and the surrounding area is brought out to an incorrect surface height.

GETTING IT FLAT

Now that the panels are all straight and in perfect alignment, are you ready to spray paint? That depends. Are there any minor door dings or other blemishes present? Do the doors have a series of vertical lines in them, where some other car door came in contact with yours? Is the overall texture of the vehicle somewhat rough? If the answer to any of these questions is yes, then you still have work to do before spraying any paint. You will need to break out some more sandpaper and block sand the entire vehicle until all such imperfections have been eliminated.

Sanding With a Long Board

Like a short wheelbase vehicle (such as an ATV) on a rough road, a small sanding block will simply ride over an already wavy panel. The panel will become smoother, but it will still be wavy. A long wheelbase vehicle, like a limousine, will bridge the high and low spots in the road, smoothing out the ride for the occupants. The same effect happens when you use a long sanding board instead of a short sanding block. Using the longest sanding board or block available with progressively finer sandpaper is the key to achieving the straightest and flattest surface upon which to apply paint.

Sanding Body Filler Repairs

Regardless of the type of surface you plan to paint over, whether it be body filler or an existing paint finish, some sanding will be required. This phase of any automobile paint operation is just as critical as any other. Remember that every blemish or surface flaw will be magnified by paint coats.

Top layers of body filler are initially sanded with 80- to 150-grit paper to smooth and flatten rough spots and to get the surface close to an even texture. Then, 240-grit paper is used to make that finish even smoother and flatter. Sanding must be done with a sanding board or block. After every two minutes or so, feel the surface with your open hand to judge your progress. Any irregularity you feel, you'll see with paint on it, so keep sanding and checking the area until it's smooth and flat and perfectly blended with surrounding surfaces.

Operate sanding boards and blocks in all directions. Do not simply maneuver them in a back and forth direction from the front to the back. Move them up and down and crossways diagonally, rotating the board or block as necessary for ease of operation. This multidirectional sanding technique will guarantee that all areas are sanded smooth without grooves or perceivable patterns.

Once you've made the area flat with 240-grit paper so there are no remaining high spots, wrinkles, grooves or ridges, use 320-grit paper to remove lingering sanding scratches and other shallow imperfections. Up to this point you've been shaping the body filler until it is flat, and it blends with panel areas adjacent to it. Now, with finer sandpaper grits, you will focus on texture smoothness.

Much of this finish sanding can be done with a small DA sander. If you're not experienced using this device on an auto body, practice before you go to work on your vehicle. Although DAs may not appear to be moving at all, they can remove a lot of filler material in a hurry.

When satisfied that your filler repair has been sanded to perfection, use 320-grit paper to gradually develop a well defined visual perimeter around the entire repair area. This "ring" around the repair should expose a band of bare metal about an inch wide and then successive bands of equally

The doors on this sedan, like those on the pickup bed side earlier in this chapter, are relatively straight in the front to back, while contoured from top to bottom. To maintain this straightness, a long board is used to sand front to back, while moving up and down along the door.

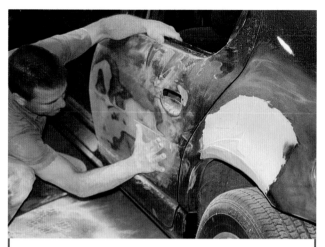

Due to the irregular pressure of your hand, you should not sand without using some type of a sanding block. Using your hand alone with tend to make the panel wavy as more pressure will be applied by your fingers and less in the area in between them. However, feeling the panel with your hand periodically while sanding will give a good indication of high and low spots.

wide exposed rings of primer, sealer, primer-surfacer, and paint. Because undercoat and paint products consist of different colored materials, you will be able to see your progress clearly. The object, in essence, is to develop sort of a layered valley of smooth walls between the top surface of the body filler area and the top surface of existing good paint. This allows fresh applications of undercoat material to fill to the same thickness as those same materials existing on the rest of the car's surface.

This approach will allow you to apply final color coats in thickness equal to the rest of the paint finish for the best possible blend, color tint and texture identical to surrounding paint finishes. This process is referred to as "feathering in." Subsequent coats of primer-surfacer mate-

Prior to the application of any body filler, the various layers of sheet metal, primer, and paint are quite evident on the rear quarter panel of this sedan. The very smallest dark area is where small rods were temporarily welded to the panel so the body worker could straighten a dent with a slide hammer. The next larger area is where the paint has been sanded off to expose bare metal. Outside of that is the original primer or sealer used beneath the factory paint. Next is the paint that has been scuffed to enhance adhesion of the primer-surfacer, and finally the untouched original painted surface.

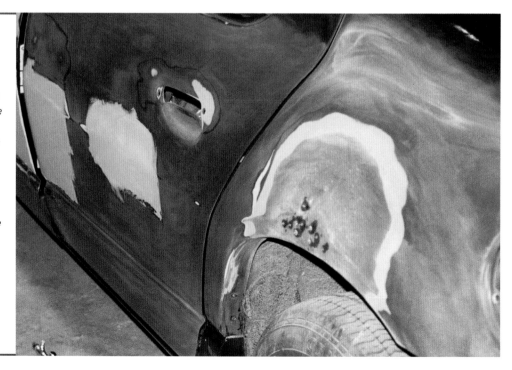

BODYWORK

rial will also be sanded to a point where the only depth difference between an existing painted surface and a repair area will be the actual thickness of the existing paint.

Cleaning Sanded Surfaces Before Undercoat Applications

Once you've sanded or scuffed the surface as required, you'll need to clean it thoroughly to remove all surface contaminants. Painters normally use air pressure to blow off layers of sanding dust from body surfaces, as well as between trunk edge gaps, door edges, and doorjambs.

Next, they use wax and grease remover products to thoroughly wipe down and clean body surfaces. Each paint manufacturer has its own brand of wax and grease remover that constitutes part of an overall paint system. You should use only those wax and grease remover products deemed part of the paint system you will be using.

Dampen a clean cloth (heavy-duty paper shop towels work great) with wax and grease remover and use it to thoroughly wipe off all body surfaces in the area to be painted. The mild solvents in wax and grease removers loosen and dislodge particles of silicone dressings, oil, wax, polish, and other materials embedded in or otherwise lightly adhered to surfaces. To assist the cleaning ability of wax and grease removers, follow the damp cleaning cloth with a clean, dry cloth in your other hand. The dry one picks up lingering residue and moisture to leave behind a clean, dry surface. Use a new towel on every panel, wipe wet, and dry *thoroughly*.

To ensure super clean and dry surfaces, go over finishes with an aerosol glass cleaner after a wax and grease remover.

The ammonia in such glass cleaners helps to disperse and evaporate moisture, as well as to pick up missed spots of wax or dirt residue. Instead of wetting a cloth with glass cleaner, spray the material on surfaces and wipe it off with a clean, dry cloth.

In the paint booth, as a final cleaning chore just before spraying any paint product, wipe off body surfaces with a tack cloth. As mentioned earlier, these specially made cloths are designed to pick up and retain very small specks of lint, dust, and other particles. Although wax and grease removers work well to get rid of contaminants like wax and grease, tack cloths work best for removing tiny pieces of cloth fiber and other items that could easily cause imperfections in paint finishes. Take the tack cloth out of the package, open it fully, and let it air out before use.

Go over every square inch of body surface that will be exposed to paint product application to be certain that all traces of lint are removed. This should guarantee that debris is not blown over onto painted surfaces during the paint process.

Tack cloths have a limited life span. Therefore, you need to refer to product instructions to determine how many times you can use them effectively. Do not try to get more out of them than recommended. Once tack cloths are saturated with lint, debris, and residue, they will no longer pick up new debris. In fact, they may spread accumulated materials absorbed from other cleaning jobs.

APPLYING PRIMER-SURFACER

Primer-surfacer products are generally saved for those body parts that have undergone repair work or suffer very

Wax and grease remover is not only preparation for the final coat of paint. It must be used prior to sanding, prior to application of body filler, and prior to application of primer-surfacer. It can be sprayed on or wiped on with a clean cloth.

The wax and grease remover is then wiped off with a second clean cloth. Heavy-duty paper shop towels are excellent for this use, as they are disposable and sure to be clean if you haven't exposed them to dirt. With reusable towels or cloths, you can never be certain they're clean. Laundered shop towels will occasionally contain a metal shaving.

Even primer-surfacer should be carefully mixed to ensure proper application. Using a calibrated mixing cup makes mixing primer-surfacer with reducer quite easy. Be sure to read the mixing instructions to verify the correct ratio.

After thorough mixing by stirring, place a paint strainer in the spray paint cup, and pour in the primer-surfacer. Never pour any kind of paint product into a spray paint cup without a strainer. Strainers are usually free from where you purchase your paint. Not using one may cost you a spray gun if a speck of dirt or debris gets lodged in an orifice that you can't clean.

minor or shallow sheet metal scratches. Primer-surfacers are *not* a replacement for body filler. Layers that are applied too thick will shrink to accentuate sanding scratches and other imperfections.

After you have successfully sanded and smoothed a top coat of glazing putty filler material, spray two or three coats of primer-surfacer onto the repair area. Then use 320-grit sandpaper to smooth that surface initially. After that, final finish sand with 500-grit sandpaper. You might find that the first three coats of primer-surfacer did not produce the results expected. Very fine sanding scratches or a shallow low spot may remain. In those situations, apply a couple more light coats of primer-surfacer and sand with 320-grit and then 500-grit sandpaper.

To aid in detecting the progress of primer-surfacer sanding, spray a light layer of SEM's Guide Coat over the surface. Sanding will immediately remove this coating from high spots and highlight low spots. In place of the Guide Coat, flat-black paint (or actually any contrasting color) can be applied in very light coats.

Older primer-surfacers were rather heavy, so overspray was not much of a problem, but, with the new high-build primers, that is no longer the case. It is necessary to bag or otherwise mask any area of the vehicle that is not going to be painted. On the bright side, because primer-surfacer will be sanded, there is no need to spray the job in a spray booth. A clean, dust-free area should be sufficient.

Because the high solids content in primer-surfacers can easily flake off masking paper onto work surfaces, it is best to remove masking sheets used during primer-surfacer applications. Sanding dust will accumulate on the vehicle's surface

and in gaps between doors and trunk lids anyway, which will require a complete cleaning with air pressure, wax and grease remover, an aerosol glass cleaner, and tack cloth before any color coats can be applied. After applying and sanding primer-surfacer materials, you can begin definitive masking for sealer applications and actual paint spraying.

Roller-Applied Primer

In order to reduce the amount of VOCs spread into the atmosphere during surface preparation, PPG has developed a primer-surfacer that can be applied with a small roller. This roller-applied primer-surfacer is a high-build product that when mixed with a catalyst will yield the same results as a conventional primer-surfacer without a spray gun or additional solvents. PPG's SX1060 primer is mixed with SX1061 catalyst in a 4:1 ratio.

SX1060 must be applied over an epoxy primer, so it will not completely eliminate the spray gun. However, for localized repairs, or for anyone who may be required to rent a spray booth for conventional applications, this product should prove to be a great asset.

PREPARING FIBERGLASS

Repairing damaged fiberglass requires resin, catalyst, and fiberglass mat products, except on newer Corvettes, minivans, and other vehicles made with a product called Fiber Reinforced Plastic (FRP). Those units require specific repair

continued on page 83

3 With your bodywork complete, the area masked off, primer-surfacer mixed and loaded into the paint gun, and a respirator on, you can spray the primer-surfacer onto the vehicle. With no door handles in the way, it is much easier to get even application. When spraying the lower edges of the vehicle, it is essential to bend over or kneel down so you can see what you are actually spraying, to ensure even coverage.

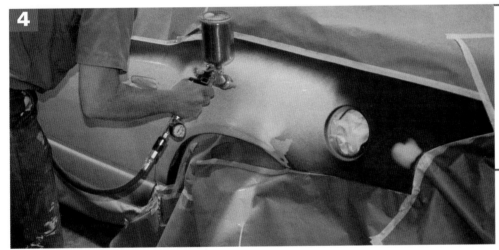

4 Don't spray primer-surfacer all the way to the masking paper, as that would create a harsh line at that point. Instead, taper the primer-surfacer from a heavier application at the actual repair to a very thin dusting before reaching the mask line.

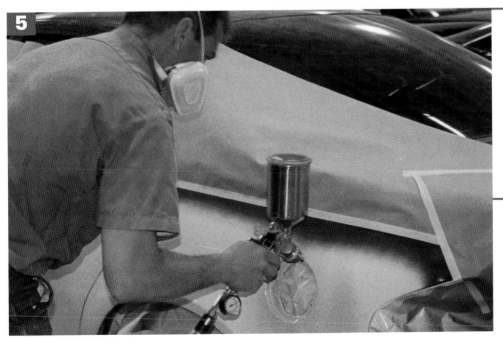

5 The gas filler door has been removed. Since the inside of the filler opening is going to receive primer-surfacer, and therefore paint as well, it should be cleaned and scuffed, just like any other panel. Tending to details like this separates the pros from amateurs.

BODYWORK

Although it is a very light guide coat application, the thin misting of black on the light gray primer-surfacer will aid in highlighting high or low spots when block sanding. (Any contrasting color will suffice.) Most hobbyists should probably apply the guide coat a little heavier. As you sand the panel, low spots will remain dark, while high spots will quickly lighten.

This detail photo of a portion of a truck door shows how lightly the guide coat is applied. With the dark and light primers being fairly even prior to sanding, it will be easier to determine the high and low spots when block sanding begins.

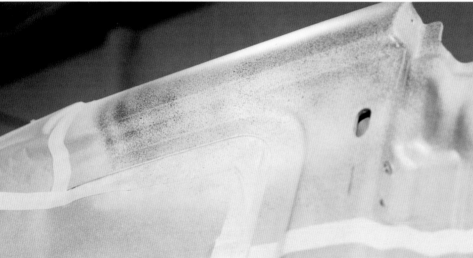

Primer-surfacers will be sanded, so it is not necessary to spray them in a spray booth. There will be some overspray, however, so the immediate area surrounding the repair area needs to be masked off. Masking tape is first applied to the top edge of the inside of the bed, with about half of the tape width sticking up above the surface. Masking paper will later be attached to this to cover the inside wall and floor of the bed.

2

Masking tape is then applied to the inside edge of the taillight opening. On this particular vehicle, the taillight opening will not be painted, so it is masked off.

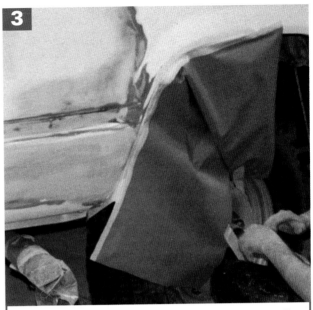

3

As the square paper is fitted around the round wheel opening, it will become necessary to fold the paper over to get it to fit properly. With tape along the inside of the lower portion of the bed side and the tailgate opening, additional masking paper is taped in place to avoid overspray on the chassis components or the inside of the bed.

4

Masking paper is then taped into place along the wheelwell to cover the wheel, tire, and inner fender.

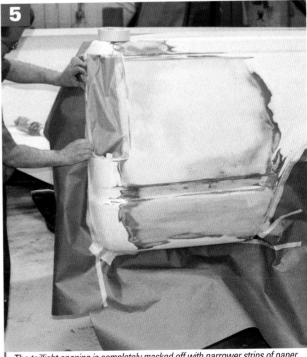

5

The taillight opening is completely masked off with narrower strips of paper.

6

Two more wide strips of masking paper are used to cover the front half of the bedside, and another to cover the inside of the bed. Be sure to tape any seams in the masking paper.

7

Apply primer-surfacer with each pass extending past the actual repair area slightly and onto the masking paper. In this case, paint will cover the repair from around the back edge to the edge of the wheelwell, so the primer-surfacer must be applied there as well.

8

continued from page 78

materials unique to their physical makeup and chemical design. Some auto body technicians prefer to cover finished fiberglass repairs with a skim coat of glazing putty to ensure against pinholes, as air bubbles in resin are common and pinholes on the surface are sometimes impossible to avoid.

Aside from any special product instructions, primer-surfacer is mixed and applied to fiberglass repairs in the same way as for sheet metal surfaces. Use 320- and 500-grit sandpaper to smooth the surface. Masking about two feet in all directions will be sufficient as long as you maintain controlled primer-surfacer sprays.

After sanding the primer-surfacer material to perfection, blow off the dust and mask the car. Use wax and grease remover for thorough cleaning, followed by a wipe down with an aerosol glass cleaner. Then wipe with tack cloth and spray the appropriate sealer. When you've reached the flash (drying) time, tack off the body again, and paint.

Above the wheelwell, the primer-surfacer will taper as mentioned previously. Notice how the painter holds the spray gun perpendicular to the surface area at all times, with the air line held back away from the vehicle.

BODYWORK

Many panels such as doors and deck lids are made up of an outer skin lapped over an inner panel or framework. Where these panels overlap, apply seam sealer to prevent moisture from seeping between the two panels and starting a corrosion problem. Seam sealer should be applied after all bodywork and sanding has been completed, but prior to applying sealer.

Automobile painting consists of a series of tasks that ultimately combine to produce a quality paint job that looks great, feels smooth, adheres securely, and lasts a long time. How good each step looks depends on the step that came before, and poor work anywhere along the line will detract from the end result. In other words, make sure you complete each stage of the painting process thoroughly and to the very highest level you can achieve. If you mess something up, take the time to fix it just right. Remember, the time you spend painting the car will be nothing compared to the amount of time you'll spend enjoying it once you're done. The car will be a rolling testament to your skills. Let the world know you're good!

Auto body surface preparation encompasses those jobs that actually get surfaces ready for paint. These tasks include dismantling some parts, removing old paint, and rust applying primer material finish sanding, and cleaning surfaces with wax and grease remover and tack cloths.

PART REMOVAL

Experienced auto painters and auto enthusiasts can always seem to tell which cars have been repainted and which have not. Yet the goal of every auto painter—going for a stock look—is to finish the job so that no one can tell his or her work is not the very paint put on at the factory.

Tiny strips of paint overspray on window moldings, door handles, or light assemblies are telltale signs that an automobile has been repainted. Closer inspection of the surface finish next to these overspray blemishes might reveal slight sanding scratches, which indicate bodywork has also been done. To a prospective buyer or car show judge, these imperfections raise red flags. A buyer may suspect that the vehicle has been in an accident and perhaps suffered substantial, now-hidden, damage. The car show judge will deduct points because the work is sloppy.

To guarantee that no overspray accumulates on mirrors, door handles, key locks, trim, reflectors, and other removable body accessories, serious auto painters carefully remove and store them. Removing the items alleviates overspray concerns, allows for controlled and thorough body preparation, and prevents paint build-up along their edges.

If you come across items for which you cannot determine a proper removal procedure, consult a service manager at a dealership, a professional auto body repair shop, or an auto paint facility. It makes no sense to take chances on breaking parts when help is just around the corner.

Another good source for this information is a factory repair manual for your vehicle. A dealership can probably help you obtain one for a late-model car or truck. For older vehicles, the Internet and eBay are good sources. Aftermarket

When painting a pickup truck, to avoid looking like an amateur, you must remove the bed so that the front of the bed panel and the back of the cab can be painted. Taking a short cut by not removing the bed, especially in a color-change repaint, is a sure way to announce that the job was not performed by a professional.

Rather than risk getting overspray on any of these panels, they were removed from the vehicle. Removal is usually faster than masking. In a professional body shop, getting the finished vehicle back to the customer in a timely manner and without customer complaints is the name of the game.

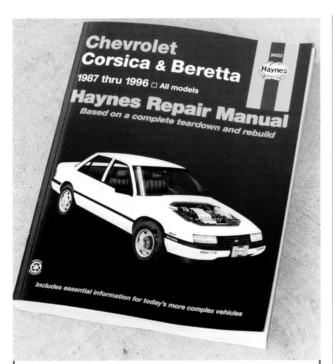

If you are not familiar with automobile assembly and disassembly, purchase a repair manual for your vehicle. The correct way to disassemble many components and their subassemblies is not always obvious, but it's simple once a manual shows you the correct procedure.

Removing parts is a phase of the project in which big gains appear to come quickly. Don't let your eagerness to tear into it rush you: before you start, create a good, sensible plan for removing and storing everything, so you can get it back together properly. Have plenty of large coffee cans and boxes on hand when you start the project. Use a heavy felt-tip marker to label boxes. Use one box for each general car section; for example, driver's side front fender and door, passenger side taillight, side light and reflector, and so on. Be certain to put small screws and nuts back onto the part after you remove it. That way you'll have ready access to them, and know their proper location when it's time to put everything back on.

Bolt On

Most auto body accessory parts such as door handles and mirrors are secured with screws, nuts, or bolts. Some emblems, badges, and trim on newer cars are attached with adhesive or double-backed tape. Before prying or yanking on something, carefully inspect it to determine just how it's mounted. You'll need to replace everything you break, and that costs money, and with rare parts, it may also take time.

If a screw or bolt has a head your screwdrivers and wrenches won't fit, don't fudge it—you could damage the tool or the fastener or both. GM, Ford, Chrysler, and AMC use bolts with multipoint Torx-heads, shaped somewhat like an asterisk or star. You'll need Torx drivers or ratchet bits to remove them. Tool houses and auto parts stores should carry them.

Some door handles are removed by loosening a heavy-duty screw located on the door edge horizontally in line with the handle. The handle is then pulled out from the door skin so the linkage arms can be dislodged. Most other door

publishers also make manuals for a wide range of vehicles. Auto parts stores typically carry these. Be sure to skim the book first to make sure it contains the information you need. A good manual will come in handy for other repairs too.

The door handle and mirror on this SUV have not yet been removed, and if repair is limited to the front fenders and hood, they won't need to be. At this point, the vehicle is on the frame rack for some frame straightening. It doesn't always take a big accident to bend the frame. One sign is that the vehicle no longer tracks properly. If you suspect frame damage, have it checked out before you paint to avoid unnecessary adjustments, scratches, and expense.

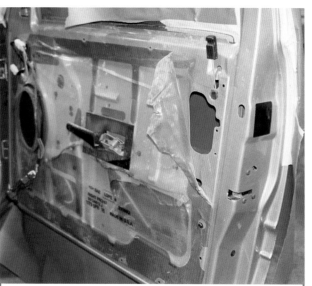

Inside door handle mechanisms are usually secured with two to four small screws. On older vehicles, it will be necessary to remove the inside door handle prior to removing the interior door panel, while on newer vehicles, the panel usually slips off over the handle. With electronic door locks, it is often best to leave the mechanism in place, but, it must be supported so that wires don't get damaged.

With the interior door panel removed, we get a glimpse of the inside of the door. Shown are the window riser mechanism, the connecting rod to the door latch, and wiring for power door locks. (Don't pinch your fingers!)

handles are secured by two screws or nuts accessed from inside the inner door space. Their removal requires that interior door panels be taken off first for access to the handle support.

Interior door panels are secured either with screws or clips. You will have to examine the door panels on your car to deter-mine how they are attached. If no screws are visible anywhere around the perimeter of the panel, chances are good that it's secured with plastic clips pushed into retainer mounts. They are simply pried loose. But before you start prying, be sure to remove armrests, window cranks, and door handles.

This taillight looks to be secured from inside the trunk, as no screws are apparent from the outside. Remove the bulbs from their sockets first (usually a twist and pull operation), and then remove the screws or clips securing the taillight lens.

Just behind (above) the cable in the photo and accessible through the opening in the radiator trim panel is a headlight adjusting screw. Assuming that your headlights are properly aimed prior to your painting project, avoid adjusting or removing this screw.

Armrests are commonly secured by two large Phillips head screws. Window cranks on older cars are kept in place with a small C-shaped metal clip that snaps off the crank's operating shaft for removal. Newer cars may have pop-off plastic caps that run from the swivel knob to the shaft. Use a small-bladed screwdriver to gently pry off caps to access screws or nuts that hold cranks in place.

Door handles on older cars are removed just like their matching window cranks, by removing their C-shaped metal clips. Newer car handles will have a screw or two holding them in place. After removing the screws, you might have to pry on the handle housing to pop it loose from the door panel opening in which it rests. Linkage arms from the handle to the door latch mechanism will have to be taken off as well.

Light assemblies are normally secured with screws located on the back of the housing assembly. Taillight units are removed from inside trunk or hatchback areas or pulled

This photo reveals a couple of different types of weather stripping. Sealing the outer extremes of the door and the body is a stiff rubber molding that is commonly glued into place. In this example, it appears that it has been damaged, and that someone made a shoddy repair. A softer, more flexible type of weather stripping (sometimes referred to as wind lace) fits around the inner door opening where the inside and outside panels of the body come together. The two body panels (inner and outer) come together to form a flange that the weather stripping slips onto.

straight out from the outside. Some lights may require you to remove lenses first by taking out two of four Phillips or Torx head screws. Reflectors should be easily removed by loosening screws located at either end of the lens or from inside the corresponding compartment.

Grilles may be a bit tricky to remove. Automotive engineers have gotten quite ingenious with hiding mounting screws and clips in such ways that it is sometimes almost impossible to figure out how they are held in place. Look for Torx, Phillips, or Allen head screws around the perimeter edge of grille sections. Although many grilles consist of a combination of parts, entire assemblies can sometimes be removed as single units if all the right screws are loosened. Separate pieces are held together with special clips.

Leave headlights in place if possible, especially if their current light beams are correctly adjusted. Should you decide that they have to be removed, do not touch the two screws that have springs beneath them. These are the directional adjustment screws used to move the headlight up or down, or right to left.

Bumpers on older cars are a snap to remove. Their support bolts are in plain view and there is generally no question as to how they are dismantled. Newer car bumpers are not always that easy to figure out. Since many of these units consist of a number of different parts, it may appear that they couldn't possibly be removed. Splash guards and other urethane accessories may cover them to the point that the only visible part of the assembly's support is located under the front or rear section of the car. Take your time removing bumpers, and enlist a helper if necessary. These units are heavy and you should take

precautions so they do not fall on you while you're under the car loosening support bolts.

Adhesive

Once the interior door panels are removed, you will notice a piece of plastic or other material between the panel and door skin. This is a vapor barrier. Its function is to prevent water from entering the passenger compartment after it has seeped past window trim moldings. Be sure to keep those vapor barriers intact. You can simply roll them up to the top of the door and tape them out of the way.

If you need to paint door edges, you will have to remove weather stripping. As with other body parts, you will have to examine the stripping closely to see just how it is secured. Some stripping is attached with adhesive. You'll have to remove it with an adhesive remover unless it is stout enough to withstand being pulled off. You may be able to use a heat gun or blow dryer to loosen the adhesive as you pull off the weather stripping.

Other kinds of weather stripping are secured with plastic pins with large heads inserted into prefabricated holes. The protruding parts of these pins are pressed into holes around the doors' perimeter edges.

Body side moldings and other trim pieces are secured to car bodies in several ways. Some feature protruding pins that snap into retainers; others have pins that are secured from the inside with flat metal retainers, and many are simply glued in place with adhesive or double-backed tape. To determine how these parts are secured to your car, you will have to gently pry up on an edge to inspect the back. Be very careful while doing this, because many plastic pieces are brittle and will crack if pried too far.

Since the replacement door has no holes for screws or bolts, the body side molding is probably held in place by adhesive, or it may have a peel-off backing. Either way, you need a thin putty knife or similar tool to pry it carefully from the vehicle. Take care when removing trim, as you'll usually have to replace it if it breaks.

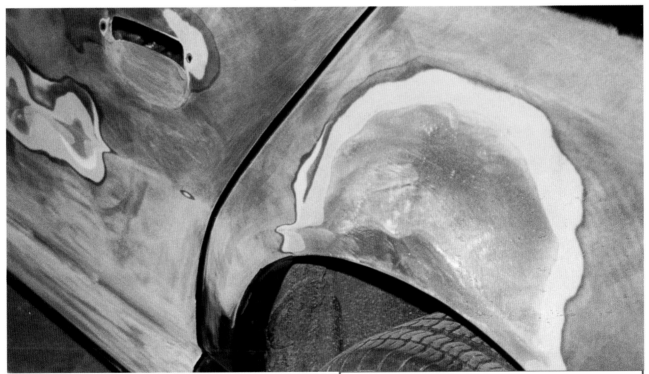

PAINT REMOVAL

The amount of old paint you need to remove depends upon the paint's condition, whether the vehicle requires bodywork, and how extensive the paint job will be. New paint can be applied over old paint, if the existing finish is sanded until all oxidized paint material is removed and the

This photo shows the original damage to this sedan. Where metal work is required and filler will be applied, the paint is removed completely with a DA sander. Outside of this area, paint is removed, but the original primer or sealer is left intact. These two areas will receive the heaviest coatings of primer-surfacer, although it will be built up in thin layers, rather than one thick coat. The large gray area has been scuffed lightly to offer good adhesion however, the original sealer is still intact.

The center roof section of this Dodge truck is going to be replaced. To facilitate removal, the rear glass has been removed. Some of the sealer used for sealing the glass is still stuck to the metal, so it is removed with a grinder. The outer roof panel is spot welded to the inner roof panel where the two come together at the window. Those spot welds will be drilled out or ground down to remove the outer roof panel.

surface is left flat, even, and smooth, and the original paint is not lacquer-based. If the original paint is lacquer based, the area to be painted will need to be taken to bare metal and a compatible undercoat applied for the top coat being used, otherwise the new paint will suffer adhesion problems. If the car needs bodywork, you'll have to take that area down to bare metal so that the filler material has its best opportunity to bond completely.

Painting decisions are easy when the vehicle needs bodywork or has deep paint blemishes. But if the old paint looks dull and oxidized, and you simply want to repaint it to look nice, here are some questions to ponder: Is the existing paint too thick to support a new finish? Is there rust anywhere on the body? Does the entire car need a new paint job, or will repaint efforts to a couple of panels do the trick? Put some time into deciding how much painting you need to do.

The best way to remove paint depends on the condition of the vehicle's existing paint surface. Cars with excellent bodies that require no sheet metal repair should have paint removed using the mildest method. This would probably be a chemical stripper or mild paint-stripping scouring-type pad.

Sanding

The Eastwood Company offers Strip Disc kits that include three 7-inch stripping discs and a cushioned backing pad that attaches to angled sanders (buffers) with 6,000-rpm

maximum speeds. They are advertised to strip paint quickly and completely without creating excessive heat, and their design will not harm valuable body panels. They are recommended after you've removed the bulk of old paint with a chemical stripper. An assortment of chemical strippers is available at auto body paint and supply stores. Be sure to read label instructions and plan to wear recommended protective equipment.

High-speed rotary sanders with coarse discs remove paint in a hurry. These work great for bodywork because the rough sanding scratches left behind make an excellent surface for filler to bond to. High-speed sanders and coarse discs also work well to remove rust.

One caution with power sanding tools is that they generate a lot of heat. If you keep the tool in one area for too long, the sustained friction can generate enough heat to warp the panel. The risk of warping is greater on new cars, with their relatively thin panels.

Media Blasting

Another way to remove old paint is by sandblasting, or more common today, media blasting. This equipment works especially well for older cars with surface rust. Sandblasting media works fast to remove paint and traces of rust caught in tiny cracks, crevices, and pits. You will have to contend with messy cleanup after your work is done, but the extra work is well worth the effort, as you'll discover that old paint and rust removal is done quickly and thoroughly.

Sandblasters require controlled use with a compatible pressure and media combination. Too much pressure mixed with harsh media will cause sheet metal warping problems and other damage. For safest results, remove all accessories, as sandblasting will take off chrome and paint, and it can quickly pit glass. Remove all vulnerable body parts or protect them with tarps or other suitably heavy material. Test the material first to be sure the sandblaster doesn't power through it.

Sandblaster manufacturers and suppliers offer charts that indicate which media should be used at what pressures for different kinds of jobs. Media are rated according to their size—the lower the number, the smaller the particle size. For use on car parts and bodies, typical ranges would be from number 40 (0.016 inch) to a smaller size of number 12 (0.004 inch). Media also come in work mixes that combine different amounts of various sized particles. Consult a salesperson at a sandblasting equipment store or jobber at an auto body paint and supply store for help in selecting the proper media.

As important as media size is the pressure at which the material is blasted. Since media can be propelled at speeds from 200 to 400 miles per hour, you had better be sure that pressure settings are correct to prevent unwanted body

This 1932 Ford cowl is a prime example of some vintage tin that needs to be cleaned up somehow, before it's reincarnated in a hot rod woody project. A dip in chemical stripper will remove all of the rust, leaving like-new metal, which will then be treated with epoxy primer. With a manageable size piece like this, the cowl could be dipped into some sort of vat filled with epoxy primer to coat the inside edges. Having the cowl media blasted instead of chemically dipped would leave the original paint in those tiny crooks and crevices. Were there any paint left, that might be a better option.

damage. In addition, you need to protect yourself from sandblasting media. Always wear heavy-duty leather gloves, long sleeves, and a quality sandblasting hood.

It is also recommended that you wear a NIOSH-approved respirator. Certain media materials, like silica, produce dust particles that could be harmful to your respiratory system. Along with respirators and gloves, sandblasters and media can be purchased at auto body paint and supply stores. Home-use sandblasting equipment can range from $40 sandblasting guns that siphon media from a bucket, to a first-class unit costing around $400.

Various sandblaster nozzle sizes require air compressors with specific horsepower. For example, a 3/32-inch nozzle requires a 2- to 3-horsepower air compressor to supply 7 cubic feet per minute at 80 psi. A 1/8-inch nozzle needs a 3- to 5-horsepower air compressor to supply it with 15 cubic feet per minute at 80 psi. Charts continue up to a 5/16-inch nozzle, which calls for a 40-horsepower air compressor to supply 125 cubic feet per minute at 80 psi. Again, check the charts at places that sell sandblast media to be sure the nozzle size, media, and air pressure that you plan to use will work in combination for your job.

Chemical Stripping or Dipping

If you want to start with fresh metal prior to repainting, whether you are resurrecting a vehicle that has been sitting outside in the elements or one that has been kept inside, a chemical stripper is the best method. Unlike media blasting, which may leave the sheet metal warped or pitted, chemical stripping will remove all of the layers of primer, paint, wax, grease, dirt, and whatever else may be on it. When the stripping process is complete, you'll have shiny, bare metal. Yet there are some drawbacks to dipping a metal body or component. When the piece is dipped (submerged), the rust removal liquid gets into all surfaces, cracks, and crevices, exposing all to the environment. If you can access all of these surfaces and apply epoxy primer, you will be able to ward off rust quite successfully. However, unless you are dipping a single layer of sheet metal, chances are that you will not be able to apply epoxy primer to all of the bare surfaces. If you are in a dry climate, you may not have any problem, however, if you are in a humid climate, rust will eventually form on this bare metal.

If you are stripping a fender or other relatively small component, you can strip it yourself with a product known as aircraft stripper. It would be best to remove the panel to be stripped from the vehicle if at all possible, as the stripper is much more difficult to mask than paint. When using paint stripper, be sure to use a proper respirator and rubber gloves. If the product is strong enough to remove paint, you can imagine what it will do to your skin and lungs.

For best results, use 100-grit sandpaper or a ScotchBrite pad to scuff the panel. This will break open the seal of the existing paint, and allow the stripper to soak in to the paint it is supposed to remove. Apply the stripper as directed by the manufacturer. Allow the stripper plenty of time to work into the paint and begin loosening it. As the paint begins to loosen and bubble up from the surface, you can scrape it off with a putty knife. As top coats come off to yield undercoats, you may need to apply more stripper.

When you've stripped the entire surface, you must neutralize the effects of the stripper with lots of water. If the stripper is not neutralized, it will attack any primer or other paint coats that you may apply. After the area has been thoroughly neutralized and rinsed with water, the surface must be completely dried. It should then be wiped down with wax and grease remover, and then coated with an epoxy primer to prevent rust from forming on the bare, albeit clean, sheet metal.

If you desire to have an entire body hulk or more than one single panel stripped down to bare metal, you would be well advised to have it dipped by a professional service that specializes in this type of work. To find a company that does this, you may have to ask auto restorers in your area, or look in *Hemmings Motor News* for advertisements. When you find a company that does this work, you should call them ahead of time to see if you need to schedule an appointment to drop off your car body or parts. Sometimes there is a waiting list. The wait may be longer if you are bringing in a complete body hulk and several other pieces, while if you just have a few small pieces, they can usually fit them in with other jobs.

You can also ask for an estimate to have your pieces dipped. Most companies will have a set price for doors, hoods, and deck lids, etc. They are familiar enough with vehicles to know what it is going to take to strip a small Model A Ford roadster, compared to a large mid-1950s Cadillac. A recent estimate for a 1956 Ford pickup cab and doors was just under $500, to give a basic idea of the cost.

Prior to taking your parts to the stripper, you need to disassemble them as completely as possible. If you take off the doors, hood, and deck lid, you will get a more compete stripping job than if you leave these items in place. You also need to do some investigation to find out if there is any body filler in the vehicle already. This can be done with a magnet or a grinder. If the magnet doesn't stick to what should be a metal surface, there is at least some amount of body filler present. If you are contemplating taking the part

in question to a stripper anyway, doing some grinding ahead of time won't hurt anything. If body filler is present and is thicker than about an ⅛ inch, you should grind it out before going to the stripper. Anything less than an ⅛ inch can usually be removed by the stripping process. Bear in mind that only metal pieces should go into the chemical dipping tank.

The stripping process consists of two different dipping operations. The first dip is into a "hot tank" filled with a caustic solution. This removes wax, grease, and paint from the metal. Depending on the number of layers of paint or other chemicals on the metal, this process will take about four to eight hours. After the parts are removed from the hot tank, they are thoroughly rinsed with plain water for another three to four hours to remove the caustic solution. With that done, the pieces and parts are dipped into a second vat filled with a de-rusting solution. At this time, the material is connected to an electrical charge in just the opposite manner from chroming and powder coating. In those processes, the current draws the chrome and powder material onto the material, while here the electric charge pulls rust away from the metal. Depending on the condition of the metal and the amount of rust, this process takes from 20 to 40 hours. When removed from the de-rusting vat, the parts are thoroughly rinsed with plain water to neutralize any continuing effect of the de-rusting solution.

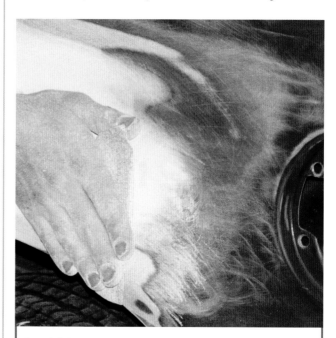

Scotch-Brite pads work well to scuff existing paint or for a final smoothing effort. Available in three different levels of coarseness, the coarsest would be appropriate for scuffing paint before applying a sealer. The finest would be more appropriate for final smoothing prior to applying primer-surfacer.

When this process is complete, a phosphate coating will be left on the dipped pieces. This will retard rust somewhat, however, the part should be rinsed clean and coated with an epoxy primer as soon as is practical.

SANDING

By the time you finish any necessary bodywork, prepare the surface for paint, and wet sand the finished painted surface, you will be intimately familiar with your vehicle's body. Don't worry, you cannot sand too much, or get your car too smooth. You can however, sand too deep (into the layer below), or in a pattern (leaving a wavy panel). When you are sanding, you should use the largest sanding board or block that will fit into the area that you are sanding. You should also sand in every different direction that you can think of to avoid sanding grooves or other deformities into your vehicle. Anyone can sand, but not everyone does it correctly.

Sanding Existing Paint Surfaces

Applying new paint over old paint without properly scuffing up the old surface is a mistake, especially when dealing with factory paint jobs that were baked on at 450 degrees Fahrenheit. Situations like this commonly result in new paint flaking off because it does not have an absorbent base to adhere to. The super hard baked-on paint jobs do not always allow new paint to penetrate their surfaces.

Although painting over a perfectly good paint job might appear to be unnecessary or foolish, some enthusiasts may want to change a solid color scheme into a two-tone blend, or business owners may need to add certain bands of particular colors so new vehicles match the rest of the fleet. For whatever reason, paint surfaces that will be painted over must be scuffed first.

Fine grade Scotch-Brite pads work great for scuffing baked-on paint finishes. The comparatively rough finish left behind makes a great base for coats of sealer. You could also use 500- to 600-grit sandpaper to scuff shiny paint finishes. The overall purpose is to dull all shiny surfaces so that new layers of material have something to grab onto. There is no need to scuff or sand in one direction only. You can, and should, sand in all directions to be sure all surface areas have been roughened up satisfactorily.

GETTING IT SMOOTH

When you have completed all the bodywork or rust repair and have all the panels straight and with the proper gaps, you are not necessarily ready to start spraying paint. The body panels all need to be smooth as well. Walk around the entire vehicle, looking closely at its surface. Any and all imperfections that you can see now, while it is in primer or scuffed paint, will be magnified by the new paint.

Even if there are no imperfections, does the entire vehicle feel as if it has a texture to it? A coat or two of paint is not

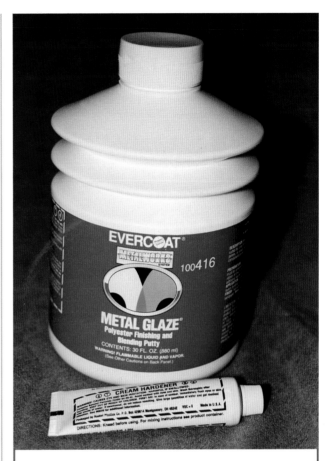

Spot putty is somewhere between body filler and high-build primer-surfacer. It is much too thick to apply with a spray gun, but it is finer than typical body filler. It is similar to body filler in that it is mixed with a hardening agent and then spread onto the body to fill minor scratches or pinholes.

going to smooth out the finish. The only way to eliminate this rough feeling is to block sand the area that still feels rough, whether it is a small area or the entire vehicle.

Finer Paper

If you have block sanded the entire vehicle with 400-grit sandpaper, you may still have some sanding scratches that will show when painted over. You will need to go over the entire vehicle with 600-grit sandpaper to eliminate them.

Using Spot Putty

There may still be some slight imperfections. Slight pinholes in body filler, or extremely minor scratches, may be filled with spot putty. This is a substance somewhat thicker than primer-surfacer, but thinner than body filler. It comes in a squeezable bottle, is mixed with a cream hardener, and can be applied with a small body filler spreader. It should be used for only the tiniest imperfections, so only a small amount is needed. After allowing the spot putty to

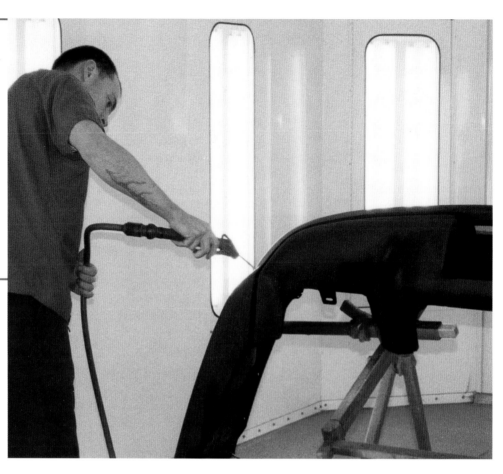

Before applying sealer to this refurbished flexible bumper/fascia, the painter washed and scuffed it with a ScotchBrite pad to remove any contaminated substances. It was then cleaned with wax and grease remover. As a final step prior to application of sealer, the painter uses an air nozzle to blow out any lingering dust particles or moisture. It is much better to blow out water drops now than with air from your spray gun while spraying paint.

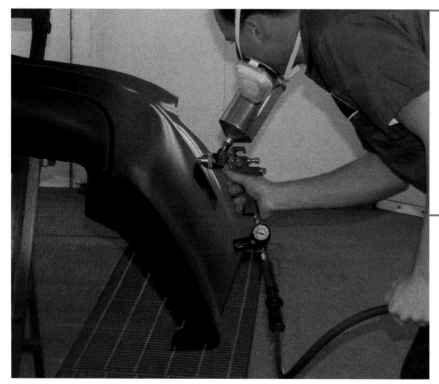

With the surface area clean and dry, this flexible panel is ready for sealer. Since no bodywork was done, there is no need for primer-surfacer to smooth out the surface. Years ago, a painter would mix a flex additive with the sealer, the base coat, and the clear coat; however, that is no longer necessary with improved paint products. In this case, sealer will be applied, and by the time the spray gun is emptied, cleaned, and the base coat is mixed, the sealer will be ready to be top coated.

dry according to the product directions, you can sand it with 600-grit or finer sandpaper.

Even Finer Sandpaper

If you are working on a restoration or show car project, you may choose to block sand the entire vehicle with 800-grit sandpaper. Depending on how elaborate you desire to get with your paint job, you could also graduate to 1,000-grit sandpaper, but only after you have used the 800-grit on the entire vehicle—jumping too quickly to a much finer paper leaves you sanding much longer to remove scratches.

APPLYING PRIMER AND SEALER

Epoxy primers and sealers do not have to be sanded, unless runs or imperfections develop when you apply them. In those cases, use a fine-grit sandpaper to smooth blemishes. Then touch up spots with a new coat of material. As previously described, epoxy primers are sprayed onto bare metal finishes to waterproof and protect them. Most auto restorers apply epoxy primer products, like PPG's DPLF40, to bare metal items once they have removed old paint and rust. Others prefer to apply body filler directly to bare metal and then seal repairs after they've applied and sanded primer-surfacer products.

For those body panels or vehicles that will receive complete new paint jobs only, primer and sealer materials are sprayed in a paint booth after masking. Because those items will receive no body repair or body filler applications,

For the most part, this body hulk is ready for an application of sealer and then paint. Rust has been removed, any necessary bodywork completed, and primer-surfacer block sanded.

their surfaces are essentially ready for paint. Therefore, treat this paint phase as you would a normal top coat application. After masking, clean surfaces with wax and grease remover, aerosol window cleaner, and a tack cloth. Then, mix the primer, or sealer product according to label instructions, don appropriate painting attire, and begin.

For those jobs requiring only a part of a vehicle to be shot with primer or sealer, you should lay large strips of masking paper over unaffected areas such as hoods, roofs, and trunk lids to protect them from overspray. Use the minimum recommended pressure and fan the spray gently to cover bare metal spots. Feather them into adjacent areas by slowly releasing the paint gun trigger toward the end of the passes. Practice this technique on something other than your car first.

Complete repaint jobs, in which no bodywork has been performed and existing paint has been scuffed, are also considered ready for paint. They need to be masked and then shot with a sealer, as recommended by your auto body paint and supply jobber or by the information in the paint manufacturer's application guide. These sealers will not have to be sanded, unless you botch a spot and have to sand out runs or other imperfections. Once the sealer has cured according to label directions, you can apply paint.

CHAPTER 7

MASKING

To prevent unwanted paint from landing on body sections adjacent to those being painted, they must be protected with masking paper and tape. Although an initial estimate of the masking needs for your vehicle may appear to be rather limited and easy to accomplish, you must understand that less than meticulous masking will almost always result in obvious spots of overspray.

Some paint overspray can be cleaned off or painted over, but trim pieces and other assorted body items marred with thin strips of paint on their edges may not fare as well. A conscientious buyer or detail-oriented judge will quickly notice small lines of paint on windshield moldings, key locks, door handles, emblems, lights, and reflectors. To them, overspray on any item proves that an automobile has been repainted. They may wonder whether it has also seen extensive bodywork, from a collision or advanced rust. Was this paint job something a conscientious owner did to make the car look its very best, or is it an effort to hide serious flaws? And if the former, why did he or she settle for sloppy work?

Next to color matching, masking is perhaps the most meticulous and exacting chore required of an auto body painter. Since your auto body paint and supply store will mix paint blends and tints, your most precise work revolves around masking. To make the job as simple as possible, be sure to use only those tape and paper products designed for automotive paint masking. Devise and follow a systematic masking plan, and then allot enough time to complete those tasks with strict attention to detail.

OUTLINING

It is not always easy to lay down a perfect strip of ¾-inch masking tape along edges of trim or other body parts. Around curves, especially tight ones, this kind of tape material tends to bunch up and fold, causing flat spots instead of smooth and evenly flowing contours. Masking rounded items is even more difficult when sheets of masking paper are attached to tape strips. As a matter of fact, placing paper and tape together along exact edges in one move is not easily accomplished on any body part.

Professional painters rely on quality workmanship and effective time management to make money. To them, it would be foolish to waste a half-hour masking trim when only five minutes would be needed to remove the part. Likewise, rather than hassle with a piece of tape and sheet of paper to mask along a section of window trim, they lay down a thin strip of Fine Line brand masking tape first and then attach wider strips of tape and paper to it—a much less meticulous task.

Placing a thin ⅛- to ¼-inch strip of plastic Fine Line masking tape right along molding or trim edges is easy because of its manageable size and texture. It gently follows

The grille and bumper on this Ford pickup are quite massive, so the painter removed them rather than attempt to mask them. With those pieces out of the way, masking the radiator, its supports, and headlights is fairly simple. Wide masking paper can be taped to the radiator support and draped down over the front of the truck. A second sheet can then be attached to it to reach to the floor. Removing the bumper and grille also allows for thorough painting of the surfaces to which these pieces are attached.

On a total repaint of a vehicle, such as on this Ford pickup, there was no need to remove the glass. Since most of the interior components are still in place, the window openings would need to be covered anyway, so it is best to leave the glass in place, eliminating any problems of air leaks in the future. A piece of 1½-inch-wide masking tape is first attached to the molding around the window. Masking paper is then attached to the tape, with the seam covered with more tape. Make sure that any tears in the paper are covered with masking tape also.

Masking tape is used to go around the front windshield in the same manner as the back glass. The outer edge of the 1½-inch-wide tape will be the limits of the masking, so take your time positioning the tape. After the truck is moved into the spray booth, masking paper will be attached to this tape, and any seams will be covered as well.

curves without bunching or folding, and its smooth edges are easy to match along body part edges for perfect masking every time.

The only function of Fine Line tape is masking those part edges next to body panels that are slated for new paint. You then attach additional strips of regular masking tape and paper to Fine Line. This gives you a wide margin to work from instead of the precise line of the part's edge.

Although most professional auto painters prefer to use Fine Line for outlining intricate masking jobs, you could also use ¼-inch paper masking tape. It works very well along straight sections, but tends to bunch up and fold around corners. In addition, the slightly rough texture of this material sometimes allows tiny gaps to form along masked edges, which allow paint materials to build up and form spots of overspray.

In addition to removing the bed from this pickup truck, the painter will also cover the rear portion of the frame. Even though the frame and adjacent pieces (wiring, brake lines, fuel tank, etc.) are mostly out of sight, a professional won't coat them with overspray. After the truck is moved into the spray booth, plastic sheeting will be used to cover this large area. Much like a drop cloth, it will cover the frame rails, the wheels, tires, and virtually everything else on the back half of the truck.

Side windows are taped off in similar fashion. As the edge of the masking tape will indicate the edge of new paint, it must be positioned carefully and firmly pressed into place. If the masking tape is not straight, the paint edge won't be either. If the edge isn't pressed fully into place, the edge won't be as crisp and sharp as it should be.

Another benefit of Fine Line plastic tape is that it is very thin. Painting along thick paper leaves a definite lip of built-up paint when you remove the paper. But Fine Line is so thin that the edge is minimal, allowing you to blend it into surrounding paint work easily.

WINDOWS

It's difficult to paint around windows without getting overspray on belt moldings and trim pieces surrounding the glass. The surest way to avoid overspray is to remove the glass and trim. Barring that, use plastic tape to outline outer molding edges next to those panels to be painted. Attach strips of wider masking tape and paper anywhere along the plastic tape's width; just make sure there are no gaps between the inside edge of the Fine Line and the wider tape.

You only need one strip of masking paper to cover windows, as long as it's wide enough to reach from top to bottom. Fold paper as necessary to make it fit neatly along the sides. Use strips of tape to hold the paper in a secure position and to cover any resulting gaps. A single sheet of automotive masking paper will prevent paint from bleeding through to underlying surfaces. If you have chosen to use a masking material other than recommended automotive masking paper, you might have to apply two or three layers.

Masking paper does not always come in widths that fit window shapes exactly. Most of the time, especially with side windows, you end up with a tight fit along edges and bulges in the middle. To avoid bulges, fold excess masking paper so that it lies flat. Not only does this make for a tidy masking job, it prevents bulky paper from being blown around by air pressure from a paint spray gun. All you have to do is lay one hand down on an edge of the paper and slide it toward the middle. With your other hand, grasp the bulging paper and fold it over. Use strips of tape to hold it in a neat fold.

Whenever masking, always remember that paint will cover everything that it touches. Very small slits between tape and masking paper will allow paint to reach the surface below. Lightly secured paper edges will blow open during spray paint operations and allow mists of overspray to infiltrate underlying spaces. Therefore, always run lines of tape along the length of paper edges to seal off underlying areas completely. This is especially important when the edge of one piece of masking paper is overlapped with another.

Windshields and rear windows are generally quite big. You might have to use two or three strips of paper horizontally placed in order to cover all glass. If you leave trim pieces in place, consider applying Fine Line tape around their outer edges before working with wider tape and paper. You must remove rear window louvers or side window air deflectors when painting body areas next to them.

Rubber moldings that lap against body panels—rubber windshield moldings along roofs, A-pillars, and cowlings—present difficult masking challenges. To make the job of placing tape directly over the molding's outer edge easier, consider putting a length of thick, nonscratching cord under it.

The Eastwood Company carries a Weatherstrip Masking Tool designed to insert long strips of plastic cord under the edges of molding and weather stripping. It raises these edges up off body surfaces to allow complete masking under them. This way, paint can reach under molding edges, instead of just up to them, ensuring good paint coverage and eliminating distinctive paint edge lines next to moldings.

If you've removed the windows and moldings, you'll have to mask off the interior compartment. Generally, exterior paint colors are applied to the middle of window openings. You could lay down strips of wide tape inside these openings and fold it over toward the inside for side windows. Along the spot-welded metal edge of windshield openings, simply apply perimeter tape and paper from the interior compartment side.

EMBLEMS AND BADGES

As with trim pieces, it is best to remove emblems and badges before painting. They are secured by clips, pins, screws, adhesives, or double-backed tape. Be extra cautious while attempting to take these items off of any vehicle. Too much prying pressure will cause them to break. Unless you can see that their protruding support pins are secured from inside a trunk space, inner fender area, or other locations, you will have to carefully pry open an edge to determine just how they are mounted.

If you are not sure how to remove those items, consult a dealership service representative, auto body paint and supply jobber, or professional auto body painter. Should an emblem or badge break during dismantling, don't despair.

Even professional auto body technicians break these plastic items occasionally.

Although most painting jobs call for removing emblems and badges, there are two occasions where they can be left in place—when you're spraying only clear coat paint or spot painting work with only a light melting coat close to their edge. In those cases, carefully mask to ensure that no overspray builds up on along their edges.

To ensure that emblem and badge edges are completely covered, mask carefully around their edges, allowing no part of the tape to extend onto the painted surface. Tape over the edges first, before masking their faces. Again, Fine Line tape may be the best material for this meticulous task. After attaching the tape's end to a corner of an emblem, maneuver the roll with one hand while carefully placing and securing the tape with your other hand. Practice is essential, so do not expect to accomplish this kind of unique masking on the first try.

Some painters make this job easier by covering emblems with wide strips of tape first. They then use a sharp razor blade to cut tape along the emblem edges at the exact point where they meet the painted body. You must use a very delicate touch to avoid cutting into paint or missing the mark and leaving an open gap along the part being masked off. If you should decide to try this technique, opt for very light passes with the razor blade, even if it takes two or three attempts to cut completely through the tape. This will allow you to avoid a deep scratch in the paint, should your hand slip.

About the only way to mask vinyl decals, like those under gasoline filler housings that say "Unleaded Only," is to cover them with masking tape and then cut off excess with a *sharp* razor blade. The word sharp is emphasized for a reason. Dull razor blades, even those that have been used to make only three or four cuts, will tear masking tape instead of cutting it cleanly. Again, use light pressure to prevent unnecessary damage to underlying paint.

DOOR LOCKS AND HANDLES

Because door locks and handles are secured right next to painted door panels, the same kind of meticulous masking is required for them as for emblems and badges. The best approach is to remove them, unless you're doing only clear coats or light paint feathering or melting in up to their edge. Removing these components is discussed in Part Removal in Chapter 6.

Door handles are best masked using tape for the entire process. Paper, even in 4-inch widths, is just too cumbersome to work with. Use ¾-inch tape to mask the perimeter edges and then 2-inch tape to completely cover the unit. If your car presents a rather unique handle, employ whatever means necessary to cover it. Use your imagination. Tape can be applied initially from the back to offer sticky edges that can extend out past upper and lower edges and can be folded over to cover the front. Remember, the most critical part of masking is along the edge, where items meet painted panels. Wide strips of tape can easily cover faces and other easy-to-reach parts.

Key locks are easiest to mask by simply covering them with a wide strip of 1-or 2-inch-wide tape, and then cutting the excess from around the lock's circumference with a sharp razor blade. Before cutting, though, use a fingernail to force tape down along the circumference to be sure coverage is complete and that the tape is securely in place.

DOORJAMBS

Many novice painters forget to mask doorjambs before spraying undercoats or top coats. This oversight always results in overspray in doorjamb areas, including the inner side of door edges. As paint enters the gaps between doors and jambs, it bounces off surfaces to land anywhere it can. The same problem exists inside the gaps along the tops and bottoms of doors. The mess created by this kind of overspray can be difficult to remove.

Painters commonly prefer to coat doorjambs and edges first when they are to be painted along with the body. After those areas have cured, you can close the doors and paint their exterior portions without overspray concerns. You may choose to mask the doorjamb areas after they are cured to avoid overspray, however same-color overspray in doorjamb areas is not uncommon among new vehicles. To paint doorjambs, door edges, and outer door skins all at the same time, you must move the doors so you can reach their front section, which swings inward past the rear part of the fender. This movement damages wet paint on hinges.

It is much easier to paint the interior side and perimeter edges of doors while they are off the vehicle. Once that has dried, you can assemble the window and latch mechanisms, install the doors, and spray their exteriors in one sequence. When painting the exterior surface, you must still mask the jambs, even those freshly painted with the same color applied on the outside. This will keep the jamb coat even and smooth.

Some painters like to apply 2-inch tape along the edges of rear doorjambs with the sticky side facing out. Only about half of the tape strip actually goes on the jamb, and the rest is folded over, so that it is perpendicular. Another strip is placed on the rear door edge in the same manner; half of it sticks out, with the sticky side facing out. This way, when the door is closed, the two strips of tape are attached to each other to effectively seal the gap between the door and jamb.

Although it is a relatively small opening, it is still necessary to close up the opening vacated by the removal of the outside door handle, as much primer-surfacer would find its way inside the car. This opening isn't being masked off from paint application, as all of the outside should be coated with primer-surfacer, and then paint. For this reason, it has to be masked from the inside. With the door open and the interior door panel removed, two pieces of wide masking tape can be overlapped to close off this opening.

Even though there may seem to be no reason for removing the interior door panels, tasks like closing the opening vacated by the removal of the door handle make it a necessity. Some people may leave the interior door panel in place and use it to prevent paint from getting inside the car. That, however, would be a very unprofessional way of doing the work.

MASKING

100

Prior to masking the outside of the vehicle, it is wiped down with wax and grease remover. Just as paint won't stick to dirt and other contaminants, neither will masking tape. You definitely don't want the masking tape and paper to start coming loose when you are in the middle of spraying primer-surfacer, or—even worse—while spraying the final paint.

A piece of tape is attached to the bottom edge of the car from the inside, so that a piece of masking paper can later be attached to it. This will act as a skirt to prevent overspray from hitting the underside of the vehicle.

Prior to masking, you must take a moment to determine what actually needs to be masked, and what needs to be left open. From about the middle of the front door to the edge of the body where it meets the rear bumper/fascia, and from the bottoms of the windows to the bottom edge must be left open. So, first use a piece of wide masking paper to cover the front half of the front door. This wide piece of masking paper will provide sufficient coverage for the front portion of the car to protect it from primer-surfacer. Additional masking will be necessary when the top coat of paint is applied.

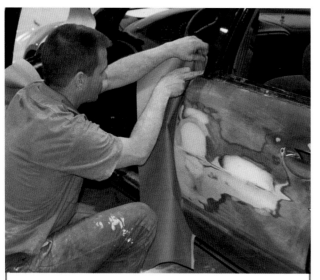

The front door is now opened and tape placed along the inner edge of the door. Masking paper will be taped to this first piece of tape and then folded to the inside of the door. This will protect the doorjamb and doorpost from overspray through the gap between the doors.

This same procedure of masking the doorjamb will be repeated on the back door as well. Taking the time to do this carefully will ultimately save more time, as you won't need to come back and sand off overspray from the doorjambs.

With a skirt along the bottom of the vehicle, masking paper is now used to mask off the windows. Primer-surfacer will not be applied above the bottom edge of the windows, or above that imaginary line as it would cross the rear quarter panel. Therefore, the masking paper is aligned with the lower edge of the window only and simply draped over the window, instead of specifically masking just the glass area.

The same technique is used along the lower door edge. For front doors, tape is applied to the front edge of the rear door to match the rear edge of the front door when it is closed. It will take a little practice and some patience to perfect these maneuvers. Tape does not always stick the way you want it to, and sometimes the air movement caused by the door closing will throw off the alignment with the corresponding strip.

You can use 2-inch tape and 4- to 6-inch paper to mask doorjambs and edges, but be careful where you place the tape edges. If you set them too far out, they may allow a visible paint line between the door and the jamb. This will be especially apparent if you paint the jambs a different color from the exterior. You will have to decide where the dividing line will be and make sure you position the tape symmetrically.

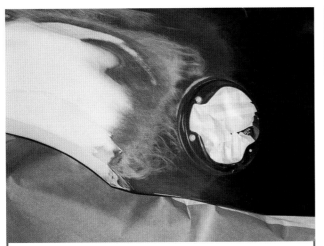

Much like the opening in the door for the door handle, the gas filler door must be masked from behind. Masking tape is now applied to the inner edge of the wheelwell to serve as an attachment point for masking paper to cover the wheel and tire. The paper is folded over as necessary to completely cover the wheel and tire, yet still be out of the way so that the wheelwell is accessible for painting.

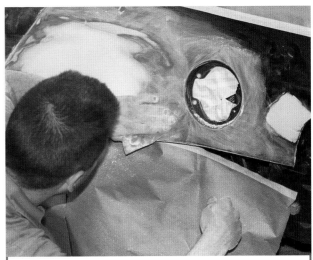

A slight blemish was found, so it was sanded down immediately, as primer-surfacer will be sprayed as soon as masking is completed. With that blemish touched up, masking is finished up by adding masking paper along the bodyline where the rear bumper/fascia abuts, and upward along the back edge of the rear quarter panel.

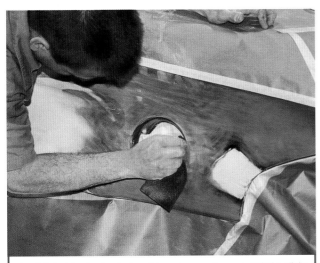

A quick double check prior to mixing primer-surfacer revealed a slight blemish in the gas filler area. It was quickly taken care of with some sandpaper. The filler to the right repaired a small ding discovered after masking began. With a little sanding, it will be ready as well.

TRIM

Body side moldings and other trim pieces do not look their best when painted over or marred with thin strips of paint overspray along their edges. Remove them for painting and reinstall them later, after the paint has dried, and you've performed all rubbing out or buffing operations. By waiting until you're done polishing, you avoid compound build-up on trim and along its edges.

Drip rail trim is generally snapped over the welded drip rail edge and then screwed tight at each end. If you dismantle this trim carefully, with the assistance of a helper on long pieces, you will avoid bending and creasing these pieces. Pay attention when masking the top inner side as well as the facing portion. Place tape of adequate width on the inner side first and then lay it down over the face. Should another strip be needed, apply it to the bottom edge first and fold excess over the front to overlap the previous strip.

On many cars, metal trim around windshields and rear windows sticks up just above the vehicle body. Take advantage of this gap to insert masking tape with the sticky side facing up. Gently slide the tape strip back and forth until you can no longer force it any deeper into the gap. Then, fold it over on top of the trim section. You may need to stand on a sturdy stool to reach top trim pieces, and you might need a helper to assist you from the opposite side. Employ the same technique for the side and bottom sections.

Applying tape to other types of trim does not require any special skill other than patience and attention to detail. Cover edges next to body panels first and faces last. Hold a roll of tape in one hand and position the extended strip with the other hand directly on top of trim sections. Be absolutely certain that trim edges are covered and that tape does not extend onto the body. Small pieces of tape that do touch body parts will block paint reaching from the surface and cause a blemish.

Always inspect your masking work after you've positioned the tape. Use your fingernail to secure tape firmly along edges. On the bottom sides of bodyside trim, you may have to lie down to place masking tape properly.

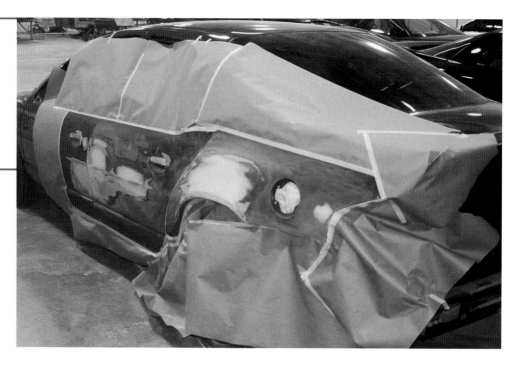

All of the filled areas on this vehicle have been sanded smooth and the masking is completed. Therefore, it is ready for a wipe down with wax and grease remover and then the application of primer-surfacer.

OTHER EXTERIOR FEATURES

Remove the radio antenna if it protrudes from a panel you're going to paint. They often unscrew from their base, leaving a large gap between the car body and remaining antenna unit. If you decide to leave the antenna in place, don't wrap it barber pole style from top to bottom. Instead, sandwich it between two vertical strips of tape—they'll cover it just as well and be much easier to remove.

Taillight and side light units are usually quite easy to remove by loosening four to eight nuts on their housings' back sides. Should you decide to mask them instead, use overlapping strips of 2-inch tape. Be sure to overlap each strip by at least ¾ inch to prevent paint seepage into seams.

Bumper designs range from out-in-the-open pickup truck step bumpers to closely fitted wraparound urethane-faced models. You must remove them to paint surrounding areas.

If you're not painting the surrounding surfaces, mask bumpers with regular masking tape and paper. If possible, insert a strip of tape between body panels and those parts touching them. Fold it over and then attach paper and tape to it. Fold paper over the top and face of bumpers. If the part requires more paper coverage, start from the bottom and fold over the top to overlap with the preceding piece.

If you intend to touch up only a quarter panel, and only the side-mounted bumper guard is in your way, consider dismantling the guard alone. These are attached to bumpers with nuts and bolts. They are flexible, for the most part, and bending them out of the way should give you enough room for dismantling them. If not, maybe that piece can be pulled away and secured with tape so you can paint below and around it.

The most practical way to mask an antenna is to run a piece of masking tape up one side and down the other, and close the edges together. The difficult part is the base of the antenna. Simply take your time and verify that all surfaces of the base are covered.

MASKING

104

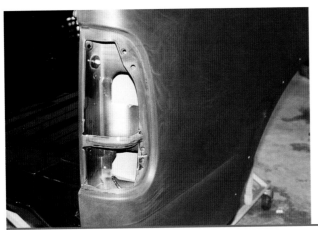

On most vehicles, taillights are much easier to remove than they are to mask efficiently. Depending on the particular vehicle, the taillight may block the flow of paint to the very edge of the panel it sits in. You must remember to disconnect the bulbs from the housings, however. On any vehicle on which the taillight lens fits over an opening, such as on this pickup bed, you will have two choices, even if you have already removed the taillight lens. If you don't mask this recessed area, it will be covered with paint. If you didn't prep the area carefully, that paint will eventually flake off, taking away from your credibility as a detail-oriented painter. The other choice is to remove the taillight lens and mask the recessed area as in the photo at right. This will save you from the tedious task of prepping an area that would simply go unnoticed anyway.

License plates and their holders are very easy to remove. If set into a housing, remove the entire unit if possible. Masking these units requires the same techniques described above for complete coverage with good overlap to prevent seepage.

Vinyl graphics, stripes, and decals are not easy to remove or store. The procedure for removing them typically destroys them. If you can't replace them, you'll have to mask them off when painting near or around them. Use thin Fine Line tape for a precision line with low paint build-up along its edge.

Meticulously mask the outer perimeter edges of vinyl graphics, stripes, and decals first. Be sure to place Fine Line tape directly on top of the item being masked and perfectly in line with its edge. When touching up or spot painting a body section below such items, you need only to mask the bottom edge. The rest can be covered with paper and regular masking tape.

However, should you need to paint areas between vinyl graphics, be sure to outline the entire scheme and then fill in with wide tape or paper, whichever is most appropriate. With a two- or three-step paint system, where clear paint will finish the job, you could remove masking after applying color coats and then cover everything, including the graphic, stripe, or decal, with clear. This effort will fill in the gap between color paint layers and vinyl to make the entire panel smooth, with no distinguishable paint edge or lip.

Be sure to confirm the effectiveness and compatibility of this procedure with your auto body paint and supply jobber, as various vinyl graphic, stripe, and decal materials may not be compatible with the paint system you employ. In addition, be 100 percent certain you want that vinyl adornment to remain on your car or truck for a long time. Once you spray clear over it, you will have to remove the clear coat before you can remove what lies beneath.

GRILLE

If you don't need to remove the grille (as described in Part Removal, Chapter 6) mask it with wide strips of paper. Attached to the top of the unit first, paper will hang down to cover most of the assembly. Use ¾-inch tape to secure paper on the sides. There is no need to mask individual contours or sections. If you have 12-inch paper and need to cover a grille that is 20 inches top to bottom, simply tape the paper edge to edge and attach the extra-wide sheet as a unit.

Intricate painting next to the grille requires that the grille be removed. No amount of masking will allow you adequate spray gun maneuverability. However, if all you need to do is paint the front parts of your ground effects system, then start masking from the bottom of the grille and work upward. When masking, always keep in mind the painting requirements for the job and the sequence you plan to follow.

The most important part of a masked area is the section adjacent or perpendicular to the area to be painted. It is the edges of those items that will expose overspray and the paint build-up edge so predominant with repaint efforts. Be sure the first piece of masking tape placed along the edges of those items is secure, adequate, and accurate.

WHEELS

Many hot rods, as well as other specialty automobiles, have painted fender wells and special wheels. It would be a shame to mar them with overspray. So, for paint projects that include fender wells, remove the wheels. Be sure the vehicle is securely supported on sturdy jack stands.

On those that command a new paint job or spot painting and already have painted fender wells, take time to cover them with masking paper and tape. Cars with normal everyday driver fender wells covered with undercoat do not need to be masked, unless you want to. On those, you can cover overspray imperfections with new layers of undercoat or black paint. The choice is up to you.

Most paint shops have covers designed just for wheels and tires. In addition, there are packages of plastic tire and wheel covers available. They fit easily and quickly over tires and wheels to protect them from overspray. If you do not have access to such items, plan to mask tires and wheels as you would anything else. Should some paint land on the tires, use thinner or reducer, whichever is appropriate with the paint system employed, to scrub them clean.

Wheels are a different story. Polished wheels will not look the same after you have attacked overspray on them with harsh solvents, number 0000 steel wool, or other abrasive. Chances are you will have to get them polished by a wheel restoration service. To save the expense and hassle, take a few minutes to mask them appropriately. Use enough paper to cover them completely, and use plenty of tape to make sure paper seams do not open from the pressure of the spray paint gun. The best protection against overspray is to remove the wheels and stow them away from the painting area.

Tape will not stick to dirty, oily, or dusty surfaces, including grungy tires and filthy fender wells. Even if tape does stick initially, air pressure from your paint gun will quickly blow it off. In that instant, paint overspray will settle on the area and mar the surface. So, before you bring your car or truck in for masking, make sure you spend plenty of time washing those areas where you need to place tape.

UNAFFECTED BODY AREAS

Even the best HVLP system produces overspray. Therefore, before you begin your project, plan to mask every part of your car that will not receive paint.

This doesn't mean you have to mask individual trim items on the driver's side when all you will be painting is the passenger side quarter panel. You will need to mask the driver's side of the car, however, or overspray will settle on it.

At most body shops, painters use large sheets of plastic to cover everything beyond the immediate painting area. They hold the plastic in place with tape so that air pressure doesn't blow it around and knock it loose or stir up particles.

In lieu of large plastic sheets, you will have to use masking paper. Think of your car as a large present. Using large sheets of paper, cover the roof, hood, and trunk lid, and secure it with masking tape. Overlap successive sheets by an inch, and seal the seams along their full length with tape. You can never mask too much.

Individual panel painting requires masking at the edge of each panel. This is a simple process. You can place a strip of tape down first and attach paper and tape to it. Or, if you have the means, roll off a section of paper with tape attached and secure it as necessary.

Paint feathering or melting requires a little different technique. Mask off panels by applying a taped sheet of paper over the area to be painted and then folding it over toward the area to be masked. This forces tape to roll over backward. So instead of a clean edge, the curved tape contour forces paint to bounce away to create a soft, gentle edge. After applying all coats, empty the paint from your spray gun except for about ¼ inch. To that, add about ¾ inch of reducer, creating a 3:1 mixture.

Remove the section of masking paper that was rolled over itself and spray the over-reduced paint mixture onto that newly exposed area. The extra reducer melts old paint and allows just a hint of new paint to infiltrate the surface. The result is a perfect blend and feathering of new paint edges into old.

For this application of primer-surfacer, only the side of the vehicle being repaired required masking, as the primer-surfacer was concentrated in one specific area. Before the actual painting, however, all of this masking will be removed. All of the rear quarter panel, all of the driver's side doors, and possibly the front fender will need to be scuffed for proper adhesion of the base coat. The painter may extend the clear coat even further to blend it into the unaffected areas.

I t's show time! You've just spent many, many hours preparing your car to receive a first-rate, beautiful, smooth paint job that will last for years and prove what you can do when you put your mind to it. But just as we didn't rush earlier steps, we're not going to hasten things now with the finish line close at hand.

How you apply the paint is every bit as important as the quality of the paint itself. Before you start spraying on your very carefully prepped vehicle, get a used door, hood, or trunk lid and practice the art of laying on paint smoothly and evenly. You're not just developing your own skills, you're also learning how your equipment performs its job. Leave the runs, drips, and irregularities on your practice panel and shoot your vehicle like a pro.

Another thing to consider before mixing the paint and filling your gun is to highlight certain time-frame recommendations and other important data that came with your paint system so you can refer to it during your job. If you prepare a small outline, including all of the painting and drying steps in sequential order, you can check off each step once you've completed it. If you like to multitask, or have kids, a cell phone or other distractions, this approach will help you to remember what you have done, what you need to do, and how much time you have to do it. Try using something other than a typical sheet of paper for this—like an off-size piece of light cardboard, or a colored sheet—and you'll be able to distinguish it quickly among any other notes or papers.

Mix your paint products according to label instructions and apply them at the recommended air pressure. Try painting with different fan patterns and pressure settings to see which combinations work best for intricate work in confined spaces, and which perform better on large panels. Practice holding paint guns at perpendicular angles to work surfaces; see what happens when you don't. Use cans of inexpensive paint, and practice until you become familiar with the techniques required for good paint coverage. When the paint has dried, practice wet sanding, rubbing out, and buffing.

Practice with your new dual-action sander to remove those coats of paint. Put a deep scratch in your practice panel and repair it, instead of practicing on your favorite car or truck. Become proficient with the tools and materials that you expect to use while fixing your special car before attacking its precious surface with power tools and harsh chemicals. Practice, practice, and practice some more. Once it looks good on your practice panel, you know you're ready for the big time.

PAINT MIXING

Because there are literally tens of thousands of different automotive paint colors, mixing the correct shade for your car is a precise science. Following stock vehicle color codes or those selected from paint chip catalogs, auto body paint and supply personnel will measure drops of color tint to the tenth of a gram to create the prescribed colors. They do this work for you as part of your paint system purchase.

Prior to spraying paint, you need to have a suitable area for mixing, reducing, and then pouring the paint into your spray gun. This spacious stainless steel-topped table provides plenty of room and is relatively easy to keep clean. A wooden workbench will provide the same results for the hobbyist, but this is a glimpse of the ideal setup. At the middle of the photo are two stands for holding gravity feed spray guns while paint is poured into the paint cup. At the back of the table are the various reducers and cans used for mixing. At the far end is a selection of pearl additives.

Also located in the mixing room is a 55-gallon drum that serves as a receptacle for excess paint, reducers, and other solvents. Any time a spray gun is cleaned, additional solvents are added to this. The body shop then has to have these products disposed of on a regular basis. For the hobbyist, disposal may present more of a problem, depending on where you live. Many paint distributors will accept small amounts of solvents from their customers, sometimes for a small fee. If it is not convenient to return the waste solvents to where you bought them, check with your local authorities to determine proper disposal methods in your area.

Custom paint mixing (when a formula is available) has always been done by weight. The paint formula provides a starting amount of base color, which is poured into the appropriate size paint can (pint, quart, or gallon). The second toner is added until the weight matches the given total for the two parts. Third and successive toners are added in the same manner until the sum of the parts equal the total amount. An electronic digital scale is much easier for this process than an old-fashioned beam scale. Kevin Brinkley mixes a pint of paint that he will eventually pour into a spray can for a customer who simply needs some touchup paint. The trouble of preparing the spray can formula quickly eats up any profit, but good customer service can generate more sales and more customers.

Paint materials are shipped in concentrated form, which helps keep the heavy pigments and other solid materials from settling. Painters then add solvents to make those products sprayable. Remember that the atmospheric conditions at which you spray the paint also affect the thinners or reducers you need to add. By shipping the paint in concentrated form and allowing end users to mix and dilute it as necessary, according to suppliers' instructions, manufacturers help to ensure that painters in any region and climate can get precisely the paint and mixture they need for best results.

In most cases, you will have to dilute concentrated paint with solvent (thinner or reducer) to yield a sprayable mixture. You must also add specific quantities of hardener to those products that call for it. Be careful—once you mix in hardener, the hardening process begins. Catalyzed paint has a limited shelf life, which your paint system's instructions will explain.

Take the following steps to be sure you get the right paint mixture. First, read the instructions that came with the paint system. Next, read the instructions that came

Once the various toners that are specified in a paint formula are combined, they must then be mixed sufficiently by vigorous agitation in a paint shaker. It will also be necessary for you to stir the paint prior to use, as the various solvents will settle to the bottom as it sits on the shelf.

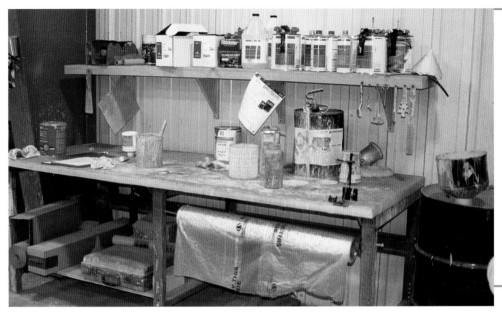

This mixing table at an auto bodyshop is comparable to what the hobbyist painter might have. At the left, we see some body filler and catalyst, along with some spreaders and a mixing board. To the right are some mixing cups and reducers. Above the bench is a shelf where the various primers, primer-surfacers, sandpaper, and various other supplies are stored. At the far right is a 55-gallon drum for waste primers and solvents.

Technological advances make today's paint products very user-friendly. If you prepare the surface correctly, mix the products correctly, and apply them correctly, they will yield a good paint job. Proper mixing ratios are included with the product information sheets and calibrated mixing cups or measuring sticks are available from your paint store.

Most body shops have special dispenser caps that allow them to pour the desired amount of paint into the mixing cup. These are a convenience, but are not necessary. You will undoubtedly find that pouring from a quart can is much easier than from a full gallon can, however. Enough sealer (in this case) for the next application is poured into the mixing cup to a predetermined line on the cup. Reducer is added until the total mixture comes to the same numbered line in the next column marking the appropriate ratio.

The mixture is then stirred for a couple of minutes, using a paint stir stick. Don't attempt to use a screwdriver for this; the blade isn't wide enough to actually stir anything, and it ruins the screwdriver. Stirring sticks are available where you purchase your paint, so make sure you ask for a few when you pick up supplies.

With the gravity feed gun securely supported in the stand and a paint strainer in place atop the paint cup, the sealer can be poured into the paint cup. For most suction feed guns, the stand isn't necessary, as the bottom of the paint cup is large enough to stand on its own. No matter what you are spraying, make sure that you use a paint strainer when pouring it into your paint cup. Also, make sure that you put the cap back on the spray paint gun and secure it properly. With the air pressure involved when spraying paint, an unsecured paint cap can make a mess. Trust me on this.

with your spray gun and air compressor. These two sources should give you a strong sense of the mixture ratio you'll need. Then, before you mix, run any questions you may have past the paint supplier from whom you got your paint. By checking and crosschecking in this manner, you'll be sure you have just the right mixture for your application, climate, and equipment.

For the mixing process itself, paint manufacturers have designed calibrated mixing sticks. According to the mixing directions, pour an amount of paint into a clean, empty can with straight sides (not a spray gun cup) up to a certain number located along one vertical column on that paint system's designated mixing stick. Then pour solvent in until the fluid level in the can rises to a corresponding number on the next column over on the same stick. Clear mixing cups with calibrations printed on them are used in the same manner as mixing sticks.

If you need a one-to-one ratio of paint to solvent, for example, pour paint into an empty can up to the number one. Then add reducer until the mixture reaches the number one on the next column over. If you need more paint for a large job, simply mix the ingredients up to a higher number—again, following the ratios your particular system and circumstances indicate.

If your paint system requires mixing paint, solvent, and hardener, it will use a mixing stick with three columns instead of two—one for each ingredient. Pour paint up to the desired number on the paint column, solvent to the

appropriate number in that column, and hardener to its corresponding number.

Not all paint systems are based on a one-to-one ratio. By looking at a paint-mixing stick, you will see that sometimes the numbers on the reducer or hardener are not twice as high up the stick as those in the paint column. Measuring sticks provide a very accurate way of mixing paint, solvent and hardener. You must follow the manufacturer's recommendations and instructions to be assured of a quality blend.

Once you've blended your paint product, use the stir stick to swish the contents around in the mixing can.

Pointed tools, like screwdrivers, don't work well for stirring. You want something flat-bottomed, and rather wide—hence the stir stick. Stir for at least two minutes. Then place a paint filter over the opening of your spray gun cup and pour in the mixture. It is important that you *never*, repeat, *never*, pour paint into your spray gun cup without using some type of filter. An impurity passed into your gun could cause it to misspray or clog, creating a lot of extra work fixing the paint surface and your spray gun.

Your paint product is now ready for spraying. Be sure to put the caps back on containers of solvent and hardener, as well as paint. This will prevent unnecessary evaporation or accidental spillage.

In the paint booth, tack off your car or truck's surface immediately and then start painting. Some paint products and colors are designed with a lot of heavy solids that could settle to the bottom of paint cups in just 10 to 15 minutes. If you were to take your time tacking and get distracted while your paint gun sat idle, solids could settle, possibly causing the color to change. This would be a catastrophe, especially with spot paint repairs.

SPRAY GUN CONTROLS AND TEST PATTERNS

Paint companies recommend specific spray gun setups for applying their products. A sample recommendation for the DeVilbiss JGV-572 base coat spray gun is "Fluid Tip—FW (0.062 inch); Air Cap #86." This would indicate a specific fluid tip and air cap that should be used with this particular paint product and would be available from the dealer of the spray gun. This is another reason why you should purchase your spray gun from a paint supply outlet, rather than a tool store that sells a variety of tools, without servicing any of them. A similar recommendation would apply to primer and clear coat spray guns by same manufacturer, Sata or Sharpe. These settings are available from information sheets and application guidelines, or from your auto body paint and supply jobber.

Most full-size production spray paint guns have two control knobs. One controls the fan spray, while the other manages the volume of paint that exits the nozzle. They are located at the top rear section of most models. About the only way to achieve proper spray patterns and volume is to practice spraying paint on a test panel. Various paint products and their reduction ratios will spray differently, especially with different recommended air pressures.

Many painters keep test panels in their spray paint booth. Usually, these are nothing more than sheets of wide masking paper taped to a wall. They can spray paint on the test panel and then adjust the gun's control knobs to get the right pattern and volume. At that point, they begin actual painting.

Periodically during paint jobs, painters may notice a flaw in their gun's fan pattern. To check it, they turn to the test panel and shoot a clean section with a mist of paint. If it looks off, they check the controls and the air pressure. If the pattern is still flawed, they disconnect the paint gun from

The two knobs located on the back of the spray gun housing are for adjusting the paint material and the airflow. Material control is usually adjusted by the knob in line with the air nozzle, while the airflow is adjusted by the opposite knob. You should refer to the literature included with your spray gun or ask your salesperson if you have any questions regarding adjusting or cleaning your spray gun. This is all the more reason to purchase a spray gun from an autobody paint and supply store, rather than a discount store. When adjusted properly, most spray guns will give great results, and if cleaned and maintained correctly they will last indefinitely.

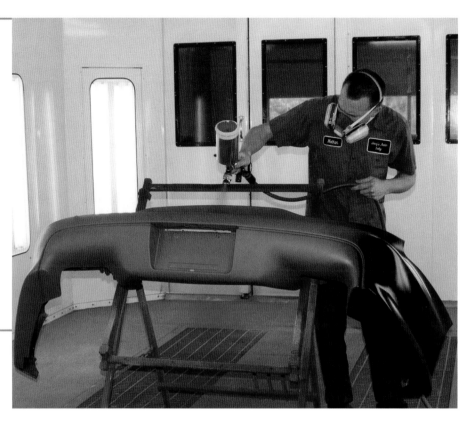

This parts holding rack is designed to tilt and adjust as necessary for the parts being painted at the time. These are common in body shops, but are probably too expensive for the hobbyist painting his or her first car. Although it is not actually the case in this photo, it appears as though the upper portion of this rack would interfere with the spray gun while the painter sprayed this bumper. This is something that you must consider when you are laying out or hanging parts to be painted. They must be situated so that you can access them completely. Anything that cannot be adequately covered will require repositioning after the part has dried to paint the opposite side or anything that was not accessible.

When positioning parts to be painted, you should attempt to position them so that as much of the part as possible can be painted from a comfortable position. This won't always be possible, but you should make it easy on yourself when you can. If you are not the type of person who exercises frequently, you may want to stretch some of those seldom-used muscles slightly before you start spraying primer or paint onto your vehicle. You don't want to have a muscle cramp or spasm while you are in the middle of spraying paint.

the supply hose and clean it. Chances are, a small port or passage has become clogged and must be cleaned before they can continue the job.

As the surface to be painted becomes more confined or difficult, as on some front end sections, painters must reduce pressure or change fan sprays to hit a smaller area. They make these adjustments with the help of the test panel.

SPRAY GUN MANEUVERING

You've secured two essential components for your project: good paint and a quality spray gun. But those essentials alone won't get you a great paint job. How you apply the paint is just as important. Spray paint guns typically work best when held perpendicular to the surface being sprayed at a distance of 6 to 10 inches; check the recommendations for your particular spray gun. PPG's *Refinish Manual* has this caution for painters: "If the gun is tilted toward the surface, the fan pattern won't be uniform. If the gun is swung in an arc, varying the distance from the nozzle to the work, the paint will go on wetter (and thicker) where the nozzle is closer to the surface and drier (and thinner) where it is farther away." Should the outer layers of the thick, wetter paint dry before the inner layers, the solvent evaporating from within will cause defects in the finish. At the far end of the arc, the paint will go on too thin to provide adequate coverage, or may be too dry by the time it hits the surface, resulting in something more like overspray than a proper coat of paint.

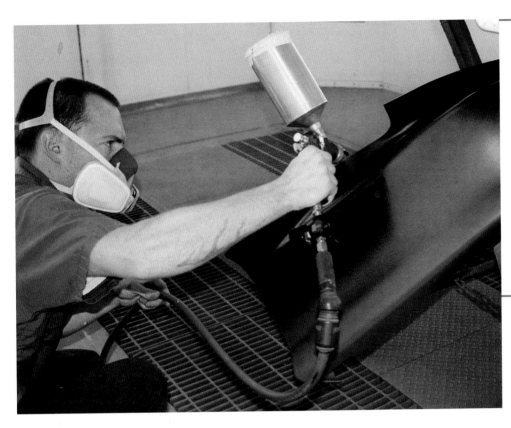

To avoid having excess paint that causes runs, and dry spots that don't cover, it is essential to hold the spray gun perpendicular to the surface being painted, even if you have to kneel down or stand on a stepladder to do this. By kneeling or standing on a stepladder, rather than just reaching and hoping, you will be in a better position to see what you are doing. Notice also how the free hand is holding the air hose well away from the surface being painted.

About the only time painters do fan the paint gun is on small spot repaints. These spots call for full coverage in the center and less paint around their feathered perimeter where it blends with existing paint. This is done with wrist action to lightly blend edges only. Practice this technique on a test panel before attempting it on your car or truck.

Because automobile roofs, hoods, and trunk lids lie in a horizontal plane, you must hold the paint gun at a horizontal angle and make smooth, even, uniform passes. To prevent paint from dripping on the body, many painters tie an old tack cloth or other absorbent and lint-free rag around the top of the cup where it makes contact with its support base. Even with paint guns that are reported to be dripless, this is not a bad idea.

Holding the paint gun so that the nozzle is perpendicular to the surface is very important. Lock your wrist and elbow, and then walk along panels to ensure a right-angle position. Do not rely solely upon your arm to swing back and forth. Move your body with your arm and shoulder steadfastly anchored. Again, this takes practice, especially when you have to move from one panel to another in a smooth, steady, and even walk.

Even fan spray should overlap the previous spray by half. In other words, the center of the first pass should be directed along the masking line: half of the paint on the masking paper, the other half on the body surface. The second pass should be directed in such a way that the top

Unless you are painting a very small part, you will need to move around to see and paint all surfaces. When you think you have all surfaces covered, it is a good idea to walk around the pieces or parts again, looking from different angles to make sure that you have indeed covered all that you intended.

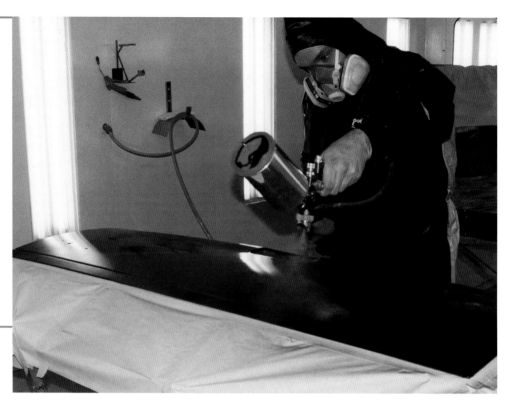

When spraying a large flat area, it should either lie horizontally or vertically, rather than at an angle. When spraying the side of a vehicle, it will basically be in a vertical position, while the top, trunk, and deck lid will be lying horizontally. Realize that, depending on your stature, you may have difficulty reaching the middle of some large panels, such as the hood or deck lid from some of the land barges of the 1950s and 1960s. In that event, you may want to remove the panel to be sure you get an even coat.

of the fan rides right along the masking line. Then, each successive pass should overlap the previous one by half. Maneuver each pass with the same speed and at the same distance away from the surface: 6 to 10 inches.

Look at your painting results. If you have practiced with your equipment on an old hood or trunk lid, chances are good that your efforts are proving worthwhile. If not, you might be experiencing runs or other gross abnormalities. Runs are generally caused by too much paint landing on the surface at one time. You may be holding the gun too close or walking too slow. Whichever, you have to adjust. Keep practicing until the paint appears to go on smooth and even without running.

SPOT PAINTING

Whether your project involves a minor body repair or complete repaint, the rules of right-angle application and controlled spraying remain in effect. The difference is in the amount of paint needed and the technique for blending new paint into old finishes.

What you want to avoid when spot painting is a raised line separating the section you painted from the old surface. One way to get around this problem is to mask along a definite edge, groove, vinyl graphic, or stripe. Depending upon the type of paint you use and the prominence of the lip or raised paint edge, some delicate wet sanding could make the scar almost invisible. Professionals opt for a different method. First, they mask an edge or stopping point with tape rolled over upon itself.

Let's say that you want to spot paint a ding repair near the driver's side taillight on the quarter panel. You've masked along a piece of body side molding on the bottom of the panel and a design groove on the top. But, toward the front and back there are no definite breaking points. To solve this problem, lay a piece of masking paper at both the front and rear ends of the repair area as if they were going to cover more of the paint surface than needed. You affix the front tape edge of the piece toward the front, and the rear tape edge of the piece toward the rear.

Now, roll the paper over the tape edge so that only the sticky side of the tape is exposed. In other words, roll the front section of paper toward the front of the car, over the secured tape edge, and roll the rear section of paper toward the rear of the car. This leaves the repair area clear and both the front and rear areas masked with a strip of tape that has been rolled back over itself.

The purpose of this technique is to create a curved section of tape that paint can bounce off of and become overspray, with only a portion of it actually adhering to the surface. This prevents the paint from forming a well-defined line along the tape, and helps it to feather into a great blend.

Now, to help that kind of situation even more, painters like to reduce paint to about a three-to-one ratio for melting. Once they've painted the spot, they will remove those rolled over strips of paper and tape, and then empty their paint gun cups to about ¼ inch full. To that, they add

Whether you are painting something as small as a gas filler door, or as large as a truck bed or complete vehicle, it is important that you remember to use wax and grease remover before every application of anything in the paint system. This includes sanding, body filler, primer-surfacer, sealer, base coat, and clear coat. You must then also spray off the entire surface with an air nozzle to make sure that no wax and grease remover or moisture of any kind is left on the surface.

¾ inch of reducer. This makes for a very hot mixture, a blend that will loosen earlier paint and allow just a tint of the new paint to melt in. The results are great, as it is difficult to find where the new paint starts and the old paint leaves off. If any nibs remain, you can wet sand them smooth, unless you've used uncatalyzed enamel paint.

The most important thing to remember about spot painting is that there is a valley that has to be filled where you removed the old paint and sealer. It might only be one to three mils deep, but nevertheless, it has to be filled if the overall surface is to be flat, even, and smooth. New sealer and primer-surfacer will fill up most of the valley, with paint filling in the rest and then blending with the adjacent surface.

The reducer-rich paint mixture literally opens up the existing paint to let a touch of new pigments fall into place and blend with the old. This is the very last step of a paint job, after the appropriate flash time has passed for the final spray paint pass for the center of the repaint.

Warning!!! Before attempting this kind of spot repair technique on your car, confirm its value with your auto body paint and supply specialist. It works great for some urethanes and lacquers, but may not fare so well with certain enamels. It all depends on the brand and type of product you use, the paint currently on your car, the color, and what additives, like metallic or pearl, are involved. There is no clear-cut rule to follow and each case is unique.

FULL PANEL PAINTING

Automobile and paint manufacturers advise auto painters to repaint complete sides of certain cars, even if the only problem area is minor body repair on a single panel. As ridiculous as this sounds, there is a method to the madness. This type of overkill repaint involves those vehicles factory-painted with pearl or other special additives. Tricoat or candy finishes are also extremely difficult to match with new paint because of the complex interplay of coatings that produce the finish's unique look.

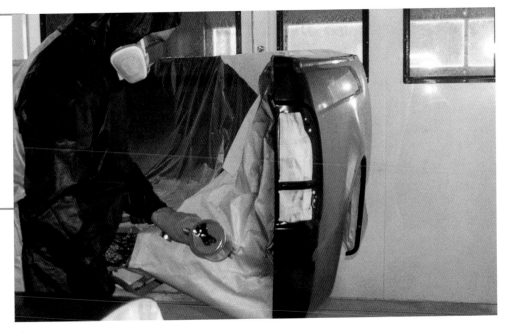

Paint the edges of an area first and then the main surface. That way, overspray helps cover the main area and you can apply less paint there. If you get the main area painted to the appropriate thickness first, then do the edges; the extra paint from the overspray may cause blemishes on the main surface.

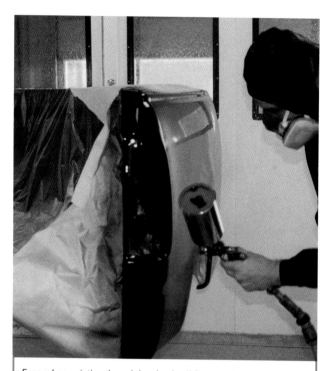

Even when painting the subtle wheelwell flare, position the spray paint gun so that it is perpendicular to the area that bulges slightly from the main panel. The flare varies in width from about 1 inch to about 2 inches wide, so it is not a large area, however, it is still important to apply the paint evenly. Remember that when using a base coat/clear coat paint system, the base coat should be applied only to achieve complete coverage. Gloss will come from the clear.

To find out whether your finish is amenable to spot painting—new-style paint schemes are more likely to be difficult—check with your local auto body paint and supply store.

Painting just a panel or two is generally no big deal with noncustom paint products. Masking can begin and end on definite body design breaks. You can see what has to be painted and know that virtually everything else has to be masked. But, what if your car or truck is a little on the old side and you are concerned about matching the new color with the old? Who wants a door and fender to look like new, while the quarter panel, hood, and roof look old and oxidized?

Many times, a complete buff job on old paint surfaces makes them look just like the new paint that was just sprayed onto doors and fenders. In other cases, you must spray a blend to feather in between the new paint and the old.

Feathering in is similar to the melting-in process described earlier: melting-in describes this process on a single panel, whereas feathering is blending surrounding panels to match the one that was repaired or refinished. After a panel is completely painted, you remove the masking from surrounding panels and spray a light coating of heavily reduced paint and reducer onto the existing paint. This works well for certain products, but not at all for others. Check with your auto body paint supplier to see if your new paint can be feathered into the existing paint in this manner.

To blend in panels with compatible paint finishes, painters complete their main job and then take off strips of masking from adjoining panels. With a heavily reduced

Kneeling helps this painter see where he's applying the clear. Notice how he took the time to mask the inner wheelwell and the inside of the bed of this pickup truck.

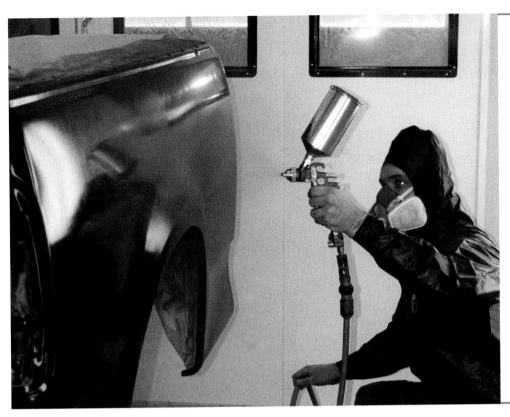

With the edges covered, the rest of this bed side can be coated with clear. After each coat of clear has had sufficient time to flash, all the dust, dirt, and nibs can be lightly sanded out if necessary prior to the next coat. In collision repairs, two or three coats of clear would typically be applied with little to no sanding between coats. Custom show car painters do lots of sanding with extremely fine sandpaper between coats of clear to achieve those mirror-finish paint jobs that cost tens of thousands of dollars. Sanding between clear coats is what makes the difference between a good paint job and a great one. You decide what best suits your needs.

paint mix, they gently melt in a feathered edge. These edges may extend out to 6 inches. When the paint finishes are incompatible for melting, painters must rely on a perfect color match between adjacent panels.

If you want a multicolor paint job, or custom touches like flames or scallops, refer to Chapter 9, Extra Details. Although they can be added later, you may be better off including them as part of the original paint scheme. Pinstriping, lettering, and other graphics are also discussed in Chapter 9.

FLASH TIMES

Paint dries as its solvents evaporate and its pigments cure. You cannot spray additional coats until the solvents from the first coat, and each successive coat, have had adequate time to evaporate. This is critical! If you spray a new coat of paint over one that has not had time to flash (dry), you will be trapping solvents underneath the new layer. But they will not remain harmlessly in place. Instead, they will pass through the overlying material causing blistering, checking, crazing, cracking, dulling, lifting, sagging, or other such imperfections on the top coat.

Flash times are clearly indicated on all information sheets and application guides for all paint products. Second and final coats may require longer flash times than initial coats. Read and follow the directions for the individual paint system employed. They are not all the same. This goes for undercoats, top coats, and clear coats.

CLEAR COAT FINISHES

Along with offering better protection for metallics and other paints, clear coats reduce the amount of color material needed for a good finish, thus reducing some of the overall solvent needed and helping manufacturers stay within governmental guidelines. Clear coat finishes are also good for smoothing out sharp paint lines left behind along custom graphic paint edges. Painters also use clear to help feather in repaints along adjacent panels and old paint perimeters.

Applying clear is no different from applying other paints. You have to maintain a close eye on your work so that each pass is uniform. Exterior body parts, like door handles and key locks, can be masked for clear paint applications without as much concern about overspray blemishes as with color coats. This is because it dries to a clear, invisible finish. Beware not to spray clear until the last color coat has dried for the recommended period. Spraying clear too early will trap the color coat's solvents and lead to the same finish problems described in the Flash Times section.

TRI-STAGE FINISHES

Originally reserved for custom jobs or high-end vehicles, tristage paint systems are becoming more common. Whether custom or original, tristage finishes include a base coat, color coat, and clear coat. The base coat gives the color coat a compatible base and also influences its appearance. For example, a purple coat sprayed over a silver base

With the body repaired, this pickup truck is moved to the paint preparation area. Primer-surfacer has been applied to about the rear third of the bed side. To blend the color, base coat will be applied from the very rear edge to about the front of the wheelwell, with full coverage centering over the repaired area and feathering out from there. Clear coat will cover the entire bedside to further blend the repaired area into the old.

It is much easier (less work), faster (again less work), and less expensive (less materials) to thoroughly wash the area to remove contaminants than to take the chance you'll have to strip and repaint it. This entire bed side will be washed and dried before it's scuffed.

To ensure good paint adhesion, the freshly washed bed side is scuffed with 400-grit sandpaper. Since base coat will be applied to approximately half of the panel and clear coat will be applied to all of it, the entire panel must be scuffed. After the panel is scuffed, it will be cleaned again with wax and grease remover and masked completely before it's painted.

Flexible panels such as this front bumper/fascia can be painted with the paint used for the rest of the vehicle. To prevent the paint from cracking, older acrylic enamels and lacquers required flex additives, while contemporary urethanes don't need them. Where required, the flex additive must often be included in the undercoats, as well as the top coats. For best results, get the latest recommendations from your autobody paint and supply jobber.

will have a different tint than the same color sprayed over a white base.

As you would with any other paint, you apply base coats to cover all intended new paint surfaces. After the recommended flash time has elapsed, spray on color coat using the techniques described earlier. When you've sprayed the correct number of color coats and the proper flash time has passed, proceed to the clear coat stage. Be sure to clean your spray gun according to the methods described earlier, and the paint and spray gun manufacturers' instructions.

Once the final coat of clear has dried for the recommended period, you will be able to wet sand blemishes and buff areas that need extra polishing. The clear coat finish will prevent wet sanding or polishing from distorting the blended color achieved between the base coat and color coat.

PLASTIC OR FLEXIBLE ASSEMBLIES

A great many different kinds of plastics are in use today on all types of automobile parts and assemblies. They range from Acrylonitrile Butadiene Styrene (ABS) to Thermoplastic Olefin (TPO) and Sheet Molded Compounds (SMC) to Reaction Injection Molded Plastic (RIM). Each has its own place, from rigid grillework sections to flexible bumper covers.

If you are using lacquer or enamel paint, such as on a vintage restoration, any flexible components should be sprayed with paint containing a special additive that allows it to flex along with the part. You may also have to use special undercoats in addition to top coat additives. The only way to be certain that the products that you use are compatible and designed for painting the parts you intend to spray is to check with your auto body paint and supply specialist. If you are using a base coat/clear coat paint system, however, flex additives are no longer necessary due to the flexible characteristics of today's urethane products.

The same caution applies to rigid plastics. Some materials are compatible with normal painting systems, while others may require specific undercoats. By using the designed paint system and proper additives, along with the recommended preparation techniques, you will be assured that newly applied paint coats will not peel, crack, or flake off. In rare cases, you cannot repaint certain solvent-sensitive plastic or urethane parts when the factory primer seal has been broken. In those situations, you have to replace the parts.

AFTER SPRAYING PAINT

Once you've painted the vehicle to your satisfaction, you need to complete several further tasks to ensure the overall quality of the job. Once the paint has dried sufficiently, you must wet sand nibs smooth and carefully remove the masking tape to prevent unnecessary paint edge peeling or
continued on page 122

119

Repairing Imperfections and Problem Solving

The following common paint finish problems, their causes, and remedies is excerpted with permission from PPG's *Refinish Manual*.

Orange Peel: Film that has the physical appearance of an orange peel.

Cause: *Film lacks the ability to flow smoothly. Rough substrate transmits irregularities to subsequent top coats.*

Corrective Action
Checklist:
Check if defect is on whole unit or in specific area.
Check other units on line to determine if pattern exists.
Check for low air pressure.
Check for under reduction.
Check for proper film build.
Check for improper gun distance.
Check reducing solvent and viscosity.
Check smoothness of substrate.
Check if defect is specific to one color.
Check for excessive temperature.

Dry Spray: A rough, textured surface often confined to a small area.

Cause: *Paint lacks ability to flow properly.*

Corrective Action
Checklist:
Check if defect is on whole unit or in specific area.
Check other units to see if a pattern exists.
Check if defect is specific to one color or many colors.
Check for proper film build.
Check for excessive film build.
Check for improper gun distance.
Check reducing solvent selection and spray viscosity.

Sags or Runs: Tiers or curtains of paint on vertical or inclined areas.

Cause: *Paint's inability to uniformly hold to a vertical or inclined surface, producing excessive build-up.*

Corrective Action
Checklist:
Check if defect is on whole unit or in specific area.
Check other units to see if a pattern exists.
Check if defect is specific to one color or many colors.
Check for excessive film build.
Check for excessive fluid delivery.
Check for improper gun distance (too close).
Check solvent selection (too slow).
Check for insufficient air pressure.
Check for excessive application overlap.
Check for too short flash time.
Check for low spray room temperature.
Check temperature of paint.
Check temperature of unit.
Check for proper reduction.

Color Match: Finished panels do not match color standard.

Cause: *Variations in application and/or paint materials.*

Corrective Action
Checklist:
Check other units on line to determine if pattern exists.
Check for complete hiding.
Check for variables in spray application.
Check lines and equipment for contamination from previous color.
Check for improper mixing.
Check for proper agitation.
Check gun pattern.
Check gun distance.
Check equipment setup.

Fish eyes: Small rounded indentations that resemble a fish's eyes.

Cause: *Foreign substances that do not blend with paint.*

Corrective Action
Checklist:
Check if defect is on whole unit or in specific area.
Check other units to see if pattern exists.
Check for oil in air lines and spray equipment.
Check airborne contamination in spray area.
Check for possible contamination in paint materials.
Check for painter contamination, skin oils, perspiration, greasy foods, etc.
Check for any oils or contamination that might get into paint or spray area.
Check for proper cleaning procedures prior to refinishing.

Dirt: Small bumps deposited in, on, or under the paint film.

Cause: *Foreign particles entering wet paint film.*

Corrective Action
Checklist:
Check if defect is on whole unit or in a specific area.
Check other units to determine if a pattern exists.
Check paint mixing/filtration process.
Check spray environment (booth).
Check preparation process of unit, tacking, solvent wash, etc.
Check painter's clothing.
Check spray equipment.
Check used paint filters for contamination.
Check for use of antistatic wipe or spray products.

Peeling: Top coat peels off when unmasking.

Cause: *Top coat layer or paint separating because of lack of physical bonding.*

Corrective Action
Checklist:
Check if defect is on whole unit or in specific area.
Check other units to determine if a pattern exists.
Check film build.
Check for contamination such as oil, sanding residue, overspray, water, solvent cleaner residue, etc., on substrate prior to top coat application.
Check for nonsanding or primer-surfacer.
Check for case hardening of substrate.
Check for poor surface preparation prior to top coat application.
Check for masking tape contacting painted surface.
Check solvent selection (too fast).
Check for thin sealer film builds or no sealer.
Check for incompatible products.

Soft Paint: Easy to mar or penetrate film with fingernail.
Cause: *Insufficient cure of paint film.*
Corrective Action
Checklist:
Check if defect is on whole unit or in specific area.
Check other units to determine if pattern exists.
Check for improper film build.
Check hardener (old, improper, or contaminated).
Check for improper mixing ratio.
Check for improper heat during cure time.
Check for improper airflow.
Check flash or dry times.
Check solvent selection (too fast).
Check for excessive humidity.
Check for cool temperatures.

Gloss/DOI: DOI is the sharpness by which images are reflected in the surface of a top coat finish. The images are usually evaluated for 90-degree angle. Gloss measures the amount of light reflected from a paint surface read at 20- and 60-degree angles.
Cause: *Poor DOI is caused by an unsmooth or irregular top coat surface and/or low gloss. Low gloss is caused by improper topcoat application process, or improper solvent selection.*
Corrective Action
Checklist:
Check if defect is on whole unit or in a specific area.
Check other units to see if pattern exists.
Check film build (too low).
Check solvent selection.
Check heat during cure process (too low).
Check airflow during initial cure.
Check reduction ratio (over reduction).
Check for uncured undercoats.

Die Back: Loss of gloss after application.
Cause: *Improper evaporation of solvent, or poor initial cure.*
Corrective Action
Checklist:
Check if defect is on whole unit or in a specific area.
Check other units to see if a pattern exists.
Check for too fast a solvent selection.
Check for cool temperature during cure.
Check for lack of airflow during cure.
Check for improper film build.
Check for improper flash times.
Check for incompatible products.

Solvent Trap (Popping): A "goose pimple" or volcano appearance in paint film which, on close examination, frequently has small holes in the center of the bumps.
Cause: *Improper evaporation of solvent from wet paint film during initial cure or force dry.*
Corrective Action
Checklist:
Check to determine if defect is on entire unit or just in a specific area.
Check for high temperature in first part of force dry.
Check other units on line to determine if a pattern exists.
Check for correct reducing solvent.
Check if defect is specific to one or many colors.
Check if defect is most prevalent on horizontal surfaces.

Check for excessive film builds.
Check for high fluid delivery.
Check for low air pressure.
Check for high viscosity.
Check for too much overlapping in film build.
Check for proper flash and purge times.

Mottling: Spotty, nonuniform, blotchy appearance of metallic paint.
Cause: *Uneven distribution of metallic flakes.*
Corrective Action
Checklist:
Check if defect is on whole unit or in a specific area.
Check other units to see if a pattern exists.
Check if defect is specific to one color or many.
Check for excessively high fluid delivery.
Check atomizing air pressure.
Check gun pattern.
Check gun distance.
Check equipment setups (fluid delivery).
Check solvent selection.
Check reduction, viscosity.
Check flash and dry times.
Check temperature in spray environment (too cool).
Check temperature of unit being sprayed.

Sand Scratches & Bull's-eyes: Objectionable sanding pattern imperfections that show through the finished paint film.
Cause: *Imperfections due to soft primer, improper sanding techniques, and low top coat film build. Excessive film builds with improper flash times.*
Corrective Action
Checklist:
Check if defect is on whole car or in a specific area.
Check other units to see if a pattern exists.
Check if defect is specific to one or many colors.
Check for correct sandpaper grit (too coarse).
Check topcoat film thickness.
Check for proper featheredge technique.
Check for uncured primer.
Check for poor quality solvent used in undercoats.
Check flash and dry times.
Check for excessive primer film builds.
Check for proper gun technique and atomization.
Check for underreduced primer-surfacer (bridging scratches).
Check for sanding before primer-surfacer is cured.
Check film builds of sealer or no sealer.

Overspray: Paint materials from another unit falling on adjacent surfaces.
Cause: *Misdirected spray droplets or dry spray.*
Corrective Action
Checklist:
Check to determine if defect is on entire unit or in specific area.
Check other units to see if a pattern exists.
Check for correct booth air balance and flow.
Check for sequence of panel application.
Check gun technique.
Check if defect is specific to one color.
Check air pressure (too high).
Check for over reduction.

continued on page 119

other accidental finish damage. Read the sections on wet sanding and buffing before removing any masking material.

Uncatalyzed enamels cannot withstand wet sanding or polishing. With this kind of paint system, what you see is what you get, unless you later decide to sand a completely cured but blemished panel down to the substrate and repaint it to perfection.

Certain lacquer and urethane paint finishes can be wet sanded and polished to remove nibs, flatten orange peel, and otherwise smooth small blemishes. This work is normally done on clear coats, as opposed to actual color coats, and may require additional light applications of clear. For this reason, professionals seldom remove masking material until they are pleased with the entire paint job and are satisfied that they've remedied all imperfections.

Drying Times

Automotive paint has to dry. If not allowed to do so in a clean environment, the wet finish can be contaminated by dust, dirt, or other debris. Professional painters always leave freshly sprayed vehicles in paint booths until enough time has elapsed for the material to cure completely, according to the paint manufacturer's recommendations.

For example, PPG recommends their DCC Acrylic Urethane paint systems be allowed to dry 6-8 hours at 70 degrees Fahrenheit, or be force-dried for 40 minutes at 140 degrees Fahrenheit. Force drying requires portable infrared heaters or high-tech paint booths equipped with heating units. For its Deltron Base coat and Clear coat systems, PPG lists specific drying times for air drying, as well as force drying, each of the system's components. As stressed earlier, proper drying is essential to prevent future coats from being damaged by trapped solvents.

Factory paint jobs with urethane paint products and those that are suitable for force drying are baked on body surfaces at temperatures around 450 degrees Fahrenheit. This can be accomplished only while cars are in a stripped condition. Otherwise, plastic, rubber, and vinyl parts would melt. Cars that are still equipped with these items cannot be force-dried at temperatures above 160 degrees Fahrenheit. Excessive heat can also damage the vehicle's computer.

There are other factors you must consider when using heat lamps and other force-dry methods. Initial flash times are extremely important. Most paint products must air dry for 15 minutes or longer on their own to let the bulk of their solvent material evaporate. Too much heat too soon will evaporate this solvent too quickly, causing blemishes.

Some paint finishes have a window of time during which you must wet sand or recoat. Wait beyond that period and you may have to scuff sand and clean the surface again, before applying touch up coats to get proper adhesion.

Wet Sanding

You must confirm ahead of time that the paint system you use is compatible with wet sanding. Your auto body paint and supply jobber can do this while you are discussing your paint needs at the time of purchase. Each automotive paint manufacturer has its own set of recommended guidelines it advises painters to follow. What may be good for PPG's Deltron system may not be so good for a BASF or DuPont system. In fact, you might even be advised to completely disregard wet sanding and opt instead for polishing to guarantee a perfect finish with the type of product that you have chosen to use.

Not every type of paint system can be wet sanded. Enamels, for example, cure with a sort of film on their surface, which will be damaged if broken by sandpaper or harsh polish.

Lacquers and some urethane products can be sanded with fine sandpaper soon after they have cured. Although it is not recommended that you wet sand color coats, you might be able to lightly sand off nibs, providing you are prepared to touch up the spots with a light color coat. Wet sanding yields its best results on clear coats that are then polished.

If epoxy primer has been applied to keep moisture from penetrating through to the metal surface below, parts may be wet sanded to achieve the ultimate in smoothness prior to spraying color coats and clear. You can also wet sand painted parts. (The paint serves as a sealer to keep moisture from the metal below.) Using progressively finer sandpaper, 1,500- to 2500-grit, soaked in water, sand in a circular motion using light pressure on the sanding block. A slight amount of car washing soap added to the water lubricates the sandpaper. It is critical that you do not sand through the paint.

Base coat/clear coat paint systems generally call for a number of color coats and then clear coats. Especially with candy finishes, sanding directly on the color surface will distort the tint and cause a visible blemish. Wet sanding for them is done on clear coats only. Your wet sanding efforts should be concentrated on clear coats in order to not disturb the underlying color coats. Wet sanding clear coats will bring out a much deeper shine and gloss when followed by controlled buffing and polishing.

Painters use very fine 1,500- to 2,500-grit sandpaper with water to smooth or remove minor blemishes on cured paint finishes designed to allow wet sanding. Only sandpaper designated wet or dry must be used, however. Those kinds that are not waterproof will fall apart and be useless.

As with all other sanding tasks, you have to use a sanding block. Since nibs of dirt or dust are small, fold sandpaper around a wooden paint stir stick instead of using a large hand block. Their one-inch width is great for smoothing small spots. Use only light pressure for this type of delicate sanding. Be sure to dip sandpaper in a bucket of water frequently to keep the paint surface wet and reduce the amount of material buildup on the sandpaper. Add a small amount of mild car washing soap to the water bucket to provide lubrication to the sandpaper. The sandpaper should also be allowed to soak in water for 15 minutes before wet sanding.

If certain blemished areas need a lot of sanding, you may need to apply new coats of clear. This is why you should leave masking material in place during wet sanding.

In some cases such as on show cars, the entire car body may be wet sanded to bring out the richest, deepest, and most lustrous shine possible. Because they anticipate extensive wet sanding and polishing operations, painters of these cars make sure that they have applied plenty of clear coats.

Removing Masking Material

To many enthusiastic automobile painters, removing masking paper and tape to reveal a new paint job or quality spot paint repair is like opening birthday presents. It is always a pleasure to see a finished product, especially after viewing it in primer for any length of time. However, unlike the wrapping paper on presents, masking materials must be removed in a controlled manner to prevent finish damage.

As we've discussed, paints have solids in them that build up on car bodies. Especially on jobs where numerous color and clear coats were applied, the thickness of the paint can bridge the lips along masking tape edges. What will occur, in some situations, is the formation of a paint film on a car body that continues over to include the top of the tape. If you pull the tape straight up, it could tear flakes of paint from the body surface.

To prevent paint flaking or peeling along the edge of masking tape strips, painters pull tape away from the newly painted body area, (as opposed to straight up off the panel),

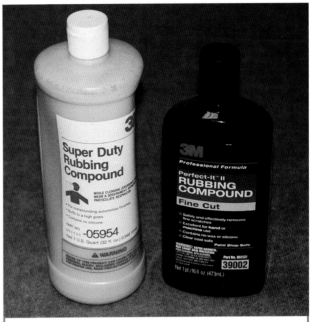

Rubbing compound can be used to "rub out" minute imperfections or orange peel in the final layer of paint. Available in different formulas, it works like extremely fine sandpaper. Even though a vehicle with orange peel in the paint can be shiny, it will have a much higher gloss if the orange peel is buffed out and the surface is that much flatter.

and back upon itself to create a sharp angle at the point tape leaves the surface. This sharp angle can cut extra-thin paint films so they don't cause flakes or cracks on the finish.

When they've applied several color and clear coats along a masked edge, meticulous painters often use a sharp razor blade to cut the paint film between the panel surface and tape edge. If you damage the paint while removing the masking material, you will have to sand and repaint as needed.

Rub Out and Buffing

As with wet sanding, not every type of paint system can stand up to vigorous polishing or rubbing out. With single-stage urethane, for example, buffing with a gritty compound will only dull the surface and ruin the finish. In contrast, polishing a catalyzed urethane (base coat/clear coat) or cured lacquer can make the finishes much more brilliant, lustrous, and deep shining.

A wide variety of polishing compounds are available for new paint finishes. Auto body paint and supply stores carry the largest selection. Some are designed to be used by hand, while others can safely be polished with buffing machines. Foam pads work best with prescribed compounds and buffing machines limited to slower rpm, while pads made with cloth material are better suited for other compounds and machine speeds. Be sure to get what is appropriate for your paint.

Polishing products come in a wide variety for many applications. You can apply them by hand, or by machine with a wool buffing pad or a foam pad. Polishing products are available in a variety of compounds, or grits. If you are polishing by hand, you would typically use a coarser compound than with an electric or pneumatic buffer.

PPG manufacturers its own brand of rubbing and polishing compounds for its paints. In addition, companies like 3M and Meguiar's produce several varieties of polishing products, all of which carry labels with specific instructions for their intended use and application.

Basically, rubbing compounds include relatively coarse polishing grit material. They are designed to quickly remove blemishes and flatten paint finishes. Because these compounds contain grit, they will leave behind light scratches or swirls. Therefore, after using compound to flatten orange peel or produce a higher surface luster, you will need to buff or polish the paint finish with a very fine grit material. Especially with dark colors, this may involve exceptionally soft finish-buffing pads and wax.

As refinish products have changed over the years, some ideas that seem like common sense are no longer valid. Manufacturers of the new urethane paint products often suggest polishing with 2,000-grit compound using a foam pad. This should minimize swirls and yield a satisfactory finish the first time around. If swirls are still present, you go back to a slightly coarser compound to remove the swirls, then use the finer 2,000-grit again. With older technology, painters would start with the coarse rubbing compound, then work up to the finer stuff, instead of this seemingly backward procedure.

Although paint finishes may appear dry, especially those that include a hardening agent, they may not be ready for buffing right away. You must allow sufficient time for all solvents to evaporate before smothering them with

polishing compound. Application guides and information sheets will generally list the recommended time. The information sheet for PPG's Polyurethane clear, for example, states, "Allow 16 hours before polishing either air-dried or force-dried DCU 2021."

By hand, use a soft, clean cloth for rubbing out and polishing and follow directions on the product label. Many auto enthusiasts apply polish in straight back and forth movements from the front to back of vehicles, instead of circular patterns. They profess that polishing panels in this manner greatly reduces their chances for creating swirls.

You need experience practicing with a buffing machine before using it on your car's new paint job. Practicing will help you avoid a paint burn—polishing through the paint finish down to primer or bare metal. Buffers with maximum speeds of about 1,450 rpm are best for novices. Machines with faster revolutions require more experience. Be aware that even the slower 1,450-rpm buffers are quite capable of causing paint burns if you don't pay close attention to what you're doing.

To use a buffer, first spread out a few strips of compound parallel to the floor about 4 to 6 inches apart. Cover an area no bigger than 2 square feet. Operate the buffing pad on top of a compound strip and work it over that strip's area, gradually moving down to pick up successive strips. The idea is to buff a 2-square-foot area while not allowing the pad to run dry of compound. Keep buffing on that body section until compound is gone and all that remains is shiny paint.

124

Buffing pads can be operated back and forth, as well as up and down. Always keep them moving. Just as with power sanders, a buffer left in one spot can rub through the paint. Be exceptionally careful buffing near ridges, gaps, and corners. If you hit those surfaces with the buffer, all of the buffing force is expended on a very small, focused area and it will burn through the paint very quickly. Instead of running the buffing pad on top of ridges, run it just up to their edge and stop. Some painters prefer to mask edges, ridges, and corners with strips of masking tape to protect them against accidental buffing burns, and then remove the tape and buff them by hand. This might be a good idea for the novice.

If you have to buff in tight areas, such as near door handles, throttle the machine on and off to lower the rpm speed. Slowing the pad in this way will help to reduce the possibility of paint burns. Be sure plenty of compound is spread over the area. For extra-confined spaces, apply compound by hand with a soft, damp cloth.

Make sure you don't drag power cords for electric buffers and air hoses for pneumatic models over the paint finish. A good way to keep them under control while buffing roofs, hoods, and trunk lids is to drape them over your shoulder. To prevent buckles, zippers, snaps or rivets on your clothing from scratching the car as you move alongside it, wear an apron. A long sweatshirt may also work. If possible, simply avoid clothing with these hard, sharp features.

Power buffers will throw spots of compound all over your car, clothes, and nearby surfaces. Be prepared for this kind of mess by covering adjacent cabinets or workbench items with tarps or drop cloths. Always wipe buffing compound thrown by the buffer off the paint as soon as possible, as it can damage the new paint if it is allowed to dry.

As cloth buffing pads become covered with compound, or every three passes, whichever comes first, use a pad spur to clean them. With the pad spinning, gently but securely push a spur into the pad's nap. This will break loose compound and force it out of the pad. You will be surprised at how much material comes off of pads, so be sure to do your pad cleaning away from your car and anything else that you don't want covered with compound or pad lint. You cannot clean the buffing pads too much.

Overspray

Polishing and buffing efforts usually work well to remove very light traces of overspray from hoods, roofs, and trunk lids. Extra-heavy overspray residue may require a strong polishing compound for complete removal. For severe problems, consult your auto body paint and supply jobber.

If you've been meticulous with your masking, most overspray problems, if any, will involve items like tailpipes, fender wells, horn units, and other low down pieces. You could spend a lot of time removing overspray from painted items, like fender wells, or spend a lot less by simply covering overspray with black paint or undercoat. If this won't work for some reason, e.g., a show car with matching-color fender wells, you'll have to sand, polish, or possibly even repaint affected areas.

Overspray on chrome might be easily removed with a chrome polish, like Simichrome. Heavy concentrations may require number 0000 steel wool with polish. Chrome items commonly prone to overspray include tailpipes, wheels, bumpers, grille pieces, and trim. The best way to avoid overspray problems on these accessories is to mask them properly with plenty of tape to secure paper edges so puffs of paint spray cannot infiltrate the masked space.

Remove paint overspray from glass using the solvent appropriate to the vehicle's paint system. Dab some solvent on a clean cloth and rub off overspray. If that does not work, try using number 0000 or finer steel wool and solvent. In extreme cases, you might have to use a razor blade and a delicate touch to scrape overspray off glass.

Caution: Some newer windshields are made with acrylic ingredients that even fine steel wool may scratch. If you are not sure whether your car's windshield is solid glass or an acrylic, check with a dealership service department, auto glass business or your auto body paint and supply jobber.

OVERVIEW

The way the paint looks on your vehicle depends on what happens before you spray it, and afterward. To get the results your hard work deserves, make sure the surface is perfectly flat, smooth, and free of dirt and particles before you spray. Have the painting steps and drying times within reach throughout the process so you can keep track of what you've done, what comes next, and how much time you have to do it.

Take your time to smooth nibs with fine 1,200-grit wet sandpaper. Use a sanding block with plenty of water. Be prepared too, in those wet sanding instances, to buff out or polish the spots smoothed with sandpaper. Polish will remove sanding scratches to leave the surface blemish-free and looking crisp.

Practice with a buffing machine and avoid ridges and other surfaces that concentrate the machine's power over a very small area. Be sure to remove spattered rubbing compound so it doesn't create blemishes when it dries. With masking paper still in place, you can add light coats of clear as necessary, or touch up spots that need that kind of attention. This is essentially your last chance to fix mistakes or repair blemishes.

By all means, take your time removing masking paper and tape. Be certain to pull tape at an angle away from the newly painted surface and also at a sharp angle over itself to prevent damage to the adjoining paint. Where paint coats are numerous and consequently thick, have a sharp razor blade handy to cut paint that may look like it is ready to peel off with the tape.

It's best to decide whether you're going to paint your vehicle in one color, multiple colors, or with flames or scallops before you buy your paint, yet nothing says you can't add these extras later. Either way, you should concentrate on getting the vehicle painted properly before you add additional colors or graphics.

Realize that anything other than a monotone (one-color) paint job will require more work. Except when doing detailed airbrush work, you'll have to mask the entire vehicle for each color of paint you spray. If you have masked the vehicle properly one time, you can do it again, but this may be more than the first-time car painter wants to try.

I highly recommend a base coat/clear coat paint system if you choose a paint scheme of more than one color. That way you can apply two coats of clear over the first color. If you get any overspray from the second color on the first, you can sand it out of the clear without damaging the underlying color coat. After applying the second color (and third, if applicable), apply two or three additional coats of clear over the entire vehicle.

The author treated this longtime daily driver to a monochromatic paint job. The entire body was stripped to bare metal prior to several undercoats and ultimately a single-stage top coat. The bumpers were sandblasted to remove the chrome, and then were coated with epoxy primer and matching top coat.

Airbrushed artwork adds some color to this otherwise monochromatic hot rod. If you're planning on artwork, use a base coat/clear coat system so the artist can sand any mistakes out of the clear without touching the color coat. Allow the paint enough time to dry fully before adding any sort of artwork.

This street rod sedan makes good use of its two-tone paint. On this somewhat large vehicle, a monochrome paint job may be too much of any one color, yet it looks good with its two shades of gray. Notice how the colors change at a distinct body line, which made masking for each color relatively easy. Although difficult to see in the photo, the seam between the two colors is covered by a subtle pinstripe.

Flash and drying times are also critical to a successful multicolor paint job. Applying masking tape or masking paper to freshly painted surfaces that have not yet dried adequately will cause you much more work. Product information sheets will provide a specified time to allow the paint to dry before taping. Likewise, clear coats must be added within a specified time, or the base coat will need to be scuffed and additional base coats added.

PART OF THE PAINT SCHEME

Flames, scallops, or a multicolor paint job such as the tricolor paint schemes from the 1950s, are usually considered part of the overall plan. Although any of these can actually be added after the initial paint application, they would still be considered part of the paint scheme when describing the car to someone. Graphics, on the other hand, are often added later. Even when graphics are painted on, their application is somewhat different from the main body surface paint.

Two-Tone Schemes

If you are repainting a vehicle that originally featured a two-tone paint scheme, it may seem natural to include the second color this time around as well. If that is the case, you should study your vehicle very closely before removing or priming over any of the existing paint. Where does the primary color stop and the secondary color start? Is there a piece of trim that covers this seam, and will that trim piece still be used after the paint job? Does the trim cover all of the paint seam, or is some of it left out in the open? Which color are the doorjambs? How well you duplicate the original color transitions will have a great impact on your overall paint job. It is better to have a high-quality monochrome paint job than a mediocre two-tone finish.

Whether you are duplicating a stock paint scheme or developing one of your own, look at other vehicles that are two-tone to see where the paint colors change. Graphics are a different story, but on a normal two-tone paint scheme, the colors almost always change underneath a piece of trim, or at a body line, rather than in the middle of an otherwise uninterrupted body surface.

Think about how you would mask the area that is to be a different color and realize that it should be the same on both sides of the vehicle. This will help you realize that you need to take advantage of body lines and natural breaks when designing a two-tone paint scheme. If you are going to be hiding a paint seam under a piece of trim, be sure to split the width of the trim evenly with each color. If the trim is an inch wide, this leaves a half-inch for each color. You should be able to align the trim accurately enough to cover this, however, if the trim is narrower, you will have less room for error in masking or trim installation.

It doesn't really matter which color of a two-tone paint scheme you paint first, though many painters would paint the portion that's easiest to mask first, so that once it's painted, they can mask it off quickly and proceed to the second color. For example, if you were painting a large four-door sedan maroon, with a dark gray secondary color below a body line that runs approximately through the middle of the doors, it might be easier to paint the lower area, mask it off, and then paint the rest of the car, rather than painting the top, hood, trunk and half the doors, and then masking all of that off to paint the lower portion. While painting the gray area, you would mask the color boundary with masking tape and the bulk of the car with plastic masking material. Once painted, you would mask the gray area with masking paper and tape.

This 1937 Ford coupe essentially has a tricolor paint scheme, although there are actually only two colors. The layout of the upper portion of black paint is nicely done; it begins with the grille in the front and extends across the hood and the top and down throughout the trunk. The good points about the lower black section are that it begins at the louvers in the hood sides and echoes the shapes of fenders on its lower edges. These two colors abut one another with no pinstriping or trim, so the masking had to be exact.

A couple of other situations may call for a multicolor paint job performed after the initial paint application. Commercial vehicles, for example, have custom paintwork on top of the manufacturer's paint. For large national accounts, vehicle manufacturers usually paint the vehicles as required by the purchasing company, however, smaller companies are required to make their own paint additions. For this type of job, you must first identify the original paint. Clean the area to be painted with wax and grease remover, then scuff the original paint with 1,000–1,200-grit sandpaper; clean again with wax and grease remover. Masking is as required for the company scheme, sprayed in a paint compatible with the original finish.

Another sort of multicolor paint job involves repainting only one of the two colors to freshen up the finish. For example, the lower color might be chipped and dinged, while the upper color remains virtually flawless.

Flames

On the right vehicle, flames that are laid out properly, utilize the right colors, and are applied properly, look great. However, there are probably more flamed paint jobs that don't look as good as anticipated. Some flames look good, some don't, while others are purely hideous. If you are having any doubts about the proper flame layout or colors to use, avoid them completely . . . or at least until you feel that you can't live without them any longer. There is simply no reason to deface a great paint job by applying a mediocre set of flames.

If you are contemplating flames for your hot rod or road rocket, it's a good idea to check out vehicles similar to yours that have flames. The first goal is to find a pattern or layout that you like. Although flames are not required to be perfectly symmetrical, they should be balanced from one side to the other in their layout and intensity.

Flame patterns can be long and narrow, or big and bold with short tips. Choose what looks best to you and flows with the lines of your vehicle. Remember that real flames would naturally be progressing upward if the burning object were sitting still, or toward the back if moving. Therefore, don't aim flames downward or toward the front of your car—you laugh, but there are examples of both cases!

When flames will extend across more than one body panel, assemble the panels prior to painting in the exact spots where they'll remain after final assembly. If you don't do this, your final panel adjustments—to get everything to open and close smoothly and the panel gaps even—will pull your paint scheme out of alignment. You don't want to have to choose between a misaligned paint job and a hood that won't shut right.

To balance the flame layout from one side to the other, you must find the centerline of the vehicle. Run a strip of ⅛ inch Fine Line tape down this centerline from the front to the back of the vehicle. If the flames will be extending in multiple layers across a large area, such as a hood or roof, this large panel should be sectioned off with tape running from side to side. The length of the flame tips can be balanced in this manner.

Before beginning the layout procedure, you must decide if you want merely balanced flames, or if you want them to be symmetrical. For symmetrical flames, the flames should be laid out on one side of the vehicle in ⅛-inch Fine-

Although these flames use traditional colors on a black vehicle, they are more contemporary in their layout, with thinner, wispy licks. As you can see, these colors jump right off this Model A Tudor's black paint. Traditionally, flames would begin with red, then orange, then end up with yellow, and maybe even some white at the tips. The colors of these flames seem to be reversed in order as they progress along the vehicle.

These flames are broader and don't include the very front of the vehicle, originating instead from the hood side louvers. Although this hot rod isn't black, it features traditional flame colors.

Line tape. Then spread a large piece of pattern paper (or several pieces taped together) over that flame layout. There must be no bubbles or pockets in the paper. Tape down the pattern paper and mark several reference points that can be identified on each side of the vehicle. Next, trace over the flame layout with a pounce wheel, which will poke tiny holes in the pattern paper. (A pounce wheel is like a small pizza cutter, except that the cutting wheel has teeth.)

When you've traced over the entire flame pattern, carefully remove the pattern paper, flip it over, and position it on the other side of the vehicle. Use the reference points marked earlier to align the paper on the vehicle. With the pattern paper aligned and secured to the vehicle, spread drafting pounce, carpenter's chalk line chalk, or talcum powder over the paper and lightly brush it into the holes made in the paper by the pounce wheel. When you've dusted all of the holes with powder, remove the pattern paper. Then, using ⅛ inch Fine Line tape, lay out the pattern by connecting the dots.

More experienced flamers may choose to lay out the flames freehand. As long as balance from side to side is maintained, this method works just as well. Using ⅛-inch Fine Line tape, lay out the first flame that intersects the centerline of the vehicle. Start at the tip of the flame, work forward to the belly, and then across the centerline. Form a pattern that is a mirror image of the first side. The overall style of the flame pattern begins to take shape as you lay out the mirror image of the first flame.

With the layout phase completed, the masking can begin. Overlap the original outline with ¼-inch masking tape, applying the excess to the area to be masked off. The ⅛-inch Fine Line tape will serve as the actual edge for the flames. Use masking tape in ¾-inch or larger sizes to mask the remaining area. Overlapping the masking tape in a

Notice how the flames on this roadster extend from the hood, across the cowl, and onto the door. Since the flames extend across multiple body panels, it is imperative that all panels align properly before flames, scallops, or any other artwork is applied. A careful observer will notice how these flames are mostly all yellow. However, they are much brighter in the front than toward the back. The painter did some very careful fading with these flames, and added some highlights at the tips.

continuous fashion will make the tape easier to remove as a sheet later, rather than removing each strip of masking tape. Use the largest tape available to cover the area to be masked; however, be sure no masking tape enters the flame area, and that all of the area to be masked is covered. After the entire flamed area has been masked, the rest of the vehicle can be masked using masking paper and tape. Be sure to extend the masking paper down below the bottom of the vehicle to avoid getting any overspray on the underside.

To ensure that the painted flames adhere well, you will need either to scuff the area to be flamed or apply an adhesion promoter. Consult with your paint and supply jobber to determine the best procedure for the paint system you are using. Next, use an air nozzle to remove any dust or dirt that may have accumulated, wax and grease remover to clean the surface once again, and finally a tack cloth to pick up all remaining lint or dust prior to spraying.

With the vehicle masked and the surface prepped, apply the flame colors you've selected. Depending on the area (size) of the flames, you may use a full-size production gun, a detail gun, or an airbrush. Fading is done by varying the air pressure and applying less than full coverage, and is defi-

The first step in painting flames is to determine which panels will receive them and in what shape or layout. On this particular Camaro, the owner had just had the entire car repainted but wanted some flames to adorn the side panels. The owner decided that the flames would be limited to the front fenders and doors. The front fascia, hood, rear quarter panels, and rocker panels were masked off. In addition to the flames, this area will be coated with clear, so the bare panels are scuffed slightly with 1,000- or 1,200-grit sandpaper to provide proper paint adhesion. The flames are laid out using ⅛-inch Fine Line tape. Randy Lenger

nitely a practiced art. You simply aren't going to get it perfect the first time out.

If you have doubts about what colors will work best with your vehicle, consult a few pros and other enthusiasts whose paint jobs you admire. Red, orange and yellow

2

To transfer the layout of the flames from one side to the other, layout paper is taped to the vehicle so that the paper is touching the vehicle over the entire surface that will be flamed (or scalloped). Next, you must make reference marks on the paper so you can place it accurately on the opposite side of the vehicle later on. The paper will be taped to the vehicle inside out when it goes on the opposite side. Using a soft pencil, trace the layout of the Fine Line tape, which you can feel through the layout paper. Trace along the approximate center of the tape, or one of the edges—it doesn't matter which, as long as you are consistent when you do the other side. Randy Lenger

3

Before taping the pattern to the opposite side, trace the penciled outline with a pounce wheel. For best results, the paper should be laid flat on a piece of drywall or something with a similar hardness. This allows the spurs of the pounce wheel to poke tiny holes in the paper. With the layout paper positioned correctly on the opposite side of the vehicle, tape it securely into place. To trace the flame pattern, pour carpenter's chalk line chalk into an old sock or shop towel that is tied up on the open end. Gently rub the sock or towel over the tiny openings in the layout paper, leaving a tiny bit of chalk on the body of the vehicle. If you look closely, you will notice a blue haze from the chalk left on the layout paper. Randy Lenger

flames are very traditional for a black vehicle. Ghost flames, which appear only from certain angles, have become popular on some newer vehicles, such as the PT Cruiser. There is really no limit to the style and colors to choose from—just be sure the combination you settle on complements your vehicle's existing paint, and is something you'll be happy to look at for many years.

Once you've applied the flames and they have dried, remove the masking paper and tape with the same care you used on the rest of the vehicle. Properly clean the surface one more time and then give the whole car two or three coats of clear. For traditional flames, apply a pinstripe over the junction of the flame colors and body color. Without this pinstripe, traditional flames simply aren't complete.

Scallops

Scallops, like flames, date back to the early days of hot rodding. They have become slightly more common than

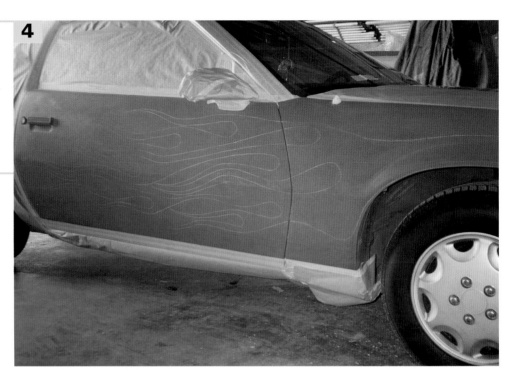

4 After dusting the entire flame layout with the carpenter's chalk, carefully remove the layout paper, leaving the layout intact. Apply Fine Line tape directly on top of the chalk, duplicating the layout from the opposite side. Randy Lenger

5 With the flame layout outlined with Fine Line tape, mask off the areas between the flames with masking tape. Also mask the rest of the vehicle with tape and masking paper. As you may have already imagined, this masking process takes lots of time and patience. A blunder here could cause lots of problems and extra work later on. Randy Lenger

flames among the custom car crowd, yet their popularity tends to rise and fall more frequently.

Generally, though not always, scallops are one solid color. Since they are also more of a geometric shape, and therefore easier to lay out, scallops are probably easier than flames for the first time painter.

There are two main layout questions as you plan your scallops. First, how many points should there be, and should the bellies of the scallops be pointed, rounded, or square with rounded corners? Second, should the tops or the bottoms of the scallop be parallel and to what should they be parallel? How to answer these questions depends on the vehicle you're painting. What looks good on a 1982 Chevrolet Malibu may not work as well on a 1949 Buick.

Just as with flames, when scallops extend across multiple body panels, you must assemble the panels to their final position when you lay them out to be sure the scallops don't

6

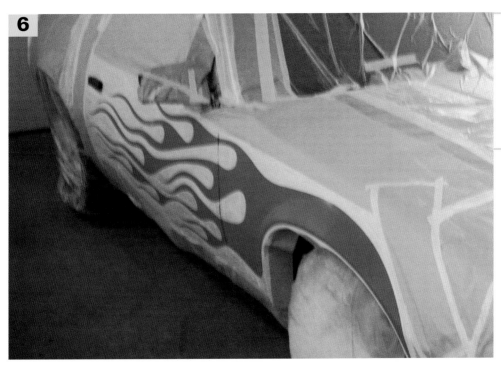

Masking paper is used to mask the area that will be directly in the line of spray, while plastic sheeting specifically designed for masking will be used to cover the rest of the vehicle. Randy Lenger

7

With layout and masking completed on both sides of the vehicle, clean the areas to be flamed with wax and grease remover one last time prior to painting. Randy Lenger

8

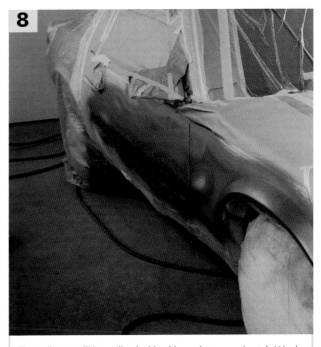

These flames will be outlined with a blue stripe approximately ¼ inch wide. Traditionally, flames are outlined with a pinstripe to cover the seam or bump where the extra layer of paint ends. This pinstripe always leaves a slight bump if applied in the traditional manner, yet it covers the bump caused by the extra layer of paint from the flames. The pinstripe outline, the body of the flames, and the rest of the door and fender panels will be smooth under a coat of clear. Randy Lenger

get pulled out of alignment through later panel adjustments. Don't lay out the scallops until all your panel gaps are even, and moving panels open and close smoothly and properly.

To balance the scallop layout from one side to the other, you need to locate the vehicle's centerline. When you've taken appropriate measurements to determine the centerline,

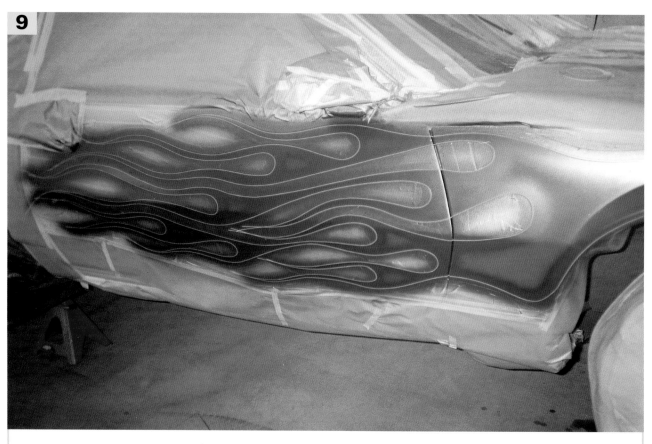

9

Although it looks like lots of blue paint, when the job is finished, this will result in a ¼-inch-wide outline of the flames only. Most of the blue paint seen here is actually on the masking paper between the flames. The red in the flame area is from the original red paint on the car. Randy Lenger

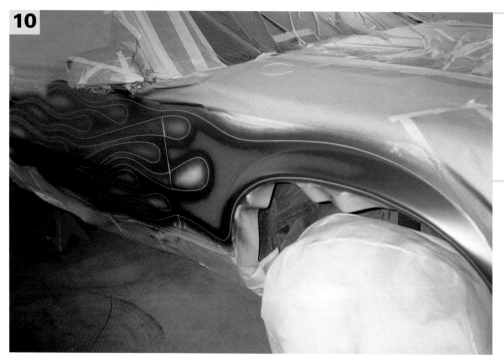

10

The blue paint is now allowed to dry according to the "time to tape" on the instructions for the type of paint being used. Do not try to rush this drying time, as applying additional tape to wet paint will cause more problems later.
Randy Lenger

11

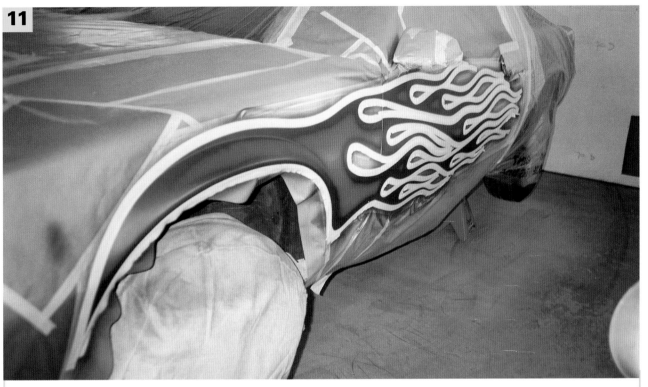

With the outline color dry, apply masking tape so that ¼ inch of the blue paint is now covered. Maintaining a consistent width is time consuming, yet very critical in the overall finished appearance of the flames. Randy Lenger

12

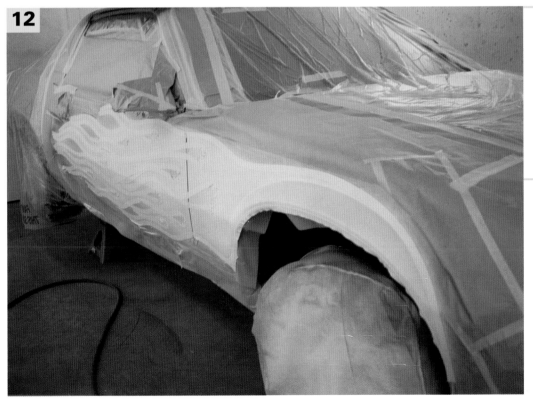

To help make the flames "pop" or jump off the vehicle, apply a white base coat. Depending on the desired effect, you could use a silver or gold base to provide more of a candy color. Randy Lenger

13

The color of the bulk of the flames (yellow) is now applied. These flames will be solid yellow with a few red highlights (to be added later), so the flamed area is simply painted with the desired yellow paint. If the flames were to fade from one color to another (or several), that would be done at this point. For instance, on traditional flames of red, orange, and yellow, red would be applied at one end of the flames with yellow being applied at the other. As the red and yellow overlap in the middle in varying amounts, the orange is developed. For most applications, there would not actually be any orange paint in the flames. Randy Lenger

14

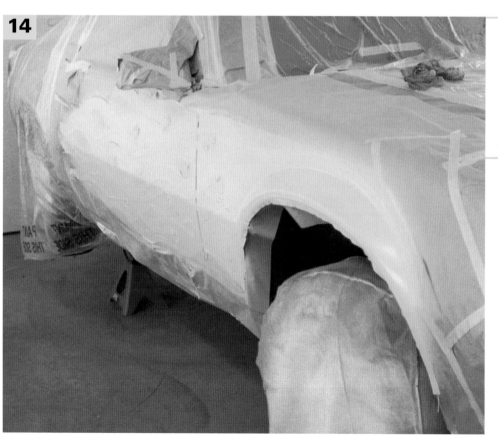

Between the labor-intensive chore of masking and the downtime required for drying between coats of paint, a "simple" set of flames can cost more money and require more time than many would believe. Randy Lenger

15

To give the flames some additional dimension, the tips are highlighted with some red. No additional masking is required for this, but you must concentrate on what you are doing to avoid putting too much red in the flame tips. Complete coverage is not the goal at this point, but rather a gentle fogging of red.
Randy Lenger

16

As when the blue was applied earlier, this looks like a lot of color. Again, most of it is on the masking paper and will be gone soon.
Randy Lenger

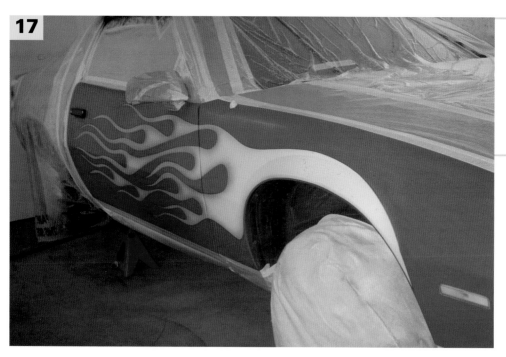

17

With the painting of the actual flames complete and adequate drying time elapsed, the masking paper is removed from the flames. Now we get to see what the flames actually look like. Randy Lenger

18

To provide durability and gloss, clear is applied to the fenders and doors, the area that had been scuffed previously. If necessary, the clear could be buffed to blend it with the clear on the rest of the vehicle. Randy Lenger

run a strip of ⅛-inch Fine Line tape down it from front to back. Additional guidelines may be applied in similar fashion to provide reference points from which to measure as you add the scallops.

As scallops cascade across the hood or down the side of the vehicle, they form a repeat pattern, rather than the free-flowing design of flames. When you're satisfied with the layout on the first side, duplicate it on the other side using the pattern method described in the flames section, or freehand.

With the layout phase completed, the masking can begin. Overlap the original outline with ¼-inch masking

19

Ghost flames require the same amount of work (layout, masking, and painting) as regular flames, but they don't always show up. Ghost flames should not be confused with outline flames, which rodders paint on their vehicles at the primer stage to see how they look. You can try different things at the primer stage because changes are so easy.

tape, applying the excess to the area to be masked off. The ⅛-inch Fine Line tape will serve as the edge for the scallops. Use ¾-inch or larger masking tape to mask the remaining area, and then mask the rest of the vehicle. Be sure to extend the masking paper down below the bottom of the vehicle to avoid getting any overspray underneath the vehicle.

You must either scuff the area to be scalloped or apply an adhesion promoter to ensure that the painted scallops adhere properly. Consult with your paint and supply jobber to determine the best procedure for the paint system you are using. Use an air nozzle to remove any dust or dirt that may have accumulated, wax and grease remover to clean the

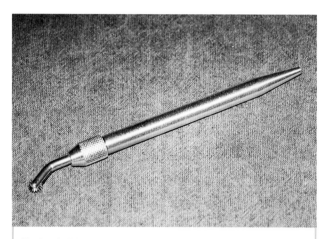

The head of this pounce wheel includes a small wheel with tiny spurs on it. If rolled along a piece of masking paper, these spurs would leave tiny holes in the paper. The paper could then be used as a pattern to transfer the same flame or graphic outline to the opposite side of the vehicle. Using reference marks to properly align the pattern, drafting pounce or talcum powder can be spread over the pattern paper. The pattern paper can then be removed and Fine Line tape used to connect the dots of powder.

surface once again, and finally a tack cloth to pick up any remaining lint or dust prior to spraying.

Spray the scallops. After the proper drying time, carefully remove the masking paper and tape, clean the surface again, and apply two or three coats of clear.

PINSTRIPING

Pinstriping can be a simple stand-alone accent to a single color paint job, or a finishing touch to most any multicolor paint scheme. Before the days of the automobile, painters applied pinstripes to the spokes of covered wagon wheels. They have endured as a design feature ever since, on almost any type of vehicle, from bicycles to children's wagons to cars and trucks. In some contexts, they're virtually mandatory. For example, you should always pinstripe traditional flames or scallops; otherwise they simply are not finished. Pinstriping provides a finished appearance to flames or scallops, covering the otherwise unattractive seam of color where the flame or scallop meets the vehicle's main paint finish. It can also serve to conceal slight irregularities in the edge of the paint.

Common on factory paint jobs, pinstriping is usually a single or double line approximately ⅛ inch wide and running along the beltline of the vehicle, in a contrasting or complementary color. Since pinstriping is an accent, painters often choose a bright color, such as orange for a maroon vehicle, or purple on a black vehicle. You most likely would not choose a two-tone paint job using equal amounts of these colors, but in the thin width of a pinstripe, it all works well.

Artists of the 1940s and 1950s popularized another type of pinstriping on hot rods and lead sleds. This pinstriping features short sweeping lines, curves, and arcs, rather than one or two long lines wrapping around the vehicle. These short lines of one more colors are intertwined, overlapped, and connected to create some interesting artwork. Although they rarely constitute an actual picture, they do invite some interesting interpretations on occasion if viewed from different angles.

The most common paint for pinstriping or lettering is One-Shot Sign Painter's enamel, which is available from larger art supply stores or some auto body paint and supply jobbers. It is relatively inexpensive, so with just a few primary colors and some extra mixing jars, you can produce virtually any color. Before applying pinstriping paint, clean the surface with a wax and grease remover applied and a clean cloth, and wipe it off with a second dry cloth.

Sign painter's enamel is compatible with most other paint surfaces. Different reducers are available to speed up or slow down the enamel's drying time. Due to the relatively small area to which it is applied, it is usually allowed to air dry, although a blow dryer can speed up the process.

Brush

Until fairly recently, all pinstriping was done with a brush specifically designed for the purpose. Known as a pinstriping dagger, this brush is normally only about four to six inches long. By dipping the tip of the brush into enamel, and then slightly squeezing the brush hairs, you can apply the pinstripe at the desired line thickness.

Striping Tool

A somewhat recent development in the art of pinstriping is a mechanical striping tool. For anyone applying an accent stripe, this is a much easier method than brush painting. You could do curves or freehand shapes like flames or scallops with it, but you would need to practice a fair amount first.

A mechanical striping tool is made of a small cylinder that can be attached to any of a collection of heads. The cylinder holds the paint, while the head applies it to the surface. The heads have either one or two wheels, providing either a single or a double line. The wheels are available in different widths for lines of different thickness, but they will always be parallel or concentric if you use a head with two wheels.

GRAPHICS (Afterthoughts or Additions)

Graphics can vary from the adhesive graduated shading on a 30th Anniversary Corvette or a checkered flag pattern currently common on a variety of stock production vehicles, to an airbrushed mural of any design. As you plan your paint scheme, keep in mind that a body side molding or

These scallops improve the look of this Track-T roadster immensely. It would still be a fun car to drive, but without the scallops, it would simply not have the eye appeal that it does. The length of the points appears to be in good proportion to the size of the vehicle. Scallops are much more geometric than flames, and as such there seems to be less room for error when it comes to laying them out. If the points are too long or too short, the scallops simply will not look right.

Notice how the bellies of these scallops are more square (albeit with rounded corners) than the Track-T example. Also, compare the colors used. Some painters would opt for greater contrast between the vehicle and scallops. The points are also more similar in length to the body portion of the scallop than is traditional.

stainless steel trim adds the same type of accent as a graphic. Examine each of the design and paint features that catch a viewer's eye and consider whether, taken together, they improve the overall look or make it too "busy" or cluttered.

Painted

A base coat/clear coat system is best for any painted graphics or artwork, as it allows you to sand overspray or other mistakes on subsequent layers out of the clear without damaging the underlying color coat. Before adding any artwork, clean the entire area with wax and grease remover. Surface preparation will depend upon the media being applied, so read the instructions provided, or check with your paint and supply jobber.

Just as with flames, all affected panels need to be in place when laying out the scallop pattern. Painting them with misaligned panels leaves you the lose-lose choice of having poor panel fit or disjointed artwork.

141

Although it is difficult to tell for sure what color it is against the red paint, the accent pinstriping looks good on this early Mopar coupe. Simply following an existing body line, this thin pinstripe "finishes" the paint job on this otherwise monochromatic vehicle. When applying accent pinstriping along a body line be sure to place the striping slightly to one side or the other of the body line to keep it from rubbing off.

Unless you do an enormous amount of striping and lettering, these half-pint cans of One-Shot Sign Painter's enamel will last for quite a while. Larger cans are available. With three basic colors, red, yellow, and blue, you can mix your own custom colors quite easily, although a wide variety of colors are available premixed. Also shown is a Grumbacher pinstriping brush. Before using any lettering or striping enamel, make sure that you have some enamel reducer or mineral spirits available for cleanup. You should also wipe down the area to be striped or lettered with a wax and grease remover to make sure that your work stays on the vehicle where it is supposed to.

Vinyl Adhesive

Although diehard hot rodders or customizers would laugh at the thought, vinyl adhesive graphics are becoming popular. A new generation of car enthusiasts appreciates their improved materials, low cost and versatility. Many enthusiasts prefer to spend a hundred bucks on a vinyl graphic they can remove if they grow tired of it, rather than investing five to ten times that much for artwork that would require almost as much again to remove and that can otherwise outlast the vehicle.

Today's computer graphics and vinyl technology make it easy for almost anyone to create high-quality artwork for a fraction of the cost of hiring an airbrush artist. These advances have also made vinyl adhesive graphics more common as an OEM item. To repair a stick-on graphic, you typically purchase a replacement from the dealer's parts department.

Now that you've produced a beautiful paint job, you don't want to detract from it by refitting dirty parts. Unless you cleaned and polished the parts when you removed them, now is the time to detail everything before restoring it to your vehicle's now pristine body. You will also want to clean up the engine compartment, interior, and trunk—including vacuuming out sanding dust—to bring them up to the same high standards. Windows that are clean on both sides, a dust-free dashboard, spotless doorjambs, scrubbed tires, polished chrome, a well-groomed interior, grease-free engine compartment, and a tidy trunk space all work together to complement new body paint and make the automobile look, feel, and smell like new.

Install the clean, detailed parts systematically so you don't have to take anything back off to fit another component. Certain trim sections, for example, are designed to be put on first with an adjacent section covering part of their edge. Likewise, you may need access to the inner side of the door panel to refit trim or a handle; install those items before replacing the interior panel. Look at all of the components that need to be added to a particular panel or section of the car and figure out the proper sequence for fitting them before you start. This way you won't have to redo anything and risk scratching the paint in the process.

GLASS

Glass requires special care because it's breakable and heavy enough to dent as well as scratch your vehicle. Since the paint should be cured by the time you begin installing glass, consider laying strips of wide masking tape along window frame edges to guard against accidental bumps that could cause paint scratches or nicks. Be sure to use automotive masking tape because generic tape might leave adhesive residue.

To avoid galvanic corrosion, make sure any metal clips holding glass panels in place are mounted correctly and do not come in contact with sheet metal body panels. Be careful installing them too, to avoid chipping or scratching the paint. Even the smallest paint chip can allow moisture and air to reach the metal and start the rusting process. Once started, especially on areas hidden by trim, oxidation will spread under layers of paint unnoticed until severe metal rust damage causes bubbles, cracks, or other problems.

Along with recognizing the importance of preventing paint chips while installing glass, you should be concerned about watertight seals all around window perimeters. Not only are water leaks annoying, they create ideal conditions for corrosion damage on metal panels and rot or mildew in upholstery and carpeting.

Quite honestly, bodywork and painting are filthy, dirty jobs. Between body filler dust, primer overspray, and water spots from washing and wet sanding, your freshly painted vehicle would be a real mess if it was not detailed when the painting is finished. Sure, the paint might look good, but it won't really matter if the glass is not sparkling and the tires are dirty. The only way to make the best of your new paint is to clean the glass (inside and out), scrub and treat the tires, and polish the chrome.

With the carpet pulled back out of the way, we can see how the taillight housing on this 2000 Chevrolet Malibu is held in place. The black plastic wing nuts are simply unthreaded from the inside, and the taillight housing is pulled away from the outside of the car. There is enough slack in the wire that the bulb and its twist-off socket can be removed from the housing from the outside of the trunk. To reassemble, the bulb is reinserted into the housing and the housing secured to the car body with the wing nuts previously removed. The carpet would then be placed back into its correct position and secured with two plastic nuts that thread onto the metal studs shown in the photo.

Fixed glass panels, like windshields, rear and some side windows, are held in place by various means. These means vary not only by window type, but also by vehicle make and model. Some feature clips, others rely on thick rubber molding, and many call for strips of butyl- or urethane-based sealers. If you are not familiar with auto glass installation, seriously consider hiring a professional to complete the work for you. Most auto glass businesses offer mobile service, sending a specialist to your location to complete the work.

Rear window glass on pickup trucks and hatchbacks oftentimes is set inside grooves along the inside perimeter of heavy rubber moldings. Another groove runs around the outer molding perimeter. Once the molding is fitted around glass, the installer inserts a cord into the outer perimeter groove and pulls it taut. While one person holds the glass and molding unit in place from outside the vehicle, another person starts pulling the cord from inside the vehicle. As the cord pulls away from the rubber it also pulls its edge back, allowing the molding to fit around the panel edges forming the window opening. Thus, the edges of the window opening gradually replace the rope in the groove. Professionals typically wrap the rope so that both ends meet in the middle of the bottom groove. The inside person pulls one end of the rope, then the other end, easing the bottom lip on first, and then inching up each side and around each top corner, toward the middle of the top groove, at which point the rope pulls free and the last portion of molding pops into place.

Installing fixed glass units with urethane sealer actually adds a degree of structural strength to some automobiles. Windshields and side-mounted fixed glass units on newer cars and vans are commonly secured by continuous beads of urethane sealer. In some cases, a bead of butyl material is used instead of urethane. Butyl has a strength of approximately 5 psi, while urethane boasts adhesion strength of approximately 500 psi.

If you performed extensive bodywork by a window opening, you may want to use a butyl bead to secure the glass in case you have to remove it for adjustments to the sheet metal or window. Since butyl is not nearly as strong as urethane, you'll be able to remove the glass again much more easily.

Before installing a fixed-glass unit, ensure that its supportive body opening is completely clean and free of contaminants. Then, lay a bead of butyl material around the window opening. For butyl-only installations, make a full bead. If you will also use urethane, slope the butyl bead away from the glass at a 45-degree angle toward the body. Then add urethane material to fill the triangular void left in the butyl bead. For either kind of installation, butyl actually holds the glass in place. It's used with urethane installations because the urethane takes more time to cure.

About the only way to remove fixed glass units secured by butyl or urethane beads is to cut through the beads with a special tool made of wire. You make an opening in the bead, pass the wire through it, then attach a handle to each end. With an assistant—one person inside, one outside—you then manipulate the wire so that it cuts the bead all the way around the window. Coordinate with your assistant so that you catch the glass once it's cut free. Afterward, loosen the old bead material using a dedicated solvent available from your automotive paint supplier.

The tools and materials needed to remove and install fixed glass units are available at auto body paint and supply stores. Be sure you fully understand all installation instructions for the products that you use. In addition, have a helper available to assist you in removing or replacing glass units, as they can be quite heavy and cumbersome. If for any reason you are hesitant to tackle such a job, consider the services of a professional auto glass installer. Compared to the cost of replacing broken glass units (from $100 to well over $1,000), a professional auto glass installer's fee is minimal.

TRIM

In addition to detailing trim pieces before installing them, you might consider using an artist's fine paintbrush and compatible paint to fill in chips, scratches, or peeled sections in paint lines. Older cars generally feature metal trim pieces with painted lines that run lengthwise along grooved indentations.

If you are planning to paint the doorjambs, you must remove the plastic or stainless steel sill plates. They are typically secured by two to five screws, depending on the length. Before reinstalling them after the vehicle has been repainted, you should fully detail them. A stiff brush and some all-purpose cleaner may be necessary.

Treat vinyl or rubber trim sections to a good scrubbing with an all-purpose cleaner such as Simple Green and a soft brush. When they are dry, apply a satisfactory coat of vinyl dressing. Rub the treatment in with a soft cloth or very soft brush. Be sure to wipe off all excess. If you don't want to use a silicone-based treatment, check with the auto body paint and supply store to see if it carries vinyl and rubber rejuvenation products without silicone.

Make sure you have all of the clips and retainers on hand before attaching trim pieces. Also be sure you know where they go and how they fit—to the vehicle and to each another. Have a helper assist you in replacing extra-long pieces. This helps prevent bends or wrinkles in the trim, and also adds more control to the installation, reducing the chance that you'll scratch the paint.

When installing belt moldings around windows, do not use a screwdriver or other hard object to flip rubber edges over onto painted frame openings. Instead, use a plastic tool designed for this procedure. They are shaped somewhat like a doctor's tongue depresser and are available at auto body and supply stores and some auto glass shops.

Since door handles and key locks attach directly to painted body panels, you must install them with care so as not to scratch, chip, or nick the finish. In many cases, gaskets or seals separate hardware from the body skin. If the old gasket is worn, cracked, or otherwise damaged, do not use it. Wait until you have a new gasket to install that handle or exterior door item.

A defective gasket increases the odds that the handle will come in direct contact with the sheet metal body panel. Should the two metals be incompatible, for example one

aluminum and one steel, their contact point creates a perfect spot for the start of galvanic corrosion. This is an oxidation process produced by the chemical reaction between the two metals of different composition. The weaker of the two metals will corrode.

The screws, nuts, or bolts used to secure door handles are normally accessed through openings on the interior side of the door. You have to reach through with your hand to tighten the fasteners. Be sure to use wrenches or sockets of the correct size to make this awkward job as easy as possible. After handles and key locks are secured, you must attach linkages or cables that run to the actual latch mechanisms.

When reassembling your vehicle, make sure that you reinstall all of the bumpers that are commonly found beneath the hood, deck lid, and doorjambs. These bumpers have a great impact on panel alignment and eliminate rattles. They also cushion the panel as it closes and prevent metal-on-metal contact. If they are broken or missing, you should replace them at this time.

While this plastic trim panel doesn't necessarily secure the grille in place, it does block access to some of the screws that do. Quite often, you will be required to start removing screws and bolts at random to find out which ones are really securing the grille. There are always some surprises, but if you take a few minutes to study how some panels overlap others, disassembly and reassembly will be easier to figure out. Like most other trim accessories that are removed prior to painting, the grille and related components should be thoroughly cleaned prior to reassembly.

GRILLE

Most grille sections are secured by screws of some type. Many are tightened into metal clips, as opposed to nuts. These clips have to be positioned correctly in order to support the grille. Pay attention to the way you place clips, as they can slide around to cause scratches along the metal supports to which they fasten. Likewise, screws must line up with the center of these clips in order to work properly. Be sure you've determined the way the pieces fit together so you can install them in the required order.

Headlight buckets, housings, or trim rings are generally separate from grilles. This is so you can change a burned-out headlight without dismantling the entire grille. Remember, there are normally two screws next to headlights that tighten down over springs. These are used only for positioning the headlight beams. If you disturbed these screws, be sure you get them properly positioned again before you need to drive after dark.

As with other exterior trim pieces and accessories, you should take this opportunity to clean, polish, and detail grille assemblies while they are off your car. Touch up paint nicks, clean tiny nooks and crannies, and wax metallic parts as necessary. Use a soft toothbrush and cotton swabs to reach into tight spaces. Should painted parts look old and worn, consider sanding and repainting them. Tiny chips or nicks can be touched up with the proper paint, using a fine artist's paintbrush.

BUMPERS

Older cars and trucks feature bumpers that are relatively easy to take off and put back on. The bolts attaching them are generally in clear view and plenty of room is provided for adequate maneuverability. Newer cars, on the other hand, can require some rather intricate dismantling and installation procedures.

Many newer bumpers are actually combinations of a number of different parts. A basic frame assembly bolts onto supports that are mounted to structural members under the front or rear ends. To that frame, urethane faces,

Rather than simply throwing the trim panel in place and tightening all the screws as you install them, take the time to make sure that the trim panel is installed correctly. This particular panel spans the opening between the grille and radiator and has some hood bumpers protruding through it. You should lay the panel in place, making sure that it is not covering anything that it is not supposed to be covered. Then start all of the attachment screws, making sure that all of the screws line up with their respective holes. You may then tighten all of them.

rock shields, guards, and other items may snap into place or attach with a number of screws. Each part must be installed correctly or the entire unit may not be able to sit flush with ground effects or other body designs.

If you are not the person who originally removed the bumpers from your vehicle, or if you have simply forgotten how they are supposed to go back on, take your time during installation and do not cinch bolts or nuts down until you are sure the entire unit is assembled correctly. In some cases, shields or faces must be put on first before the bumper is secured to mounts. Otherwise, they will not fit into place. If that happens, simply loosen the bumper, pull it out, and insert the shield. Then, slip the unit back in and tighten it up.

Some front bumper assemblies are quite large, more or less encompassing the entire nose of the vehicle. To manage their size and weight, plan to have someone help you install them. In addition, most of these units feature a lot of screws and bolts that work somewhat in unison to adjust the bumper from a number of different points. To position the bumper perfectly, move from fastener to fastener tightening them gradually. If you wrench one bolt down tight too quickly you may find that one side sticks out more than the other, or the gaps are not even around its periphery. Again, this is where a helper can prove invaluable by lifting, pushing, or pulling parts of the bumper into their proper position and holding them there while you tighten the fasteners.

EMBLEMS AND BADGES

A thorough cleaning with a soft toothbrush and mild cleaner should remove accumulations of polish, wax, and dirt from tiny corners and impressions to make these items look like new. Be sure their fastening mechanisms are intact. Plastic emblems are not always easy to remove, and many times their plastic pins or supports crack during dismantling. If yours are damaged, you may have to replace them with new ones.

Chipped paint on emblems and badges does not necessarily mean they have to be replaced. You can use an artist's paintbrush, or lettering brush to repaint delicate emblem designs. Check with your auto body paint and supply jobber to determine the correct color. Unless your vehicle is a concours contender or other special classic, you might be able to match emblem colors closely with vials of auto body touchup paint. However, for those vintage, classic, or concours needs, you may have to special order the perfect type and color paint to keep emblem and badge equipment in original condition.

New emblems, badges, and other decorative body items are normally available through dealership parts departments, even those for a lot of older cars and trucks. For those parts that are not stocked at dealerships, you may have to look elsewhere for replacements. One of the best

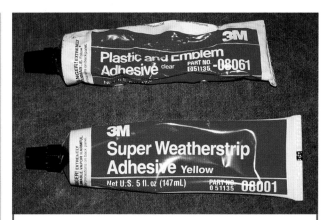

Several adhesive products are necessary when reassembling a vehicle. One type of adhesive shown here is used for installing weather stripping, while the other is used for attaching trim and emblems. Although your local discount store may sell all types of glues and adhesives, they will probably not have what you really need when it comes to gluing your car back together. Since you have gone to all the trouble of sanding, priming, and painting, you should use the correct adhesive for the job. So, go to your favorite autobody and paint supply store and tell them what you need to glue back together. They will have the correct product for your task. Most products are available in a variety of sizes, so you won't be wasting a lot. In the end, using the correct product will always win out over saving a few pennies.

sources for locating companies that specialize in hard to find automobile parts is *Hemmings Motor News*.

This monthly publication is packed full of company-sponsored and individually supported advertisements that list just about every kind of automotive-related part, accessory, and service that any auto enthusiast could ask for. Since its hundreds of pages are broken down into a number of separate categories, you should be able to find a source for the parts you need. Along with this publication, there are a lot of other magazines dedicated to auto enthusiasts, restorers, and do-it-yourself customizers. They also include sources for older car and truck parts.

VINYL TRIM

Unless you masked carefully along the edge of a vinyl stripe or decal for a spot paint job, chances are you removed the piece. Replacement vinyl stripes in all sorts of colors and widths, as well as decals, are available thorough dealership parts departments and auto body paint and supply stores.

If only one panel on your car was painted, leaving all of the rest of a vinyl stripe design intact, you might be able to purchase only the missing piece. Factory installed stripes come in sections, while individual packets of custom striping just come in certain length rolls. Especially for newer cars, check with a dealership parts department when you need to buy a certain section of vinyl stripe tape. This can save you money over the purchase of an entire roll of matching, yet generic, stripe tape at the auto body paint and supply store.

Before attaching vinyl stripes or decals, make sure the fresh paint has cured according to label recommendations. Then, use a clean cloth dampened with wax and grease remover to clean those areas where you expect to attach them. Read any instructions provided with the vinyl material.

For those pieces that are already cut to size, you have to position them before peeling off any of the backing paper. This is so you can match both ends an equal distance from body panel edges and make adjustments to height as needed. One way to do this is by securing vinyl tape sections with a piece of masking tape. You can move the masking tape around as necessary until it is securing the vinyl tape exactly where you want it. Then, tilt the vinyl tape up from the masking tape—the masking tape acts as a hinge—remove the backing and set the vinyl tape back down.

With thin stripes, you might be able to lightly lay a section down and lift it up again for repositioning. Wide stripes and decals are not so forgiving. Once their extra-strength adhesive makes contact with a body surface, they generally cannot be pulled off without suffering some sort of damage. So, take your time, have patience, and ask someone to help you with large projects.

Painted pinstripes can be matched using the proper kind of pinstripe paintbrush and slow drying enamel paint, such as One-Shot Sign Painter's Enamel. Unless you have done this before, you will have to practice on an old hood or door before trying your hand on your favorite car. The Eastwood Company offers a full range of pinstripe and lettering paintbrushes for all kinds of uses. Eastwood also sells a variety of slow-drying lettering enamel most commonly used by professional pinstripers. Auto body paints and supply stores also sell these supplies.

Although practice with a pinstripe brush may help you learn how to put stripes on straight and symmetrically, you may have trouble matching the color of existing pinstripes. Many times professional pinstripers mix different colors to arrive at new and exciting tints. Through trial and error, and some advice from a color expert at your auto body paint and supply store, you can match existing colors by following color charts and mixing drops of one color with drops of another.

In order to paint perfectly symmetrical and evenly spaced pinstripes, you might want to use stencil tape. Finesse Stencil Tape looks like pinstripe tape, except that all of the different sizes and designs are the same color. It is placed like vinyl pinstripe tape, but instead of staying on the car, it serves only as a boundary for pinstripe paint. Paint attaches to the car body between tape sections in perfectly straight and even widths. Once the paint has

dried, remove the tape for perfectly painted pinstripes. Finesse Stencil Tape is available at auto body paint and supply stores and artists' supply houses.

MISCELLANEOUS

Along with those parts already mentioned, you might have to install windshield wipers, license plates, side reflectors, trunk locks, radio antennae, luggage racks, door edge guards, mud flaps, running boards, ground effects, spoilers, weather stripping, hood bumpers, and so on. If you took them off in preparation for your car or truck's paint job, you should at least have some idea how to put them back on.

Use strips of masking tape to protect painted body areas adjacent to parts you're installing. Large cotton towels work well under newly painted doors to prevent scratches or chips as they are supported by crates or other means, while you work to secure hinges. Think of new paint as your car's skin, and treat it as you would your own. Plan ahead while replacing parts and try to anticipate potential scratch or chip hazards. Use masking tape, towels, or cardboard, to maximize the degree of protection offered newly painted parts so they do not incur scratches, chips, nicks, scrapes, gouges, or blemishes of any kind.

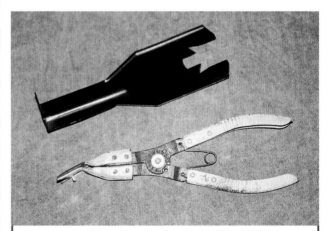

These two tools are a couple of the specialty tools that this author has collected over the years. The black piece of formed sheet metal slides behind interior door handles and window riser handles, allowing you to remove the spring clip that secures them to the shaft. Using anything else will be aggravating and most likely ineffective for the particular clip involved. It cost less than five bucks at the time, and it has paid for itself several times over by eliminating the aggravation of trying to find an alternative. The pliers-type tool is for removing windshield wiper arms from their transmission shaft. After putting several scratches in a freshly painted cowl panel, the author figured out that there had to be a better way of removing wiper arms than with a screwdriver. The local auto parts store had just what I needed, and for not much more money than the touchup paint for the screwdriver scratches.

CHAPTER 11

CLEANING, DETAILING, AND MAINTAINING

After spending considerable hours, and maybe even days, cleaning, polishing, painting, and waxing exterior body parts, you may think that your car is detailed to the highest degree. But, have you looked at the vents on your car's dashboard? Are they dusty? If you spent any time at all sanding the body of your car or truck, chances are good that more sanding dust than you had imagined has infiltrated the interior, trunk, and engine compartment. That stuff is amazing. It seems to find its way into just about every nook and cranny possible.

CLEANING

Since the outside of your automobile looks so good, why not spend a little time on the interior? Your vacuum cleaner with a soft brush attachment will work well to remove large accumulations of dust on and around the dashboard. Use a soft cloth, toothbrush, or cotton swab to clean corners and confined spaces. The vacuum cleaner's crevice attachment fits into tight spaces around seats and center consoles to remove dust and debris.

Mix a small amount of a cleaner such as Simple Green in a bucket and dip cleaning cloths into it periodically to help clean sticky steering wheels, stained sun visors, dirty door panels, and vinyl seats. You will be amazed at how much dirt gathers on your cleaning cloth.

DETAILING

Next, vacuum the trunk thoroughly. If yours is an older American car that features an open metal space with no cardboard or carpet siding and it has been neglected for far too long, detail it. Remove scale, rust deposits, and other debris with a wire brush. Use a vacuum to remove residue. Then consider applying a couple of coats of a rust-inhibiting paint as a sealer. To really make the trunk space look new and original, apply a quality coat of trunk splatter paint. Two cans are generally enough for normal-sized, 1950 to 1970 vintage American car trunks.

Trunk splatter paint comes in a few different colors. The unique part about splatter paint is that three colors are generally spit out. The base color might be gray and it will be highlighted by spots of white and black, just like an original finish. Do not apply this material to the back of the rear seats, and make sure the entire space is clean before application.

Engine compartments can present detailers with more than just sanding dust. Years of accumulated grease and oil may make cleaning it seem like an impossible chore. But an engine cleaner, like Gunk, and pressure from the wand of a self-serve car wash can easily remove the bulk of those accumulations. Be sure to cover newly painted fenders with large towels or other soft material, and keep the water wand away from the distributor and carburetor.

By the time you have fully prepped a vehicle for repainting, a vast amount of dust will have engulfed the vehicle. Using a heavy-duty shop vacuum or one at the local car wash, vacuum this dust and dirt from everywhere that you can. Having an accessory nozzle with a narrow tip will be helpful. It will be in the air conditioning and heat vents, on and between the seats, as well as under the seats and in the carpet. You should also clean the seats with the appropriate cleaner for the upholstery in your vehicle.

Even though it isn't fancy, this vinyl door panel looks much better when it has been cleaned. Pre-saturated dressing cloths work well for cleaning the dash and door panels, but since they contain silicone, use care not to get them on painted surfaces. The silicone won't really affect the cured paint, but it could cause fish eye blemishes if the affected area needs to be repainted.

Other than needing some mild cleaning and minor detailing, this trunk is not in bad shape. For the most part, some soap and water, a scrub brush, and some elbow grease could have it looking brand new. Many older vehicles have severe problems with rust in the trunk area. As wheelwell or fender panels begin to rust, they allow moisture to gain access to the trunk area. This moisture gets trapped under the spare tire and carpeting. Since it is hidden, you usually don't notice it until it is a major problem.

After that, some time with a stiff paintbrush and a cleaner such as Simple Green can make the engine compartment on your automobile look almost as good as the new paint job. You can take more time to make the engine compartment look better by painting the engine block and polishing all of those items that need it. The more you do, the better it will look.

LONG-TERM PAINT CARE

Although newer catalyzed paint products are much more durable and longer lasting than the materials used before them, you cannot expect their finish to shine forever without a minimal amount of routine maintenance. Basically, this entails washing, some polishing as needed, and scheduled waxing.

Although it may not look bad in the photo, this engine compartment could use some major cleaning. An all-purpose cleaner such as Simple Green and a small brush would work wonders for cleaning the multitude of plastic and rubber parts. Some car wash soap and water applied with a towel, then rinsed, and dried would clean up the painted surfaces, such as the shock towers and inner fenders. Some aluminum cleaner and a brush could be used to clean up the valve covers and engine components.

Even though some paint products may be advertised as never requiring wax, many auto enthusiasts and professionals believe that good coats of wax not only help provide great paint longevity, but also make washing car bodies a lot easier. It almost seems like dirt and road debris float off waxed surfaces instead of having to be rubbed off.

Unless yours is a show car that will seldom, if ever, be driven, sooner or later, nicks or small chips will appear. Along with regular maintenance, you must also repair these minor paint problems as soon as possible. If not, exposed metal will oxidize and that corrosion will spread under paint to affect adjacent metal areas.

Washing, Polishing, and Waxing

For years, farmers washed their tractors with kerosene. Not only did it do a good job of cleaning, it also afforded a measure of rust protection by forming a film over the tractor body. This procedure might be good for farmer's tractors, but it is certainly not the way you should take care of your newly painted car or truck.

Auto parts stores, some variety outlets, and even a few supermarkets sell car wash soap products. For the most part, almost any brand should be well suited for the finish on your vehicle. Many auto enthusiasts prefer to use liquids, as opposed to granular types, because they believe that just one undissolved granule on a wash mitt could cause scratches. Be sure to follow the mixing directions on labels of any product that you use.

The best way to prevent minute scratches or other blemishes in the paint is to wash the car in sections. Wash the hood, roof, and trunk areas first. Then clean the vehicle

If any paint overspray is found on the window glass, a paper towel with a bit of reducer will usually remove it. If it's excessive, you may need to use a very fine Scotch-Brite pad, or even a razor blade first. Once you've wiped it with paint reducer, remove any traces of the chemical with a window cleaner.

sides. Finish up with the dirtiest parts, like rocker panels, fender well lips, and the lower front and rear end panels.

Anytime you notice that your wash mitt is dirty or if it should fall to the ground, always rinse it off with clear water before dipping it into the wash bucket. This helps to keep the wash water clean and free of debris.

To clean inside tight spaces, like window molding edges and cowl louvers, use a soft, natural hair, floppy paintbrush. Do not use synthetic-bristled paintbrushes because they could cause minute scratches on paint surfaces. In addition,

Prior to delivery to a customer, the vehicle is thoroughly washed by hand with soapy water and rinsed with plenty of clear water. This provides the body shop one last chance to find any blemishes before the customer does. Mistakes and accidents happen, but from a business standpoint, it is much better to take care of them before the customer points them out.

After washing, the car is thoroughly dried as well. Preferences differ when it comes to the best material for drying a car. Some people use clean cloth baby diapers, while others use bath towels, while still others use "special" car drying towels. Others use a chamois, but these only work their best if the car is sporting a good coat of wax.

wrap a thick layer of heavy duct tape over the paintbrush's metal band. This will help to guard against paint scratches or nicks as you vigorously agitate the paintbrush in tight spaces, possibly knocking the brush into painted body parts such as those around headlights and grilles.

Let's talk a moment about polish and wax. Although both are designed as paint finish maintenance materials, each has its own separate purpose. Polishes clean paint finishes and remove oxidation and other contaminants. Wax, on the other hand, does no cleaning or shining. It does, however, protect those paint finishes that have already been cleaned and polished. Simply stated, polish cleans; wax protects.

Auto body paint and supply stores generally carry the largest selection of auto polishes and waxes, although many auto parts stores stock good assortments. Every polish should include a definitive label that explains what kind of paint finish it is designed for, for example, heavily oxidized, mildly oxidized, and new finish glaze. Those designed for heavy oxidation problems contain much coarser grit than those for new car finishes.

The labels will also note whether the product is intended for machine (buffer) use. Those with heavy concentrations of coarse grit are not recommended for machine use. Their polishing strength, combined with the power of a buffer, could cause large-scale paint burning problems.

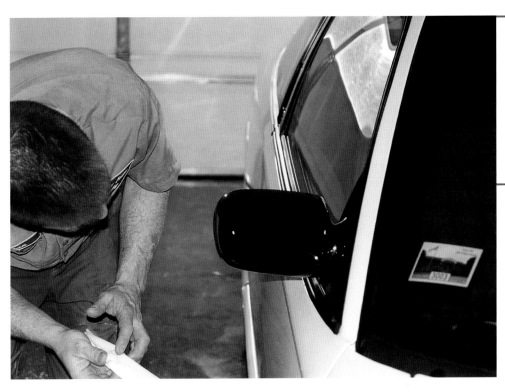

If you find small blemishes during the detailing process, touch them up with some of the same paint and a small brush. If there are small dabs of dirt on the freshly painted surface, a small dab of rubbing compound on a clean cloth can usually remove it.

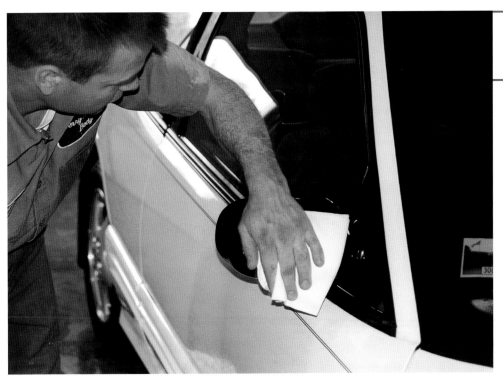

Make sure that you wipe off all of the residue from the rubbing compound.

Carnauba wax is perhaps the best product to use for protecting automobile paint finishes. Meguiar's Eagle 1, and other cosmetic car-care product manufacturers offer auto enthusiasts an assortment of carnauba-based auto wax products. There are other paint protection products available that profess to work like wax, but contain different chemical bases, which you must clearly understand before applying them to your new paint job.

Some of these (typically, they have poly or polymer in the product name) are loaded with silicone materials. Although they may protect your car's finish for a long time, professional auto painters advise against them because the silicone can saturate the paint right down to the metal and create fish eye problems if you need another repaint down the road. In some cases, silicones can even become embedded in the sheet metal itself.

If you find yourself in a quandary when it comes time to select a polish or wax product, seek advice from a knowledgeable auto body paint and supply jobber. This person should be up-to-date on the latest product information from manufacturers and the view professional painters and detailers in the field have of the products.

When to Wash New Paint Finishes

Allow plenty of time for your paint's solvents to evaporate or chemically react before washing the vehicle. For uncatalyzed enamels, this may entail a few days or a week. You can generally wash newer paints with hardener additives after one or two days, as long as you use mild automotive soap products and a gentle approach.

Because auto painters have such a wide selection of paint products to choose from and since each brand or system may react differently from others, it is always best to confirm appropriate paint drying times with a professional auto body paint and supply jobber before washing, polishing, or waxing any new finish.

How Long Before Waxing?

The rule of thumb is to wait 90 to 120 days before waxing your freshly painted vehicle. This length of time varies according to weather conditions. During summer months, while temperatures are warm and humidity low, 90 days should allow plenty of time for paint solvents to completely evaporate. Cool, wet weather reduces solvent evaporation activity and therefore requires a longer waiting period.

Light coats of quality auto wax actually form a protective seal on top of the paint finish. Even though it is quite thin and by no means permanent, this wax seal will prevent solvent evaporation. Should that occur, those vapors that need to exit paint would be trapped. As a result, they slowly build up pressure within the paint, which will eventually damage it, frequently in the form of blistering.

So, instead of protecting a paint surface, waxing too soon after new paint applications can actually cause unexpected damage. Remember, this is wax, not polish. Polish does not normally carry with it any long-lasting protective additives. Its main function is to clean and shine. Be aware that a lot of new cosmetic paint finish products are advertised as cleaner-waxes. They do combine polish and wax ingredients.

Do not use combination polish/wax products until paint has cured for at least 90 to 120 days, because the wax ingredients in these products will form a light seal over surfaces and trap solvents, just like dedicated wax-only products. If you need to polish a new catalyzed or lacquer paint job, be absolutely certain it contains no wax ingredients. Read labels to be sure, and do not be afraid to consult with an auto body paint and supply store jobber.

Repairing Small Nicks

No matter how hard you try to guard against them, small nicks or paint chips find their way onto new paint finishes much sooner than expected. For those vehicles driven on a daily basis, this dilemma is simply unavoidable. Along with rock chips that occur in traffic, parking lot door slammers are merciless. Add to that a long list of other accidental and careless mishaps and sooner or later, your new paint job will suffer some degree of minor damage. Fortunately you can repair small nicks with a minimal amount of work, providing they are small and the affected paint job is not exotic. You will need some touchup paint, a small artist's or lettering paintbrush, and masking tape.

Clean the damaged area with wax and grease remover and then closely mask off the nick, or nicks. Stir or shake the touchup paint as needed. Now simply dab your paintbrush into paint and retrieve just a very small amount of paint on the tip of the bristles. Apply that drop of paint to the nick. Do not attempt to fill in the entire nick depth with the first paint dab. Wait for a while to let the first dab set up, and then apply a second small dab.

Continue the dabbing and setting up until paint has filled the nick to just over the surface. It should be obvious before you quit that you've applied touchup paint above the height of the main finish, in other words, it should look as if you put on too much paint. Then let the new paint cure. Do not touch it for about a week to 10 days.

After a lengthy drying period, mask the nick again. This time, mask a wider area. Then use 1,200-grit sandpaper with water to gently smooth the nick area and bring the surface of the new paint down to the surrounding finish. The masking tape will prevent unnecessary sanding on the surface surrounding the repair area.

When you have smoothed the newly applied dabs of paint to the same level as the rest of the finish, remove the masking tape. Then, use polish to further blend the repair into its surroundings. If polishing scratches appear, graduate to a finer polish. Let the repair cure for a few weeks before waxing.

OVERVIEW

As long as you have your automobile torn down for paint work, why not spend some extra time detailing the extras? Not only will the effort make your paint job look its best, it will also do a lot to prolong the life of many accessory

Remember that small scratch shown on the first picture in Chapter One? It is finally being touched up with a bit of the paint from that project and a small brush. Since this is a new paint job and the paint used to touch it up is from the same can, it should match with no problems. Paint from actual touchup bottles will sometimes differ slightly.

parts. Besides, everyone knows an automobile runs better when the windows are clean.

Automotive paint jobs can last for years as long as their finishes are maintained, protected, and not abused. Frequent washing, maintaining effective wax protection, and limiting exposure to ultraviolet rays will add greatly to almost any paint job's longevity. Although the new catalyzed paint systems are more durable than most paint products employed before them, gross neglect will cause their shine and luster to fade and oxidize over time. It is up to you to maintain them in clean condition and prevent the penetration of lingering dirt, tree sap, bird droppings, airborne pollution, and mildew.

Soft wash mitts, soft cotton towels, and soft waxing applicators and cloths go a long way toward keeping paint finishes in pristine condition. Operating any mitt or cloth on your car's surface in a straight back and forth movement will also help to greatly reduce the formation of swirls or spider-webbing. Always read the labels of any car

wash soap, polish, or wax product to determine just exactly what it is intended to do. If you still don't understand, ask for help.

Quality car covers made of materials that breathe provide an excellent means for overall paint protection, especially when your car has to sit out in the sun for days on end. The sun is your paint finish's enemy. The more you can do to prevent it from suffering through endless days of baking under harsh sunlight, the longer its shine will last. If a quality car cover is not within your budget now, try parking in the shadow of a building. Or park head first in the parking lot on one day and then back in the next to alternate sunlight exposure between your car's body sides.

From beginning to end, automobile painting can be interesting, illuminating, fun, and rewarding. By the time you complete your project, you will have devoted a lot of time to sanding, masking, spraying, cleaning, and polishing. You will have spent a lot of time reading product information sheets and application guides, as well as conferring with your local auto body paint and supply jobber. You will have spent hundreds of dollars on materials, chemicals, tools, and equipment. But, you will have saved a lot more by doing the job yourself and will have also gained a lot more personal satisfaction than you ever could by simply dropping your favorite car off at the local paint shop.

With advances in chemical technology, automobile painting has become a high-tech profession. The multitude of material choices and their ability to blend or bond with similar yet unlike substances create tremendous potential, and also some risks, for the person seeking to apply his or her own paint. In this arena, you have to read labels and confirm product usage with your auto body paint and supply jobber. And, you absolutely must acknowledge, accept, understand, and incorporate all of the available safety recommendations set forth by paint manufacturers and the regulatory agencies responsible for overall worker safety. Your health, and that of those around you, is more important than any vehicle and any paint job. Protect yourself first, so you can enjoy the fruits of your labors for a good, long time.

After your job is complete, tools wiped off and put away, material carefully sealed and stored, your work place squared away and hands cleaned, stop and take a good long look at your achievement. Although it takes years of experience to become a professional automobile painter, conscientious auto enthusiasts with a keen do-it-yourself desire to learn can accomplish professional results, if they understand the basics and are not afraid to ask for help. I hope this book has given you the information and confidence to go out and give auto painting a try.

SOURCES

3M/Speedway Automotive
5320 W. Washington Street, Indianapolis, IN 46241
www.speedwayautoparts.com
317-243-6696
Masking tape, paper, and other products

Al's Metal Finishing
9660 Washburn Road, Downey, CA 90241
www.alsmetalfinishing.com
800-779-4933, 562-803-5266
Media blasting

Automotive Technology, Inc.
544 Mae Court, Fenton, MO 63026
www.automotivetechnology.com
800-875-8101, 636-343-8101
Paint booths, equipment, and supplies

Auto Restorer Magazine
P.O. Box 6050, Mission Viejo, CA 92690
www.autorestorermagazine.com, tkade@fancypubs.com
949-855-8822
"The How-To Guide for Car & Truck Enthusiasts"

Badger Air-Brush Company
9128 W. Belmont Avenue, Franklin Park, IL 60131
www.badger-airbrush.com
800-247-2787, 847-678-3104
Airbrushes and accessories

BASF/Automotive Finish
26701 Telegraph Road, Southfield, MI 48034-2442
www.basf.com
800-080-0347, 248-948-2088
Paint products

California Car Cover Company
9525 DeSoto Avenue, Chatsworth, CA 91311-5011
www.calcarcover.com
800-423-5525, 818-998-2100
Car covers

Campbell Hausfeld
100 Production Drive, Harrison, OH 45030
www.chpower.com
888-247-6937, 513-367-4811
Air compressors and pneumatic tools

CASTAIR of Minnesota
550 Flying Cloud Drive #1B, Chaska, MN 55317
www.castair.net, acplus@aol.com
888-445-9251, 952-445-9251
Air compressors

Danchuk Manufacturing
3201 S. Standard Avenue, Santa Ana, CA 92705
www.danchuk.com
800-854-6911, 714-751-1957
Chevrolet restoration parts

Dupli-Color Products
101 Prospect Avenue NW500 Republic, Cleveland, OH 44115
www.duplicolor.com
800-247-3270, 216-515-7765
Paint products

DuPont
11215 Brower Road, North Bend, OH 45052
www.info@dupont.com, www1.dupont.com
800-441-7515, 513-941-4121
Paint products

Eastwood Company
263 Shoemaker Road, Pottstown, PA 19464
www.eastwoodcompany.com
800-345-1178, 610-323-2200
Specialty tools and equipment

Finesse Pinstriping, Inc.
P.O. Box 541428, Linden Hill Station, Flushing, NY 11354
www.finessepinstriping.com
800-228-1258
Striping tape

Hemmings Motor News
P.O. Box 100, Bennington, VT 05201
www.hemmings.com
800-227-4373
Classified ads for vehicles, products, and services

HTP America
3200 Nordic Road, Arlington Heights, IL 60005-4729
www.usaweld.com
800-872-9353, 847-357-0700
Welders, plasma cutters, tools, and accessories

Imperial Restoration/POR-15
7550 E. Rice Road, Gardner, IL 60424
www.getrust.com
800-576-5822, 815-237-8678
Rust removal and restoration products

Jerry's Auto Body, Inc.
1399 North Church Street, Union, MO 63084
800-449-4757, 636-583-4757
Auto collision repair

Meguiar's
17991 Mitchell South, Irvine, CA 92614-6015
www.meguiars.com
800-854-8073, 949-752-8000
Car care products

Metro Moulded Parts, Inc.
11610 Jay Street, P.O. Box 48130, Minneapolis, MN 55448
MetroSales@metrommp.com
800-878-2237
Trim and molding products

Miller Electric Manufacturing Company
1635 W. Spencer Street, Appleton, WI 54914-4911
www.millerwelds.com
800-426-4553, 920-734-9821
Welders, plasma cutters, tools, and accessories

Mothers Polish Company
5456 Industrial Drive, Huntington Beach, CA 92649-1519
www.mothers.com
800-221-8257, 714-891-3364
Polishes, waxes, and cleaners

PPG Refinish Group
19699 Progress Drive, Strongsville, OH 44149
www.ppgrefinish.com
440-572-6880 fax
Paint products

Pro Motorcar Products, Inc.
36400 Woodward Avenue, Suite 224, Bloomfield Hills, MI 48304
www.promotorcarproducts.com
800-334-2843, 248-646-0666
Paint inspection, preparation, and application equipment

Quick Draw Brush Works Pinstriping
15445 Ventura Boulevard #912, Sherman Oaks, CA 91403
tommyitchotis@mac.com
818-348-6754
Pinstriping and artwork

Restoration Specialties & Supply
P.O. Box 328, Dept. A, Windber, PA 15963
www.restorationspecialties.com,
info@restorationspecialties.com
814-467-9842
Reproduction parts

Rudy's Custom Works (Randy Lenger)
3286 "B" Highway 100 (Old Route 66), Village Ridge, MO 63089
636-742-3060
Custom painting, flames, and artwork

Sharpe Manufacturing Company
8750 Pioneer Boulevard, Santa Fe Springs, CA 90670
www.sharpe.com
800-742-7731
Paint spray guns and equipment

Sherwin-Williams Automotive Finishes
4440 Warrensville Center Road, Warrensville, OH 44128
www.sherwin-automotive.com
800-798-5872, 800-247-3268
Paint products

Stencils & Stripes Unlimited
1108 S. Crescent Avenue #38, Park Ridge, IL 60068
www.stencilsandstripes.com
847-692-6893
Reproduction paint stencils, stripes, and decals

The Paint Store
2800 High Ridge Boulevard, High Ridge, MO 63049
636-677-1566
PPG distributor, paint products, tools, and supplies

Trim Parts
2175 Deer Field Road, Lebanon, OH 45036
www.trimparts.com, sales@trimparts.com
513-934-0815
GM Restoration Parts

Trim-Lok
6855 Hermosa Circle, Buena Park, CA 90620
www.trimlok.com
888-874-6565, 714-562-0500
Plastic and rubber trim and seals

Valspar Refinish
210 Crosby Street, Picayune, MS 39466
www.houseofkolor.com
601-798-4229
Paint products

Wyoming Technical Institute (Wyotech)
4373 N. 3rd Street, Laramie, WY 82072
www.wyomingtech.com
800-521-7158, 307-742-3776
Automotive technical school

Year One
P.O. Box 129, Tucker, GA 30085-0129
www.yearone.com
800-932-7663, 800-950-7663
Automotive restoration parts

VEHICLE PAINTING CHECKLIST

The following checklist gives the basic steps to follow when repainting a vehicle, whether it is a complete repaint or only a few panels. For the purpose of this checklist, the term 'sheet metal' will refer to any body panel, regardless of material.

NOTE: Always mask the vehicle appropriately before spraying any material. Always allow the appropriate flash and dry times before advancing to the next step.

1. Assess body damage (if any) and determine if chassis repair is necessary. Chassis repairs should be addressed prior to bodywork to ensure that body panel fit is correct.

2. Thoroughly wash the vehicle, using car wash soap. This will help eliminate adhesion problems later on, as body filler and paint products will not adhere to dirty or contaminated surfaces.

3. Remove all bumpers, trim accessories, mirrors, door handles, etc., that can be removed. Removing these items will usually be easier than masking around them. Removal will also make bodywork and painting more accessible.

4. Scuff metal surfaces with 180–220-grit sandpaper.

5. Apply epoxy primer.

6. Apply primer-surfacer. If primer-surfacer is applied within 72 hours, it can be applied directly to the epoxy primer. If more than 72 hours, epoxy primer must be scuffed using a Scotch-Brite pad before applying primer-surfacer.

7. After applying primer-surfacer, block sand with 400- and 600-grit sandpaper.

8. Apply base coat. Remove nibs of dirt and debris with 1,200-grit sandpaper. Apply additional base coat as necessary for coverage.

9. Apply clear coat. Remove nibs of dirt and debris with 1,200-grit sandpaper.

10. Final sand with 2,000–2,500-grit before buffing.

FIBERGLASS BODY/BODY COMPONENT PREPARATION CHECKLIST

With the large number of companies reproducing complete bodies and countless body components out of fiberglass, it is likely that at one time or another, you will need to prepare fiberglass for paint.

Check with the manufacturer of your particular components to verify what they recommend for their product. Each company has its own special blend of components (resins, hardeners, etc.) for producing fiberglass parts. They should be able to tell you what method of surface preparation works best with their products.

If you cannot find specific instructions for your particular fiberglass products, the following should give you satisfactory results:

NOTE: Always mask the vehicle appropriately before spraying any material. Always allow the appropriate flash (dry) times before advancing to the next step.

1. Scuff the entire fiberglass surface with 80- to 100-grit sandpaper.

2. Take the fiberglass components to a body shop, and run the components through a bake cycle at 140 degrees.

3. Block sand the entire fiberglass surface with 120-grit sandpaper.

4. Perform bodywork as required.

5. Apply epoxy primer.

6. Block sand with 180-grit sandpaper.

7. Apply primer-surfacer. If primer-surfacer is applied within 72 hours, it can be applied directly to the epoxy primer. If more than 72 hours, epoxy primer must be scuffed using a Scotch-Brite pad before applying primer-surfacer.

8. Block sand with 180- and 220-grit sandpaper.

9. After applying primer-surfacer, block sand with 400- to 600-grit sandpaper.

10. Apply base coat. Remove nibs of dirt and debris with 1,200-grit sandpaper. Apply additional base coat as necessary for coverage.

11. Apply clear coat. Remove nibs of dirt and debris with 1,200-grit sandpaper.

12. Final sand with 2,000- to 2,500-grit before buffing.